## Mountbatten Library

Tel: (01703) 319249   Fax: (01703) 319697

Please return this book on or before the last date stamped.
Loans may be renewed on application to the Library Staff.

# Molitor

# Molitor

## Ebéniste from the Ancien Régime to the Bourbon Restoration

Ulrich Leben

with a complete catalogue of the furniture

Translated by William Wheeler

CINOA Prize 1990

Philip Wilson Publishers

To my parents
and family

© Ulrich Leben

First published 1992
by Philip Wilson Publishers Limited
26 Litchfield Street, London WC2H 9NJ
in association with Editions d'art Monelle Hayot

Distributed in the USA by
Rizzoli International Publications, Inc.
300 Park Avenue South, New York, NY 10010

ISBN 0 85667 4079

LC 91 060243

Designed by Editions d'art Monelle Hayot and Roy Cole
Typeset by Tradespools Ltd, Frome, Somerset
Printed and bound by Graphicom srl, Vicenza, Italy

# Contents

# Preface

Born in Luxembourg under Habsburg rule, Bernard Molitor was an artist of German parentage who sought his fortune in Paris. Ulrich Leben, brought up in a culture of similar sensibility, expresses the *ébéniste's* hopes and difficulties as if he had himself experienced them. He understands the quest of an artist who searched the highways and byways of Europe for the soil that would best nurture his creativity.

In the artistic and intellectual crucible that was eighteenth-century France, Molitor sought artistic inspiration and the creative spirit, and met patrons and *marchands-merciers* who provided a market for his furniture.

Molitor was one of the last *ébénistes* to work for the monarchy in France, and one of the last guild masters. An artisan belonging to a world of high imagination and elegance that swiftly vanished, he possessed one of the few workshops that was not destroyed by the Revolution. A staunch royalist and supplier to the greatest of court figures, he pursued his career against all obstacles and vicissitudes. With the help of his cousin Michel Molitor, who was actively involved in the storming of the Bastille and following adoption of French nationality, he succeeded in evading serious Revolutionary suspicions during the Terror. In the era that followed he was honoured with orders from the *Directoire*, the Emperor Napoleon, King Jérôme of Westphalia and great private collectors including the duc de Choiseul-Praslin.

From the *Directoire* to the Restoration, Molitor maintained an output of originality and individuality, at the same time satisfying all the caprices of fashion. His motifs were often inspired by events of the moment, notably Napoleon's return from Egypt, while the quality of his workmanship remained firmly of the *ancien régime*.

At this time of upheaval in France, fashion fluctuated extraordinarily. *Ebénistes*, upholsterers, tailors and milliners responded to all the latest extravagances, and often outstripped them with astonishing new inventions.

Contemplation of the financial sums devoured by the Revolution invites over-simplification. The concern was actually not to spend less, but to make expenditure appear less than it was. Sumptuous furniture was made, veneered in mahogany and precious woods, but with less apparent ostentation. Even before 1789, Thierry de Ville d'Avray criticized administrative inefficiency that he was unable to change. Napoleon was no more successful in his attempts to check the excesses of the Empress Josephine.

One of Molitor's great strengths lay in his ability to supply the simplicity of style that the Revolutionary era desired. He was aided in this by the return of the *goût à l'antique*, which favoured the fine sobriety that characterized his work. He was always more at ease with mahogany and ebony pieces embellished with oriental laquer panels than with marquetry. He decorated his furniture with ormolu mounts, but the very refinement of their use typifies his supreme mastery; the individuality of his style amounting to a signature.

Molitor became more and more successful throughout his career, despite moments of acute crisis. The reason for this is twofold: he was both a gifted artist and a shrewd businessman and financier.

Ulrich Leben has used a wide variety of sources, all the more valuable as the systematic use of marks disappeared with the abolition of the guilds, making means of authentication other than by a signature all the more important. His starting-point is his key discovery of the inventory at the deaths of Bernard Molitor at Fontainebleau. This document led Ulrich Leben to two further inventories concerning the Molitor family as well as eighty documents preserved in the Archives National in Paris. He has reconstructed the life and work of Bernard Molitor with great precision on the basis of plans, records from the *Garde-Meuble*, and various prospectuses and subcontracting agreements concluded by Molitor with other craftsmen. 'The tools for the reconstruction of an *ébéniste's* work,' as Ulrich Leben writes, 'are inventories and surviving pieces, rarely autobiographical documents.'

Hence the extent to which the author has consulted the cultural, political, economic and social context of the period in which his subject lived, consultation which is proceeded by informed deduction and comparison. The study of Molitor offers a unique thirty-year continuity during a period particularly lacking in information about furniture-making. Molitor's *oeuvre* reflects the stylistic evolution of a transitional era – from the fall of the monarchy through Revolution to *Directoire*, Empire, and finally Restoration.

The present work is the only monograph ever devoted to Bernard Molitor. It is based on the author's doctoral thesis undertaken at the University of Bonn, towards the funding of which he was awarded the Confédération Internationale des Négociants en Objets d'Art (CINOA) Prize for 1990.

In pursuit of a thorough knowledge of his subject Ulrich Leben, an art historian, has completed an apprenticeship as a *menuisier-ébéniste* at Meerbusch, Germany. He thus avoids the pitfalls lying in wait for those who have only a theoretical knowledge of the written sources and lack the practical experience indispensable for a comprehensive understanding of their subject.

Austere genre though it is, the monograph is the most thorough possible source for knowledge of an artist. This one at last liberates Molitor, two centuries after his death, from the fate of the anonymous master.

Monelle Hayot

# Acknowledgements

We should like to express our sincere thanks to all those museum curators, art historians, dealers and private collectors who have so generously given us access to their collections, offered their advice and made available their photographic material and documentary sources.

**Austria**

Dr. Christian Witt-Döring

**France**

M. Daniel Alcouffe, M. Dominique Augarde, M. Christian Baulez, M. Emile Bourgey (CINOA), M. Bernard Chevallier, Mademoiselle Comère, Madame Coural, Maître Danré, Madame N. Felkay, M. Bruno Foucart, M. J. L. Gaillemin, Madame Aletta Gillet, M. Michel Germond, Mademoiselle A. M. Joly, Madame Denise Ledoux-Lebard, Mademoiselle Patricia Lemonnier, M. Patrick Leperllier, M. Loisin, M. Alexandre Pradère, Madame Tamara Préaud, M. Laurent Prevost-Marcilhacy, M. Jean-Nerée Ronfort, M. Jean Pierre Samoyault, Madame Colombe Samoyault-Verlet, M. Pierre Verlet, M. P. H. Wallbaum

**Germany**

Herr Günther Abels (CINOA), Professor Dr. Tilmann Buddensieg, Frau Anna Czarnocka, Herr Dräger, Herr Viereck, Herr Dr. Burkhardt Göres, Herr Dr. Hans Ottomeyer, Herr Dr. Meinulf Siemer, Frau Dr. Rosemarie Stratmann-Döhler, Professor Dr. Michael Stürmer, Deutscher Akademischer Austauschdienst, Konrad Adenauer Stiftung

**Great Britain**

Sir Geoffrey de Bellaigue, Miss Frances Buckland, Mr. Michael Hall, Mr. Philip Heward-Jaboor, Mr. Peter Hughes, Mr. Hugh Roberts, Mr. Adrian Sasson

**Luxembourg**

Herr Erpelding, Herr Alphonse Wiltgen

**United States of America**

Ms Shelley Benett, Mr. Roger Berkowitz, Mr. David Cohen, Mr. Theodor Dell, Mr. Henry Hawley, Mr. James Parker, Ms Gillian Wilson, Ms Ghenete Zelleke

We extend our thanks to all the members of CINOA

| | |
|---|---|
| Austria | Bundesgremium des Handels mit Juwelen, Gold-, Silberwaren, Uhren, Gemälden, Antiquitäten, Kunstgegenständen und Briefmarken |
| Belgium | Chambre des Antiquaires de Belgique |
| Denmark | Danish Antique Dealers' Association |
| France | Syndicat National des Antiquaires Négociants en Objets d'Art; & Chambre Syndicale de l'Estampe du dessin et du tableau |
| Germany | Bundesverband des Deutschen Kunst- und Antiquitätenhandels |
| Great Britain | The British Antique Dealers' Association; The Society of London Dealers |
| Republic of Ireland | The Irish Antique Dealers' Association |
| Italy | Federazione Italiana Mercanti d'Arte & Associazione Antiquari d'Italia |
| New Zealand | The New Zealand Antique Dealers' Association |
| The Netherlands | Verreeniging van Handelaren in Oude Kunst in Nederland |
| South Africa | The South African Antique Dealers' Association |
| Switzerland | Syndicat Suisse des Antiquaires et Commerçants d'Art; & Association des Commerçants d'Art de la Suisse |
| United States | The National Antique & Art Dealers Association of American, Inc. Art Dealers Association of America, Inc. & Art and Antique Dealers League of America, Inc. |

# Note on the text

The body of this book is divided into three main parts. The first part, the 'Life' covers the early life and career of Molitor, the second part, the 'Work' assesses his work and the third part is a comprehensive catalogue of Molitor's known works to date, which includes details of material, date, provenance and location.

References to works by Molitor in the first two parts of the book are followed by either a caption number (when illustrated in the 'Life' or 'Work') or a catalogue number (when not illustrated in the 'Life' or 'Work'). The caption numbers are printed in roman type; the catalogue numbers are printed in italics in parenthesis. In order to identify the catalogue number of an illustrated piece, the reader must refer to the caption.

In the catalogue, where a piece is illustrated in the 'Life' or 'Work', the caption reference is given next to the catalogue number in italics in parenthesis.

*Abbreviations used in the catalogue, notes and bibliography:*
A.D.S. Archives de la Seine
A.N. Archives Nationales
A.N.M.C. Archives Nationales Minutier Central
A.N.Y. Archives Nationales Serie Y
B.N. Bibliothèque Nationale
G.M.F. Mobilier National
M.A.D. Musée des Arts Décoratifs

References to 'doc 1–15 in the text refer to the documents in the appendix, pp. 208–227.

# MOLITOR,
## EBENISTE,

Demeurant ci-devant rue de Lille, faubourg St. Germain, dernièrement rue du faubourg St. Honoré,

Vient de fixer son Domicile rue neuve du Luxembourg, près celle des Capucines, ancienne Maison du Timbre, ayant Boutique sur le Boulevard de la Magdeleine, en face la rue Commartin ; fait et vend tout ce qui concerne l'Ebénisterie antique et moderne.  A Paris

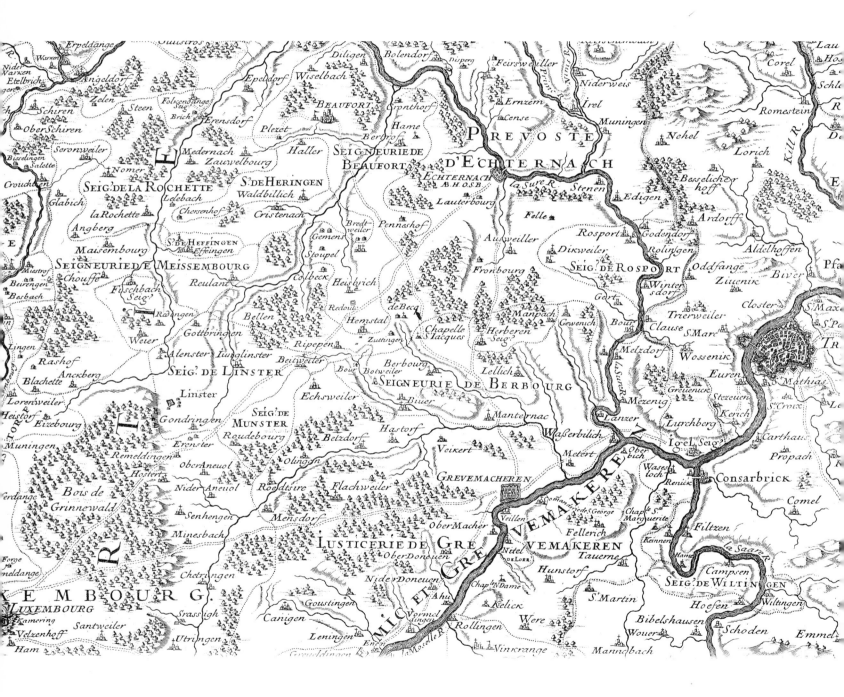

1
Molitor's birthplace – the village of Betzdorf, near the city of Luxemburg. Map by Hubert and Jallot, Paris, 1781. Private collection

# Life

Origins and family

Like many others of his generation, Bernard Molitor joined the great movement of German craftsmen away from their homeland, seeking their fortune, as often as not, in Paris, then the centre of the luxury item industry on the continent.

Molitor was descended from a family of millers who had inhabited the Duchy of Luxembourg for several generations, although their exact origins are difficult to determine, as it was the custom in church registers to record all millers under the name of 'Molitor'. Frequent moves by the miller families complicate the search still further. Millers were subjected to a complicated dependancy beyond their immediate masters – to whom they had to pay taxes and render their services; they were also responsible for collecting the *Molterschossel*, a payment taken from the villagers in their locality to be passed on to the feudal lord of the region. They were frequently suspected of keeping the monies for themselves hence, at the expiration of a mill's lease, the millers' families often preferred to move on in search of pastures new.[1]

Bernard Molitor was born in Betzdorf, a village twenty-eight kilometres northeast of the city of Luxemburg.[2] His father operated the village mill, and the local lord, Baron Philippe Evrard Mohr de Waldt, ruled over the villagers, exploiting his powers to the full.[3] The Molitors' mill was located on the

2
Molitor's place of birth, the family's mill at Betzdorf.

outskirts of the village, along the river Styr. Ancestors of the Molitor family have been traced to Haans-Haus, to the neighbouring hamlet of Hagelsdorf, and to Mertert, a village in the Moselle whence came Bernard's great-grandfather. His only documented forbears, however, are his father and uncle, the brother Nicolas and Bernard Molitor. His father Nicolas was born in 1712 and married Marguerite Lemmer, born on 13 November 1721, the second daughter of the miller Jonas Lemmer and his wife Katharina. Jonas Lemmer leased the Betzdorf mill, belonging to Charles Emmanuel de Vecquer, in 1702, and it is probable that Nicolas Molitor served as a helper; here, he began his marriage to Marguerite, a union that produced three children: Bernard, Anne-Marie and Mathias. Bernard came into the world on 22 October 1755 at around 11 o'clock and was baptised on the same day in Betzdorf church.[4]

Marguerite died in 1776, aged 54 and Nicolas Molitor went to live with his daughter Anne-Marie who had married the miller Federspiel, and now resided at the mill in Deyser. He died on 7 August 1787, with his daughter at his bed-side. The date of birth of Bernard Molitor senior is unknown.[5] Miller of the lower mill in Müllerthal, he had married the owner's daughter Sybille Schuhmacher around 1728. Two children were born from this union: Peter (1725–1805) and Michel (1734–1810), the future ebéniste's cousin who can be traced to Paris from 1773.

A number of factors can explain the young cousins' emigration. Without doubt, the principal reason for Bernard and Michel's journey was their complete lack of prospects in their present situation – poor millers without a rental contract whose fathers, mere hirelings, had advanced themselves by marrying the daughters of the millers for whom they worked. The running of Michel's family's mill eventually passed to his older brother Peter by birthright, depriving the younger brother of all means of existence. The expiry date of the lease on the mill at Betzdorf is unknown, but we do know that Michel arrived in Paris before Bernard. In 1773 he lived in the Faubourg Saint-Antoine, near the Bastille, an area enjoying the Royal privilege: resident tradesmen were not obliged to join one of the city's guilds. For this reason, numerous foreign craftsmen flocked to the quarter and Bernard Molitor seems to have undertaken his journey to Paris confident that he would meet his cousin there. The circumstances which led the two millers' sons to opt for cabinet-making remain obscure.

The Faubourg Saint-Antoine (c. 1776–1787)

For a poor but confident fortune-seeker, the attraction of Paris was particularly strong. Despite all the risks, and with a little luck and cleverness, it was easier to make a living in the wealthy French capital than it was in rural areas. In 1773 Michel Molitor's name appears among tax returns for the Faubourg Saint-Antoine, where he lived between the main thoroughfares; the rue du Faubourg Saint-Antoine, the rue Saint Nicolas and rue Charenton. His taxes came to six *sous* and he probably worked in one of the Faubourg's large workshops, while at the same time carrying out work for his own clients. In an inventory of the *ébéniste* Antoine Foullet's workshop, Michel Molitor is mentioned as an *employé artisan*.[6] Nonetheless, no precise date can be given for his arrival in Paris. Since both cousins were cabinet-makers, and as first names were not always included in contemporary records, it is equally difficult to ascertain the exact date of Bernard's arrival in Paris, although it was probably between 1776 and 1778. The move may possibly have been prompted by his mother's death, in 1776. A small advertisement in the daily newspaper *Les petites annonces, affiches et avis divers*, on 21 September 1778, in which the merits of an anti-bedbug ointment were extolled, is signed by *le sieur Molitor, ébéniste,* and has the merit of being the first printed document bearing the Molitor name in Paris.[7]

Speaking only their native German, the Molitors lived in the *Faubourg* among their compatriots, in unmarried obscurity.[8] Less than a decade later, in 1787, Bernard Molitor's name appears for the first time in the ledgers of

*ANNONCES, AFFICHES.*
*DU 21. SEPT. 1778.*          *1403*

Le fieur *Molitor*, Ebénifte, cour de l'Orme, à l'arcenal, maifon du fieur *Lelievre*, Sellier, poffede pour la deftruction des punaifes, un fecret qu'il a employé avec fuccès dans plufieurs maifons de cette ville. C'eft une POMMADE qui n'a point d'odeur, qui n'incommode perfonne & qui ne caufe aucun dommage.

the *Bâtiments du Roi*. During this period, the Molitors resided in the privileged quarter around the Arsenal where they rented both a workshop and annexed lodgings from the royal saddler Monsieur Lelièvre.[9]

It is impossible to identify with any certainty the workship in which Bernard Molitor worked, and hence the master from whom he received his training, but we can reasonably assume it to have been an important workshop in the *Faubourg*, and most probably that of J.-H. Riesener.

Molitor may have taken drawing lessons at the *Ecole Gratuite de Dessin*.[10] From very early on he seized every opportunity to familiarize himself with

3
Molitor's first known advertisement in *Les Petites annonces, affiches et affaires divers.*
Private collection

the tastes and fashions of Parisian high society and to demonstrate his ability to cater to them. The cousins' professional activities were twofold: they prepared their ointments and handwarmers 'à la Comtesse', sold through advertisements, while they executed furniture whose quality began to attract a discerning clientèle. Parisian *marchands-merciers* came to the *Faubourg* from the centre of Paris to stock their boutiques with the inexpensive, quality pieces which they then resold at a profit.

Bernard Molitor's name is found in the registers of the *Bâtiments du Roi* for 1787, recording his first official contract for works of *ébénisterie* for the Royal Château at Fontainebleau. Molitor is mentioned in respect of mahogany parquet flooring, executed under the direction of the architect Pierre Rousseau in Queen Marie-Antoinette's *cabinet de retraite*.[11] On 26 October 1787 Bernard Molitor was accorded the title of *Mâitre* in the *Corporation des Menuisiers Ebénistes de la Ville de Paris*.[12] As a foreign subject, Molitor had to pay 536 *livres* and to furnish proof of six years' apprenticeship to qualify as a Master. Upon completion of the work at Fontainebleau, it is quite possible that an established Master interceded on Molitor's behalf to sponsor his admission to the official guild of his trade.[13] Molitor was now able to obtain the much sought-after *estampille* and could open his own workship in the city centre, from which to sell his own creations. Hence, at the age of thirty-two, Bernard Molitor had successfully risen to the top of the Parisian estab-

4
Signature of Bernard and Michel Molitor in the 1796 inventory following Elisabeth Molitor's death.
Archives Nationales,
(LXXI–126)

lishment in his craft and discovered the financial rewards to be reaped from his accomplishments. On this sound footing, he established his own workshop and permitted himself to entertain the idea of starting a family.

Stylistic similarities in certain pieces force the comparison between J.-H. Riesener and Bernard Molitor, leading us to suppose that professional ties existed between the two *ébénistes*. Few documents exist, however, which might confirm this. It is, at least, certain that they were acquainted. In an 1801 experts' report, Sieurs Molitor and Riesener, as well as George Jacob, were summoned to judge a dispute between two other *ébénistes*, Claude Magnien and Xavier Hindermeyer; and there is no doubt that the Molitors lived near Riesener's large workship in the Arsenal district at the time of its heyday, from 1778–82, when numerous Court commissions were received.[14] Furthermore, Riesener supplied the furniture for the *cabinet de retraite* at Fontainebleau and Molitor may well have collaborated in Riesener's workshop before his acceptance into the Guild.[15] Certain early stamped works, for example 5 and 7, display strong stylistic affinities with furniture by Riesener and carry strikingly similar mounts. The re-utilization of these same motifs is also notable in the late works of Molitor.

There is clearly a link between the young *ébéniste*'s work at Fontainebleau, his admittance to the Guild in October 1787, and his marriage a year later in June 1788. A number of positive factors seem to have combined to

5
Mahogany veneer *secrétaire à abattant* with ormolu mounts, among Molitor's earliest creations. It is reminiscent of the work of the *ébéniste* J.-H. Riesener (cat. 48).
Bibliotheque des Arts Décoratifs, Collection Maciet

promote Bernard Molitor's sudden rise to prominence. Documents reveal that besides his artistic skills, he equally possessed an acute business sense. His use of advertising in *Les petites annonces ...* represents one of the first examples of this, and to launch his products beyond the Paris periphery, he continued to use the modern medium of the press, which was already at that time widely distributed in other large urban areas. Another factor, far from insignificant, also promoted his success and the expansion of his workshop, namely the unsparing support which he received from several well-known individuals, already firmly established in the Guild, whose friendship and assistance largely contributed to Molitor's breakthrough. The Fessard family, whom Molitor had the occasion to meet during his work at Fontainebleau, played an important role. Marin Fessard had been *Charpentier du Roi* and after his death his widow, Marie-Anne and their son took charge of all carpentry at the Château. A personal friendship developed from their joint work on the *cabinet de retraite* and it must have been during this collaboration that the *ébéniste* met his future wife Elisabeth Fessard, who was Marin's daughter.

| | |
|---|---|
| The marriage to Elisabeth Fessard | Molitor married Elisabeth, who was the same age as her husband, on 7 June 1788. In the marriage contract, the recently appointed Master estimated his fortune at a substantial 15,000 *livres* in the form of various pieces of furniture, assets and money.[16] Elisabeth, herself a widow, brought 3,600 *livres* originating from her first marriage to Bonaventure Verdier, a notary, and from her father's inheritance. Michel Molitor acted as his cousin's witness, and Marie-Anne Fessard, together with her sons Marin and Claude, famous copper engravers, as well as the harpsichord maker Pierre-Joseph Zimmerman, husband of Elisabeth's sister Rosalie-Elisabeth. Soon afterwards, Molitor established his own workshop in the Faubourg Saint-Germain at 26 rue de Bourbon, and moved in with his young bride. On 15 April 1789, their first daughter, Anne-Julie was born. She was baptised at the church of Saint Sulpice.[17] |

The Bastille was taken just three months later, provoking the first wave of emigration among the Parisian nobles beginning in July 1789. Nonetheless, Molitor's workshop seems to have continued production successfully until 1792; in the summer of which year, the *Garde-Meuble* commissioned two precious mahogany doors. On 10 August 1792, Louis XVI was overthrown, the monarchy was abolished and with it disappeared the Parisian market for luxury goods. Little is known of how Molitor fared in the years 1793 and 1794. In the capital the Terror reigned and wealthy Parisians had more pressing concerns than the furnishing of their *hôtels* or apartments. With the establishment of the *Directoire* at the end of the hostilities in 1795, life returned to something approaching normality.

One year later, Elisabeth Molitor died, on '15 Fructidor year IX (1 September 1796). Following her death a complete inventory was drawn up with an exact description of the workshop, the furniture warehouse and the private apartment where the Molitors had lived since their marriage in 1788 (*doc 4*). This document provides an accurate picture of the household of a successful *ébéniste* prior to 1789. In the description of their mezzanine-level apartment, a sound, bourgeois opulence is revealed, with the *salon* furnishings featuring a sofa and six matching *fauteuils*, painted grey and covered with a crimson and yellow-striped Utrecht velvet, plus a *secrétaire*, and a mahogany *guéridon*. There were six chairs in green-painted beech wood with fine cane trellis work, four of which were decorated with a *gerbe* motif on the back. In the cupboards there were white dishes and fine English earthenware. Silver cutlery, valued at 348 *livres* was stored in the *secrétaire*, together with a watch from Geneva, one gold and one silver pocket-watch, both made by Darliebe, and the family jewels.

On the salon walls hung portraits in oils of Molitor and his daughter, six engravings of landscapes and one depicting 'The Good Peasant Woman'. There were also four drawings, two of which were sanguines. Only one book was mentioned in the inventory, a German edition of the *Secrets des arts*. In the warehouse located on the floor above the apartment, unfinished pieces were stored awaiting bronze mounts and marble slabs. The total value of the Molitors' furniture, including the workshop stock, was valued at 9,795 *livres*. The accounts show 844 *livres* in *assignats* and 2,428 *livres* in debts owed to other craftsmen and suppliers. The entire value of Bernard Molitor's fortune, including stock, amounted to 12,466 *livres*.

From September 1795 the *Directoire* formed its first government which, after years of agitation, instilled hope for social peace and improved living conditions. The régime engendered a new, wealthy bourgeois class, eager to acquire luxury products for its comfort and to display its newly-acquired social status. *Les nouveaux riches* were in search of refined décors for their residences. They addressed themselves to those same craftsmen who had previously served the aristocracy and to those whose workshops had survived the Revolution. In view of the 1796 inventory, the value of his stock and his full order book, business was prospering for Molitor, and on 15 Prairial year VIII (4 June 1800), he acquired at auction a building in the Faubourg Saint-Honoré. He moved in the following year with his second wife.[18]

The Revolution and its aftermath

The stance taken by Michel Molitor during the Revolution was diametrically opposed to that of his successful cousin. Bernard, the master craftsman, whose clients were members of the Court or in its entourage, remained, for business as much as for personal reasons, loyal to the Crown. This was in total contrast to the pro-Revolutionary views of the worker Michel, who was in the forefront of the events of 14 July 1789. During the period from 1789–92, Bernard Molitor does not, however, appear to have

6
Commode in mahogany
veneer with ormolu mounts.
Unstamped, it is possibly one
of Molitor's earliest works,
dated *c*.1785–88, and
probably commissioned by a
Parisian *marchand-mercier*.
Wallace Collection, London

7
Console table in mahogany
veneer with ormolu mounts,
unstamped, but attributed to
Molitor on account of its
distinctive ornamentation
(cat. 86).
Toledo Museum of Art, Ohio

been in danger. On a list dated 6 August 1790, he was classified as a *'citoyen actif'*, alongside the comment *'no. 257 Molitor, ébéniste, rue Bourbon'*.[19] To be eligible for the status of *citoyen actif*, a person had to be of age and free from any type of work contract. The candidate had to pledge allegiance to the Constitution and pay a tax which was equal to three days' work. In the first years of the Revolution, prior to the Terror, it was still fairly easy to adapt to the new conditions, and Molitor survived relatively well until the aboliton of the professional Privileges and the fall of Louis XVI in August 1792.

In 1792 it is known for certain that Bernard received commissions for furniture from the Crown and the comtesse de La Marck. But after the fall of the monarchy under Robespierre, from 1793–94, Molitor was to experience serious difficulties. The Revolutionary Tribunals were instituted on 11 March 1793 and on 21 March, surveillance committees were created in each district of Paris to collect information on suspicious individuals, particularly foreigners. Various decrees were promulgated, promising rewards to those who denounced suspects. In the ensuing witch-hunts, Molitor's account books alone, divulging the names of his aristocratic clients, could have proved quite literally fatal. Some years later, in a letter to the comte de Clarac dated 1818, Molitor openly avowed his Royalist sentiments during the Terror. The letter has something of the nature of a confession and recounted the troubles that he had subsequently to face.

There was, of course, a certain pragmatism in Molitor's devotion to the Crown.[20] It was essentially founded on the professional ties between the *ébéniste* and his aristocratic clients, the Court from which he received commis-

8
Mahogany veneer, roll-top or *bureau à cylindre* with ormolu mounts. The mounts are identical to those adorning furniture delivered to the Château de Saint-Cloud in 1788, through the intermediary of the *marchand-mercier* Daguerre (see also 81, 82 and 154) (cat. 70).
J. Paul Getty Museum, Malibu, California

9
Detail of 8 showing side view.

**10**
One of a pair of ebony veneer and Japanese lacquer commodes with double doors. Instead of its customary use on drawers, the palmette frieze is an integral component of the design of the door front (cat. 28A). Private collection

sions and, not least; the *Garde Meuble*. It seems probable that Molitor took French citizenship after 1789. Without this, despite the fact that his wife was French and that he owned a substantial workshop, he was still considered a foreigner and for this reason would be a particularly easy target for the investigations of the local surveillance committee. By 1796, the extent of his fears can be sensed upon inspection of his accounts. Entries have been partially crossed out and have been scribbled with clearly deliberate illegibility. Absolute discretion was essential for Molitor and all those mentioned in the inventory. In the previously mentioned letter of 1818, Molitor complained of the dangers to which his Court connections exposed him. His eventual denunciation, was most probably the work of jealous, distrustful Revolutionaries who suspected him of wanting to flee, or of collaborating with emigrés. Molitor also mentions a summons to appear before the Revolutionary Tribunal. The trial proceedings concerning this affair have not been located, but the other documents recorded in 1796 are ample proof of the explosive situation faced by the *ébéniste*. As he later wrote to the comte de Clarac, his eventual deliverance was '*par un miracle de la providence*'.

On 8 September 1793, Bernard Molitor received a certificate attesting

11
Side view of 10. The side panels were executed in Paris after the original Oriental designs, but display inferior craftsmanship.

12
The pair to 10 (see also 102). The nest of ten drawers behind the commode doors were originally part of an Oriental lacquer cabinet which Molitor dismantled and reused (cat. 28B).
The Carnegie Art Institute, Pittsburgh

to his absence from the emigré lists and a week later, on 15 September, the General Assembly of the Circonscription issued him with a *certificat de civisme*. From 1793–96, several certificates recording oath-taking, services rendered to the National Guard and other civic obligations to the young Republic are mentioned. Receipts have been found concerning a gift to the Nation, a 'patriotic tax' and various other taxes of a more or less voluntary nature.[21] On 23 Pluviôse, year III (2 November 1795) three citizens from Molitor's neighbourhood testified that he had resided there since May 1792. This testimony was legally necessary if Molitor wanted to have his rights recorded on the list then being drawn up concerning the commissions that were registered, but not executed, before the fall of Louis XVI. All these facts point to the risks Molitor faced. Until August 1792, it was possible to appease the Revolutionaries by paying certain taxes or donating various gifts. Later, everyone was at the mercy of possible denunciation so, in order not to raise suspicions and to try and avoid falling prey to the Revolutionary Tribunal, Molitor, and those closest to him, needed to act with cleverness and diplomacy.[22]

Michel Molitor's position presented itself in a different light. His partici-

pation in the assault on the Bastille was one of the rare moments when he emerged from obscurity.[23] Since he lived near the Bastille, it is tempting to imagine that he was swept along in the heat of the moment on 14 July. On 25 April he had his name added to the official list of the Conquerors of the Bastille which is registered at the National Archives. The men who had distinguished themselves, during the first hours of the conquest of liberty, were

13
Mahogany veneer *secrétaire à abattant*. Compact in shape and resting on turned feet, the slightly, projecting central section of the fall front is adorned with a Sèvres medallion representing the disarming of Cupid (*La punition de l'Amour*) (cat. 49). Private collection

14
*Secrétaire à abattant* in speckled mahogany veneer with ormolu mounts. The recessed cornice is particularly unusual. This design for a lady's *secrétaire* is similar to pieces produced for the most important *marchands-merciers* (cat. 47). Private collection

15
Mahogany veneer commode
fitted with two doors, one of
which is double and folding.
The limited use of ormolu
decoration on the frieze rail
and canted corners anticipates
the restraint of the
Republican style during the
years 1790–92 (cat. 4A).
Private collection

soon to become national heroes. Until 1792 they received numerous decorations and titles, and as members of a special unit of the National Guard, a uniform and rifle. In 1810 a National Guard uniform was itemized in the inventory of Michel's modest estate. This official recognition allowed him to vouch for his cousin Bernard, and to support him during the Terror. A bachelor and a practising Catholic, Michel lived with the Molitor family after the Revolution.[24]

Bernard Molitor was among the few important *ébénistes* whose workshops survived the Revolution. Nevertheless, when he resumed work in 1795, he was apparently unable to overcome a certain distrust from the new social order. The Revolution had bought his rapid rise to prominence to an abrupt halt, and he was to suffer further experiences during the Convention.

The right of the
*estampille*

The right to the *estampille*, the signature stamp on furniture, had been established in 1741 in the statutes of the *Mâitres Menuisiers Ebénistes*. There are, however, signed pieces produced prior to this date. From 1741, until the period of Turgot's reforms in 1776, which were doomed to failure, the stamp was obligatory on furniture created by the Guild Masters.[25] It normally comprised the first initial and the complete name of the Master and if need be, the Guild monogram, *JME* (*Jurande des Menusiers Ebénistes*) was added. At regular intervals, inspectors carried out visits to the workshops with the aim of verifying the quality of workmanship, but despite this and outside the *lieux privilégés*, such as the Faubourg Saint-Antoine, there remained numerous means of circumventing the right to the stamp.[26]

After a first unfruitful attempt on 4 August 1789, with the Chapelier law, the National Assembly deliberated in favour of the definitive abolition of the trade association or guilds between March and June 1791. In the decree of 17 March 1791, Chapter 1 stipulated that 'All privileges of the profession are abolished. From April 1, each citizen is free to practise the trade or craft which will please him to undertake, to the extent that he acquires the necessary licence.'[27] The fees involved in obtaining a licence were so low that, in comparison with the Guilds' requirements, virtually anyone could apply. In fact, the basis of the evaluation for a furniture-maker's licence was calculated on the workshop rent or estimated annual profits. In this debate free enterprise for craftsmen was seen as the essence of the revolutionary belief that 'liberty is the soul of industry'.[28] In a free economic system the old guilds represented an obstacle that had to be removed sooner or later.

The apprentice strikes which broke out in Paris in the spring of 1791, following unfavourable economic conditions, provided the perfect catalyst for the final abolition of the Guilds. The previously unsuccessful Chapelier law, which forbade all professional bodies and trade associations was now passed and the *Menuisiers Ebénistes* were forced to submit. With their Guild's abolition, the Masters lost their exclusive right to the *estampille*. From the

16
Samples of Molitor's *estampille* taken from pieces of furniture.

date that the law took effect, each and every manufacturer could sign his furniture and put it on sale. Some Masters relinquished the use of the stamp; others, who had previously been denied the right, began to use it.[29] The *estampille*, which had been a control exercise by the Guild up to that time, now became a brand name by which an individual Master established his renown as a creator of furniture. Molitor used the stamp irregularly after the abolition of the Guild. From 1803–10 he sometimes affixed trade labels to his work.

17
*Secrétaire à abattant* in speckled mahogany veneer which was part of the commission supplied to the duc de Choiseul-Praslin. Typical of Revolutionary furniture, the grain of the wood forms the dominant motif, and the ormolu decoration (see also 88), is reduced to very specific areas (cat. 52).
Cleveland Museum of Art, Ohio, The Thomas L. Fawick Memorial Collection

Four years after the death of Elisabeth Fessard, Molitor remarried. On 25 Fructidor year VIII (12 September 1800) Renée Catherine Miray, the daughter of Marin Miray, and Anne-Françoise Hue, a wealthy bourgeois couple from Caen, became his wife in a ceremony that took place in Normandy.[30] In the marriage contract Molitor evaluated his fortune, including his house in the Faubourg Saint-Honoré, at 60,000 francs. Three daughters were born from this union: Elisabeth on 25 Vendémiaire year XI (12 October 1802) and twins Honorine and Hortense on Ventôse year XIII (11 March 1805). All three were baptised in the nearby church of La Madeleine.[31]

Business began to improve and the heavy demand for quality furniture,

18
Speckled mahogany veneer
commode with ormolu
mounts (see also 88, 90).
Originally part of the
commission supplied to the
duc de Choiseul-Praslin and
*en suite* with 17. The use of
ornamentation and veneer as
well as the detached, tapering
corner columns lend the piece
a remarkable fluency despite
the large surfaces involved
(cat. 27).
Private collection

which now emanated from private individuals as well as from the Consular government, found Molitor cramped and limited in his building in the Faubourg Saint-Honoré. In the spring of 1803 the *ébéniste* rented the entire building to a baker named Antoine Genevois and moved into the former *Maison du Timbre*, at the corner of the boulevard de la Madeleine and the rue Neuve du Luxembourg.[32] On the ground floor of this building, a vast sales area with show windows gave on to what had become a highly fashionable, elegant Right Bank promenade. The workshop faced away from the street, opening on to the courtyard.

On 11 February 1809, Molitor married his first daughter, Anne-Julie to Maître Dominique-Philippe Eloy, a notary from Perthe near Melun.[33]

Molitor's comfortable financial situation permitted him to give the very large sum of 19,000 *francs* to the young couple: 10,000 *francs* to his daughter, the equivalent of 3,000 *francs* in furniture and various *objets* as well as 6,000 *francs* from the bequest of her mother, Elisabeth Fessard. Michel Molitor died on 12 May 1810, at the age of seventy-six, in this third-floor room in the same building lived in by his cousin Bernard. The extent of his modest inheritance is known from the inventory drawn up on 21 May.[34] In 1813 Bernard Molitor moved his workshop and dwelling back to his own house in the Faubourg Saint-Honoré. It is possible that at this time the *ébéniste* considered reducing his production of furniture.

Following the death of her father, Marin Miray, Molitor's wife Renée came into a considerable part of her father's inheritance. The Molitors now also received regular income in rent from Bernard's property, as well as money from the real estate sales. Without doubt, such prosperity prompted the *ébéniste*, who was then 65 years old, to abandon his role in the workshop between 1818 and 1819, and to contemplate retiring. The sale of a series of cabinets to the kings of England and Prussia and to the restored monarchy in France, brought Molitor's career as an *ébéniste* to a prestigious close. From then on he was principally occupied in managing and increasing his fortune.

In the 1818 edition of the *Almanach de Commerce de Paris*, Bernard Molitor figured among the *Principaux Habitants de Paris non commerçants*'. In notarial documents, Molitor considered himself an '*ancien ébéniste*' or '*propriétaire*'.[35] From 1824 onwards he often stayed with his married daughter in Fontainebleau. The small, tranquil town appealed to the elderly man and reminded him of his youth. His repeated visits encouraged him to acquire a beautiful, recently constructed house with a garden on rue Marrier, in the centre of town. He moved in with his wife and daughters but kept an apartment in his building in the Faubourg Saint-Honoré, and rented the others.[36] In December 1832, Molitor married his daughter Elisabeth to Pierre-Joseph Debionne, a notary and Justice of the Peace from Fontainebleau with four children from his first marriage.[37] He dowered Elisabeth with an annual sum of 1,500 *francs*, the revenues from capital of 30,000 *francs*, furniture and a trousseau with a value of 5,000 *francs*. The marriage contract was signed in Paris in Molitor's building; as were all the transactions from then on.

Through his determination, and a deal of good luck, the emigrant miller's son had excelled in his craft and attained the heights of glory and success in the capital of luxury. Prosperous and living in refined surroundings, his daughters given bountiful dowries, no further proof is needed of his high social standing. Around noon, on 17 November 1833, Bernard Molitor died at the age of seventy-eight at Fontainebleau. The funeral took place the next day at the new cemetery.[38]

His will was read on 11 December 1833.[39] The exquisite furniture, the *objets d'art*, and the luxurious fittings that comprised his estate, attest to Molitor's wealth. A large part of the furniture was in mahogany while other pieces were in ebony, lacquer, citronwood and yew. Several pieces featured costly gilt bronze mounts. The styles reflect the best in fashion and taste from the period 1780–1820.[40]

Several bookcases are mentioned in the inventory drawn up after Molitor's death. There are also fourteen paintings, *pietre dure* and a marquetry

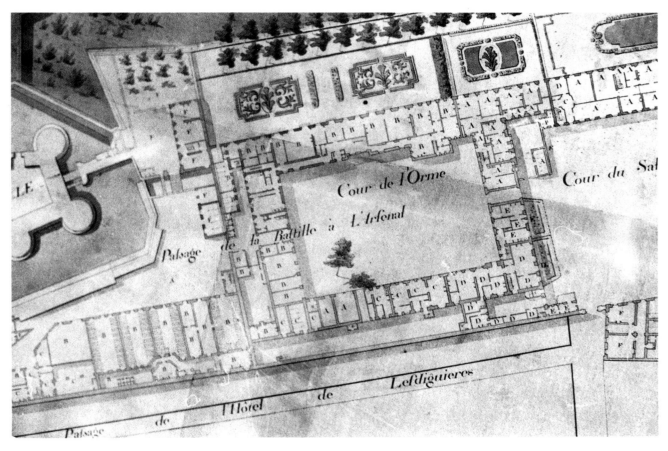

19
Michel and Bernard Molitor's rented workshop in the cour de l'Orme, located near the Bastille in the Petit Arsenal. (Premises indicated by the letter C.)
Bibliotheque Historique de la Ville, Paris

20
Cour de l'Orme in the Petit Arsenal.
Bibliothèque Historique de la Ville, Paris

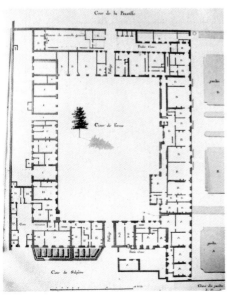

21
*Table de toilette*, originally part of the order supplied to the Choiseul-Praslin family. Its form is reminiscent of furniture made by Martin Carlin for the *marchand-mercier* Daguerre (cat. 124B). The Wallace Collection

22
Detail of 21. Marquetry tabletop inspired by English designs and remarkable for its finely-detailed execution. The overlapping ovals also demonstrate the influence of Japanese lacquer. Wallace Collection, London

picture, although their subjects are not described. He also owned some finely-framed engravings. In the dining-room at Fontainebleau a cartel clock was listed and in the bedroom, a clock is described representing Diana the Huntress. Two other clocks in bronze for which no details are given are also mentioned.

The cartel clock and that depicting Diana, were in gilt bronze on mahogany bases, covered by a glass dome. Molitor's love of fine craftsmanship manifested itself in the acquisition of bronze vases filled with artificial flowers in costly materials, lavish mirrors and a number of parlour games in exotic wooden boxes.

The *ébéniste* possessed finely decorated porcelain for all occasions. Cutlery and a complete service of solid silver tableware engraved with the initials *ABM* (Anne and Bernard Molitor) were estimated at a value of 2,786 *francs*. His wine cellar housed 1,827 bottles of various vintages. This inventory is far richer than the earlier one drawn up in 1796. The precious woods,

*fauteuils* covered in silk, porcelain, silver and elaborate mirrors described, attest to the evolution of the new bourgeoisie to which Molitor undoubtedly belonged. Before 1789, such furnishings would have been reserved for the select, wealthy few.

Molitor was one of the rare *ébénistes* of his generation who was lucky enough to finish his days in comfort. A good number of colleagues of his generation saw their work destroyed by the Revolution, and its outcome; but in his last years, while he still practised his profession, Molitor could pride himself on being the last surviving great *ébéniste* to have served the pre-Revolutionary Royal family.[41]

## Parisian progress: workshops and premises 1778–1820

Molitor always chose excellent locations for his workshops. In the privileged domain of the Arsenal, even as a sub-tenant, he was never, in effect, subjected to the laws of his trade's Guild. Molitor could produce and sell his own wares even before official election as a Master of the *Menuisiers-Ebénistes*. After becoming a member of the Guild, he established his first workshop in an appropriate area for the sale of luxury furnishing – the fashionable Faubourg Saint-Germain where many aristocrats and Parisian socialites lived. After the Revolution, he left the *Faubourg*, now deserted, to gravitate towards the new centre of society life, around the place de la Revolution (now place de la Concorde), the Madeleine and the Chaussée d'Antin.

Documents have been found which attest to the presence within the Arsenal of both Bernard and Michel Molitor from 21 September 1778.[42] Dwellings here were highly sought-after by merchants and craftsmen, eager to escape the restrictions of the guild laws. In cramped quarters, a companionable liveliness reigned among practitioners of the most diverse activities and crafts. The Molitors lived in the *Petit Arsenal de la Bastille* in courtyard number six, known as cour de l'Orme, where they sublet from Jacques Lelièvre, *sellier du Roi*.[43] The *maison* Lelièvre was situated on the left side of the courtyard coming from the cour des Salpetrière. This part of the Arsenal had been built some twenty years earlier in 1765. The exact location of their premises is marked on the map by the letter *C*.[44]

The building consisted of sixteen rooms and was among the most spacious in the *cour*. Several descriptions exist. On the ground floor was a kitchen, pantry, three large rooms and four small bedrooms. Upstairs in the *mansarde* there were five bedrooms and two attics which Lelièvre had made into bedrooms. Behind the house a courtyard extended the whole breadth of the building, with stables and two woodsheds. At the back of the courtyard a shelter had been built against the wall. This space could be used for storage, and a second floor had been built above, in which two small rooms had been installed. In 1782 Lelièvre was also sub-letting the premises to other craftsmen: Sieur Lhuillier, a pottery merchant who had his store on the premises; Demoiselle Lamy, dressmaker's apprentice; Sieur Destriches, mason; Sieur Le Barre, bridle maker and Sieur Jeune, monumental mason. The Molitors' workshop was mentioned for the first time in a complaint addressed to the police at the Châtelet concerning the theft, after working hours, of personal affairs belonging to Bernard and Michel that had been left in the workshop.[45] The workshop itself must have been located in one of the ground floor rooms, with direct access to the courtyard. If the 15,000 *francs* which Molitor had announced as his fortune, shortly before his marriage in June 1788, is taken into consideration, the room must have been sufficiently spacious to allow him to execute several orders at the same time.

In the summer of 1788, Molitor set up house with his first wife Elisabeth, on the Left Bank at the rue de Bourbon (now rue de Lille) in the Fau-

23
(previous page) *Guéridon* in solid and veneered mahogany with ormolu mounts. As Consul, Napoleon commissioned this and other pieces during the furnishing of the Château de Saint-Cloud in the spring of 1803 (cat. 98). Musée National, Château de Versailles

VUE DE L'HÔTEL DE SALMS.

bourg Saint-Germain.[46] He rented a workshop and lodgings in a building belonging to Etienne Trompette, *entrepreneur en menuiserie des Bâtiments de la Couronne*. The *maison Trompette* was situated at the corner of rue de Bourbon and rue de Bellechasse. Michel Molitor continued to live at the Arsenal, but, for the periods during which he collaborated with Bernard, he sometimes stayed with the family. The wide, airy streets of the quarter were lined with *hôtels* and gardens: the Faubourg Saint-Germain was the wealthiest and most distinguished area in pre-Revolutionary Paris. It was hence no accident that Molitor chose to move there. The opulence of life in the Faubourg gave rise to a constant demand for luxurious furnishings and precious *objets d'art* – an ideal situation for the establishment of an *ébéniste's* workshop.

The ornamental work executed by Molitor would suggest that he and Trompette, renowned for his work for the Crown, often collaborated on the creation of luxurious interiors. The names cited in Molitor's 1796 inventory were proof that the majority of his clients lived in the Faubourg or its periphery.

Molitor's workshop was situated in the ground floor of Trompette's building; a place for wood storage was to be found behind the house. Directly opposite, on the rue de Bellechasse, the Hôtel de Salm had just been

24
Engraving by Neé after a drawing by Meunier. The Molitors rented a workshop and apartment in Etienne Trompette's house on the corner of the rue de Bourbon (now rue de Lille) and rue de Bellechasse, opposite the Hôtel de Salm (now Musée de la Légion d'Honneur). Private collection

25
Small *bureau plat* in solid and veneered ebony with ormolu mounts. The pure, sober outline, the choice of wood and the exceptional quality of the mounts characterize post-Revolutionary, luxury furniture (cat. 132).
Private collection

erected (now the Hôtel de la Légion d'Honneur). Designed by the architect Pierre Rousseau for the prince de Salm, this *hôtel* represented one of the most modern private constructions of the period. The *beau monde* considered the receptions and parties given by the prince to be among the most brilliant that Paris had to offer in the years preceding the Revolution. Also close by, behind the buildings at the very end of rue de Bellechasse, near the *quais* of the Seine, and facing the Tuileries gardens, were the fashionable baths of Sieur Albert.

Molitor paid a rent of 830 *livres* for his workshop and lodgings, a sum he duly delivered every year to Etienne Trompette on 1 July. The layout of the space is included in the inventory of 1796. Situated behind a large front

26
(opposite) Detail of 25. The outer sides of the uprights are decorated with large palm fronds executed in both matt and burnished ormolu. The satinwood drawer lining contrasts admirably with the dark ebony.

door, the ground-floor workshop was lit by two large windows which gave on to rue de Bellechasse. A small room adjoining the workshop served as the Molitors' kitchen, below which lay the wine cellar. A room on the first floor, the *étage noble*, had been converted into a furniture store with two large windows opening on to the rue de Bourbon. The Molitors' best room, with a window opening on to the street, on the *étage noble*, served as the furniture showroom – ample proof of the Molitor's acute business sense.

This overlapping of professional and private lives was customary within the Guild-system, where collaborators or apprentices were received as family members. Family life for Bernard and Elisabeth was centred on rooms in the mezzanine, between the workshop and the showroom. The windows

of their *salon* were directly below the furniture showroom. There was a small attic storeroom and at the back, a small bedroom *en mansarde* had been furnished for their daughter Anne-Julie. Directly off the *salon*, the couple's bedroom was large with a window opening on to the courtyard. An anteroom completed the mezzanine apartment. On the third floor, small rooms must have been used as dormitories for certain workshop helpers.[47] The workshop was equipped with eight workbenches, six whetstones, and numerous tools; its general state was considered mediocre and the overall estimate of the value of its equipment came to 156 *livres*.[48] Eight workers could be accommodated at the same time with one or two helpers – an average size for the workshop of a Guild Master of the period.

It should be noted that Molitor worked in these peaceful conditions for only a very short time before the Revolution broke out.

On the land behind the house, the 1796 inventory reveals that the depot was stocked with large amounts of wood used for the manufacture of furniture, including a wide range of exotic timbers, for example: planks of mahogany, sheets of veneer and citronwood.[49] To carry out the inventory, the amount of local timber had to be estimated from the lengths in stock, while exotic timbers were valued by weight. The total value came to 1,132 *livres* and 16 *sous*. The types of timber listed corresponded to those noted in Molitor's accounts and to those which we know him to have used most consistently. Other materials were itemized, such as stock of pre-wrought brass used for inlays. The presence of a wide variety of marbles in the workshop is significant. The entries here include slabs of *Languedoc blanc veiné, chipotin blanc, griotte, vert de mer, marbre de couleur* and even a tabletop with inlays of *pietra dura*. It is supposed that the marble came from Berder, a supplier located in the rue de Sèvres.

The diversity of the furniture displayed was remarkable, proving Molitor's commercial prowess in being able to offer to his clients a large range of models on a regular basis. In the warehouse there were: a *bureau plat* on castors, four *secrétaires*, seven commodes, a lady's *secrétaire*, a *bonheur-du-jour*, two *armoires*, a bookcase and two dressing tables. The number of games tables is surprising; among them *tables à brelan* and *tables à trictrac*. The designation of *tables à la Pompadour* given to two tables in particular is surprising given that the Revolution was in full progress at the time. In the warehouse were stocked '*quatre garnitures de sceaux argentés pour des servantes*'. Thirteen tables are listed: *tables à manger, guéridons, tables à déjeuner*, with round or polygonal tops.[50] *Tables à manger*, similar to the dining tables known today, with four legs or a central pillar, came into fashion in the 1780s. When the English custom of taking tea became fashionable, a new type of table had to be devised, with a large, main table-top surmounted by a smaller one, designed for the *fontaine à thé* to stand on, which allowed tea to be served in the *salons*.

Special attention should be given to a *guéridon garnie en acier*. This use of polished steel was a recent innovation for *ébénistes*, and proof of their continuing interest in new materials with the aim of satisfying the extravagant tastes of a newly-rich clientèle avid for novelty.[51]

That four chairs, (not previously recognized by the Guild as *ébénisterie*) should figure in the *ébéniste's* inventory is not surprising, since all such professional strictures were abolished in 1791. One supposes that Molitor had made them himself. All the models presented a similar form and style of execution. The chairs in mahogany veneer were inlaid with brass wire which corresponded to a technique often employed on larger pieces.

Prices varied according to the elegance and style of the model chosen:

50 to 600 *livres* for a bureau, 120 to 250 *livres* for a commode, 30 to 120 *livres* for a *table à manger*. The four chairs cost 86 *livres*. The most expensive item, *un secrétaire de femme, orné de bronzes dorés au mat*, was estimated at 1,200 *livres*. The storeroom list allows us to build up a faithful picture of the workshop and of the variety of pieces produced for a demanding clientèle.

Once Molitor had achieved prominence in wealthy Parisian circles, he had no difficulty under the *ancien régime* in selling his wares. After the demise of the aristocracy, he was obliged to seek other clients outside the Faubourg Saint-Germain. The Revolution left certain parts of Paris, notably

27
Mahogany *lit de repos*. After the abolition of the Guilds in 1791, *ébénistes* were authorized to make seat furniture (cat. 156B)
Collection B.B. Steinitz

28
Cuban mahogany commode
from the Consular period. The
Egyptian terms, escutcheons
and feet are all notable for
their exceptional quality
(cat. 31).
Private collection

the Faubourg Saint-Germain, deserted for years to come. The *hôtels* of the aristocrats had been seized and put up for sale. Their owners had fled and if they returned to Paris at all, they were either impoverished or had been sentenced to death.

It was only with the establishment of the Empire that the Faubourg came to life again.[52] During the same period, other areas became equally fashionable. Already, before the Revolution, the Right Bank and the Place Louis XV (later place de la Révolution and now place de la Concorde) had been the scene of important events and brilliant festivities. With the opening in 1791 of the pont de la Nation (now pont de la Concorde), which was completed after 1789 with stones from the Bastille, a vital new link was created between the two banks of the river Seine. The nearby Faubourg Saint-Honoré became the fastest-developing quarter in Paris. The construction of the Church of the Madeleine, which had been suspended in 1790, recommenced while property speculation re-animated the area around the place de la Révolution, up towards the Champs-Elysées, over to the boulevard de la Madeleine and further north to Chaussée d'Antin. The literary salons of the Faubourg Saint-Honoré became the centre of attraction for the Parisian bourgeoisie in the post-Revolutionary period.

Not surprisingly, Molitor sought to move into this area. His aforementioned business acumen and his perception of the emergence of a new kind of clientèle told him that a change of banks and Faubourgs was in order and would lead to prosperous times in the *nouveau Paris*. Rather than his customers ordering furniture from their homes, they would increasingly buy previously prepared pieces which they would have seen in his shop. As we have seen, Molitor acquired his building in the Faubourg Saint-Honoré at auction on 15 Prairial year VIII (4 June 1800) and moved in between 6 June and 9 July 1801.[53] Strategically situated at the 'entrance' to the Faubourg, on the corner of rue Royale, the grandly designed six-storey building, with two windows in each level, had been built as an investment with a view to renting it out. One of the three terraced buildings constructed during the *Régence* by a stone merchant, the plot was unusually narrow for the quarter and the architect had sought to exploit the available space to the utmost.[54] This was not the general case for the *Faubourg*; further in from rue Royale, plots were spacious and large hôtels had been erected. Molitor's sales and showroom area occupied the whole front of the building with a large shop window, unusual for the period. The workshop had been fitted out at the back and between the two areas, leading off the shop, was the Molitors' dining-room. With a chimneypiece and windows which opened on to the courtyard, the dining-room communicated directly with the pantry, which in turn led into the kitchen. Adjoining the kitchen, behind a vestibule and a nearby office, the workshop consisted of one large and two small rooms and was probably lit by a sky-light. Overall, the plans for the building show cramped quarters on an overbuilt plot, totally inadequate for a workshop with a substantial turnover.

Despite the two rooms which the *ébéniste* had retained in a building nearby in his former workshop on rue de Bourbon (now rue de Lille) space was lacking.[55] Molitor soon realised that the rue Royale, saturated by traffic

29
View of 28 with the doors open revealing four drawers without rails. In addition to the unified effect created by the veneer, the attention to interior detail is typical of Molitor's superior pieces.

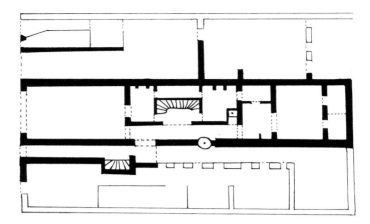

entering and leaving the Faubourg, just outside the old city gates, was inappropriate for his needs. In spite of the agreement he had concluded with his neighbour, the *charcutier* Monsieur Trianon, who let Molitor use his entrance for deliveries, the *ébéniste* decided that he must move once again. He moved to 1 boulevard de la Madeleine and rented his building on the rue Royale to the baker Antoine Genevois from 1 Germinal year XI (22 March 1803), as is related in the *Almanach de Commerce Parisien* from year XII (1803–4).[56]

The surveyor's plan for Molitor's new premises in the former *Maison du Timbre* show a building which was clearly conceived as a business premises, with large show windows on the ground floor overlooking the street.[57] The workshop was probably located in a back courtyard. The building's corner site, with a large portal on the rue Neuve de Luxembourg, permitted easy access for deliveries.[58]

This move to larger quarters was not simply motivated by Molitor's need for additional workshop and sales space, with typical foresight, he was also setting up shop in what was one of the most fashionable areas during the Consular period. The boulevard de la Madeleine was the prolongation of a great circular way which followed the old city ramparts, dating from Louis XIV, all the way to the Bastille. Besides theatres, the opera, tea salons, restaurants, panoramas and public baths, numerous shops selling luxury goods had opened at its upper end.[59] *Le Petit Coblentz*, the Royalist promenade, was also nearby. The boulevard had always been a magnet for Parisian high-life and its significance increased after the Revolution. All that was new was first presented there in the hope of receiving public approval and thus ensuring success. Molitor remained here until 1812, when he returned to his house in the Faubourg Saint-Honoré.[60]

From now on, in his personal documents, Molitor describes himself as a *marchand* or as a *fabricant de meubles*. From these designations it can be

30
Molitor's building at 9 rue du Faubourg Saint-Honoré. The plan shows that the workshop was situated behind the shop which had a showroom facing on to the Faubourg. Molitor and his family lived upstairs. (After A.N.f. 31 45/118).

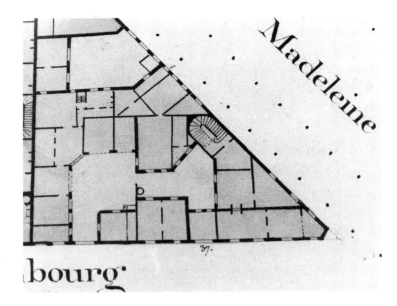

deduced that he bought furniture from subcontractors in the Faubourg Saint-Antoine, to sell at a profit, as other merchants had once bought from him. Molitor remained the director of his workshop until he was in his sixties and retired between 1818/20. A sale of cabinets to the *Garde-Meuble* is the last-documented transaction of his career.

The *ébéniste* had always rented out a part of his building on the Faubourg Saint-Honoré. However, it would seem that he had kept his workshop as, even in 1832 when Molitor was seventy-seven years old, it was still excluded from rental leases.[61] Probably he continued to practice his craft, producing pieces for his personal use, until a great age. In the inventory drawn up in 1869 after his daughter Elisabeth's death, various tools were listed. Discovered in the attic at Fontainebleau, they were thought to have come from the Paris workshop, having been transferred there when Molitor's building was rented in 1846.[62]

## Workers and collaborators

From various sources come details concerning Molitor's workers, the main document being the inventory compiled after his wife's death in 1796. Other references can be gleaned from the papers of craftsmen from whom Molitor purchased pieces and materials. In certain cases the furniture itself is helpful in substantiating theories of collaboration. The origins of certain design elements, especially on those pieces which are stamped, can also be a basis for attribution. Little is known about the craftsmen forming Molitor's team of assistants: only two are known by name. Michel Molitor is already familiar to us, and was certainly present on a regular basis. In 1796, Bernard Molitor still owed him 1,500 *livres* for work which he had produced since 1791. In an official paper concerning guardianship of the Molitors' young daughter Anne-Julie, the name of Jacques Raveneau appears as living in the Molitors' house and working in the workshop. The scarcity of information concerning employees at the time of the inventory might indicate the equal scarcity of

31
Molitor's premises at 1 boulevard de la Madeleine, rented in 1803. This corner location provided large windows for the shop area and easy access to the workshop in the back courtyard through a large gateway.
Archives Nationales F-3174

32
Commode in speckled mahogany veneer with ormolu mounts. The large base, the flanking detached columns and the high frieze are characteristic of Empire furniture. Such high quality veneer and mounts were reserved for the most luxurious pieces (cat. 26). Private collection

33
Mahogany *pupitre* with ormolu mounts, one of Molitor's later works. Winged female figures extending candle holders flank a framed painting on glass (dated 1814) which forms a screen (cat. 78). Private collection

work in the difficult years following the Revolution. Unfortunately, the letters concerning orders and employees' hours do not record the identity of the workers. With eight workbenches installed it would seem, however, that Molitor had hired at least as many workers in the most prosperous years of his production.

A number of sources testify to a link between Molitor's workshop and the *ébéniste* Félix Rémond. In 1806, when Rémond supplied a *table de toilette* to the Empress Josephine, he was residing in Molitor's house at 37 rue Neuve-du-Luxembourg.[63] The mastery of the marquetry on the side panels of this table, (which is still on display at Malmaison) is reminiscent of the shell motifs found on work by Molitor. Rémond may have been apprenticed to Molitor before opening his own workshop.[64]

Molitor's 1796 inventory and the list of his debts show that he was supplied with marble by Monsieur Berder on rue de Sèvres – Molitor owed him 110 *livres* as well as 150 *livres* to Sieur Chaille, a supplier of polished steel in the Faubourg Saint-Denis, dating from 1793. Other debts included 447 *livres* to the joiner Jean-Baptiste Demay for work supplied in the months of Fructidor.[65] 29 *livres* were owed to the locksmith Virieux while other creditors remained nameless – among them a draughtsman, a copper turner and a wood turner. The *ébéniste* and furniture tradesman Joseph Sintz was named as a second expert for the inventory, along with Etienne Trompette. As friends of the family they were named guardians of Anne-Julie Molitor, still a minor. On 5 Fructidor year IX (24 August 1801), Sintz and Molitor rendered their joint conclusions in a matter of furniture appraisal.[66]

There is no doubt about Etienne Trompette's collaboration with Molitor on the important commission to execute a set of doors for the Tuileries. The order had come about through the good offices of Sieur Auguste Renard, architect, who was Molitor's neighbour on the rue de Lille (rue de Bourbon),

34
Ebony and Japanese lacquer *bonheur-du-jour* adorned with ormolu mounts. It was bought in 1816 for the future King of England, George IV, and delivered to Carlton House (cat. 68A).
Royal Collection, by kind permission of H. M. The Queen

35
Bookcase, *en suite* with 34. It combines Empire forms with pre-Revolutionary ormolu mounts and construction techniques (cat. 68B).
Royal Collection, by kind permission of H. M. The Queen.

and certainly knew his work. Renard may, in fact, have been responsible for a good number of commissions. His brother-in-law by his first marriage was Joseph Zimmerman, the instrument-maker, who may also have worked with Molitor.

On 28 Pluviôse year VIII (17 February 1800), Molitor and J.-H. Riesener were named co-arbiters by the *Tribunal du Commerce* in a legal despute between the two *ébénistes* – Pierre Antoine Bellangé and Xavier Hindermeyer. The co-arbiters for the opposing party were Georges Jacob and Claude Mathieu Magnien. It is here, in the litigation proceedings, that the names of Molitor and Riesener appear side-by-side for the first and only time. The choice of arbiters was particularly significant for it showed that the new social order acknowledged and respected the renown of former Guild Masters, such as these four expert craftsmen.[67]

In July 1801 the joiner and wood carver Pierre-Gaston Brion is recorded as working with Molitor's workshop.[68] Another probable collaborator, although no documents exist as proof, seems to have been the *marchand-mercier*, Dominique Daguerre.[69] Before the Revolution, Daguerre enjoyed a monopoly on the sale of porcelain plaques from the Sèvres factory, plus Japanese lacquer panels and certain types of ormolu mounts. When Daguerre died in 1793, Martin Eloy Lignereux carried on his business. Molitor used ormolu mounts identical to those on furniture supplied by Daguerre, and subsequently he must also have been ordering through Daguerre and Lignereux. Certain other designs for ormolu mounts came from Thomire, and Molitor continued to be supplied by him after Thomire and Duterme took over Lignereux's affairs in 1804.

In the inventory drawn up after Michel Molitor's death in 1810, it is apparent that he had placed certain of his own pieces on consignment in Antoine-Thibaut Baudouin's boutique. Baudouin was the most famous Parisian merchant of furniture and luxury furnishing; the showroom in his mansion on rue Grange-Batelière was an essential port of call for fashionable visitors to the capital.

*Ebéniste* and business man

Molitor's professional itinerary conjures up the image of a man who, above and beyond his talents as a craftsman, possessed a predisposition to succeed in the French capital. His business acumen was confirmed soon after his arrival, with the setting up of his own workshop in the domain of the Arsenal where privileged enterprise reigned, allowing craftsmen to sell their wares directly to the *marchands-merciers*. Fourteen of Molitor's advertisements appeared in the daily *Les petites annonces, affiches et avis divers*, during the period 1778–87.[70] The first concerned an anti-bedbug ointment, safe for household use, the efficacy of which Molitor would personally attest to (*doc* 1). From 1781 he also publicized *chaufferettes à la comtesse*, handwarmers presented in a book-shaped wooden case into which a hot briquette was inserted in a tinplate box, isolating it from the touch. Fashionable ladies carried them in winter to the theatre, to mass, or used them as bed warmers. Small articles such as this were much sought-after by the *marchands-merciers* for resale. Molitor's production showed that he was capable of securing a demand in an already saturated market, where cleverness and novelty were the keys to success. After his admittance into the *Menuisiers Ebénistes* he wisely organized his workshop to sell directly to the public, thus eliminating the intermediaries and increasing his own profit margin. His work was admired: the parquet floor at the Château de Fontainebleau was much-

36
One of Molitor's advertisements in *Les petites affiches . . .*, 1782. Private collection

Le fieur *Molitor*, Ebénifte, cour de l'Orme, à l'Arcenal, a perfectionné fes CHAUFFRETTES *à la Comtesse*, faites en forme de livre, dont on peut fe fervir à l'églife, en voiture, au fpectacle & en voyage : *prix en bois de noyer 18 liv. & en bois d'acajou 24 liv.*

37
Mahogany veneer *jardinière* with ormolu mounts. Here the *ébéniste* has re-used the case of an old musical clock, placing it on a pillared stand. The ormolu decoration dating from the Restoration confirms this as a late work (cat. 153A). Private collection

acclaimed and an early testimony to his professional relations with the most renowned craftsmen and notable patrons of the day.[71]

The correlation between Molitor's work at Fontainebleau, his acceptance as a Guild Master and his marriage the following year has already been noted. The marriage contract with Elisabeth Fessard declared his fortune at 15,000 *livres*, consisting of various cabinet-making merchandise '*dettes actives, deniers comptants*' and personal property. The sum is even more impressive when one considers the short time for which the *ébéniste* had been practising as a Master. In 1789 his name is among those on the *liste générale*

*des Maîtres Menuisiers Ebénistes*. Advertisements appeared concerning his workshop in various editions of the elegant *Almanach de Commerce de Paris* before 1789.[72]

In 1784, under the direction of Thierry de Ville D'Avray, the new administration of the *Garde-Meuble* had received directives to limit spending. However, large sums were appropriated to the refurbishing of the Château de Saint-Cloud from 1785 to 1789, which were manifestly covered up in the Royal accounts. Between 1789 and 1792 important commissions were recorded by the *Garde-Meuble* attesting to the insouciance of the Royal Family and illustrating their economic priorities in the period which preceded the fall of Louis XVI. Things changed abruptly in 1792. Largely dependent on exports, the prosperity of the French luxury goods industry was directly affected by the Revolution as foreign orders came to a halt between 1792 and 1795. However, the *Almanach de commerce de Paris* began publication soon after the institution of the *Directoire* in November 1795, confirming the industry's renaissance. From 1798, Molitor regularly advertised in the *Almanach* until his workshop closed in 1818.

On 1 Brumaire year XI (23 October 1802), after his second marriage, Molitor received an advance of 9,000 *francs* on his future inheritance from his wealthy father-in-law.[73] By 1805 Molitor had absorbed all his debts and his financial situation even permitted him to lend money.[74] His subsequent fiscal dealings constituted a regular, additional source of income and continued to occupy him even after he closed his workshop. In a typical transaction, he acquired at auction a building on the rue Sainte-Marguerite in the Faubourg Saint-Antoine, in October 1816. The building had belonged to his brother-in-law before the latter's bankcruptcy. Molitor first rented, then resold it in March 1826.[75]

Several years were necessary to complete the technicalities concerning the will of Molitor's father-in-law Miray, who died in 1815. In the terms of the testament the Molitors acquired land, estates and buildings in and around Caen. Besides his share of the inheritance, Molitor also acquired further family shares at auction in 1817. This property represented yet another substantial source of income for the *ébéniste*.[76] In the summer of 1828, Molitor bought his comfortable house in Fontainebleau, with its impressive portal, a garden and storage building.[77]

Several short trips to Paris notwithstanding, he resided there on a permanent basis with his wife and unmarried daughter Honorine. The inven-

38
Detail of 37.

tory drawn up after his death gives a clear idea of the considerable fortune passed on to his heirs.

## Public Patrons and Commissions

It is extremely difficult to attribute a precise date or provenance to many of Molitor's pieces. Records concerning his pre-Revolutionary production are rare indeed – be they inventories, auction catalogues or bills. This is no doubt due in part to the relatively short period between his acceptance into the Guild and the outbreak of the Revolution. However, two Royal commissions for fine *ébénisterie* are known. Later recollections by the comte and comtesse de Clarac, and other notable contemporaries, testified that Molitor's talents, as displayed at Fontainebleau, had earned him the favour of Marie-Antoinette, although this cannot be confirmed, since all that now remains of the ledgers and documents concerning the Queen's *Garde-Meuble* are a few meagre fragments.[78] The names of private patrons are sufficiently eloquent

39
Molitor's house at 7 rue Marrier, Fontainebleau.

40
Engraving by Godefroy and Massard of Louis XVI, dated 1789. Following the fall of 1787, the annual Royal visit to Fontainebleau was cancelled.
Private collection

 LOUIS XVI.

41
Attributed to Alexander
Kucharsky. Portrait of Marie-
Antoinette *c.*1789.
Private collection

42
Detail of the marquetry table
top for the *table de toilette* (see
21 and 22) supplied to the
Choiseul-Praslin family.
The Wallace Collection

proof of the extraordinary success of Molitor's creations, but it is unusual, however, to find documented information concerning his buyers. The reputedly prestigious provenance of some works, which have been passed down within the same family for generations, can rarely be supported on paper. With the temporary closing of the *Garde-Meuble* in Messidor year V (June 1797) we lose the most important source of information for precise dating.[79] State commissions only recommenced several years later with the Consular government and the creation of a new *Garde-Meuble*.

Some commissions, however can be traced. There were several orders for the Château de Saint-Cloud by the then Consul, Napoleon, in 1803; Emperor Napoleon commissioned furniture in 1811; and between 1808 and 1812 the Emperor's brother Jérôme, King of Westphalia, furnished his Kassel residences with works supplied by Molitor. During the period 1816–20 there are records concerning two orders from George IV of England (then Regent), and later from Louis XVIII. After 1800 other pieces can also be dated with the help of existing records.

Prior to the fall of the monarchy in August 1792, two separate commissions are recorded through the intermediary of the *Bâtiments du Roi*. In 1787

Molitor received commissions for several projects concerning alterations to the interior of the Château at Fontainebleau and in 1792 he was also commissioned to make a set of double doors in mahogany for the Tuileries.

The Queen's *Cabinet de retraite:* Château de Fontainebleau 1787

The architect Pierre Rousseau, in charge of the remodelling work at Fontainebleau, secured Molitor his commission for the parquet in Marie-Antoinette's *cabinet de retraite*. Rousseau and his colleague Potain were given free rein in the choice of craftsmen.[80] The comte d'Angiviller, *Surintendant des Bâtiments du Roi*, was responsible for overseeing the financial outlay for the project. Royal spending being closely scrutinized at the time, quality at a reasonable price was all-important. The works thus provided an opportunity for young, talented craftsmen to prove their worth with an enviable Royal commission. The plans for the *cabinet* were left with Potain, *Intendant des*

*Bâtiments*, at Fontainebleau on 4 March 1787. Potain submitted them to Louis XVI a week later. With the King's approval, work was speeded up for completion before the annual royal visit to the Château, but Rousseau received a message on 29 July from Paris cancelling the visit, by which time the work had virtually been completed. Other work was carried out by Molitor at Fontainebleau over the summer of 1787. The bill for his services came to a total of 9,971 *livres*, but was negotiated to the sum of 7,549.13 *livres*. All that is definitely known of the work executed at the Château is the parquet in mahogany featuring a central motif depicting a compass card intermingled with the Queen's cypher. No documents exist describing Molitor's other work at Fontainebleau.[81]

The Tuileries doors: 1792

Mahogany doors were executed by Molitor for the Royal apartments in the Château des Tuileries. They are now lost, but descriptions exist. In the summer of 1792, Molitor received the order originating from Auguste Renard, *Inspecteur des Bâtiments* and *Deuxième architecte du Roi*, to execute two doors in mahogany with ormolu hinges.[82] This commission seems to have been planned within the scope of the modifications to the Château, intended to facilitate the imprisonment of the Royal Family.[83]

In the presence of Renard, Molitor delivered the two doors to the *Garde-Meuble de la République* on 13 Messidor year III (1 July 1795), following the Terror. On the same day, the painter Thibaut delivered 'two gilt door casings'; the locksmith Aubert 'parts of the hinges in copper and with two locks' and the joiner Trompette 'parts for the establishment of a frame for two doors'.

At the time of delivery, the value of the doors was estimated at the exorbitant sum of 20,000 *livres*. This surprisingly large amount could be explained by the rampant rate of inflation that followed the Terror. We have no record of payment for this work; the 1796 inventory records only the registration of 286 *livres* in *Le grand livre de la dette publique*, a register in which artists and craftsmen who had worked for the Crown could enter debts to be recovered.[84] Until 1797, the doors remained in the warehouse of the *Garde-Meuble*, where they had been kept since their delivery four years earlier.[85] With the institution of the *Directoire* and the transfer of government to the Palais du Luxembourg, the need arose to restore that building's former splendours and to furnish it appropriately. Money available for the purchase of furniture was limited, and the members of the government had to resort to the stock reserves of the *Garde-Meuble* in order to fit out their apartments and offices.

From the extant descriptions of the Molitor doors, it would seem that they were still considered modern when, five years after their conception, they were delivered to the *Service de Palais Directorial* on 8 Germinal year V (29 March 1797).[86] It would also seem that the doors were actually installed.

However, the Palais de Luxembourg underwent modifications in the middle of the ninteenth century and it is possible that during the renovations they were destroyed. Whatever the case, all trace of them has now disappeared. Both the detailed description drawn up upon delivery, and a later one made when the doors were transferred to the Palais de Luxembourg, agree on their sober-looking character, which invited comparison with the furniture of the Republican period.[87]

The mahogany doors were each 392 cm in height and 74 cm wide, simply but handsomely decorated with eight mouldings, eight studs and as many ormolu rosettes. The hinges were ostentatiously apparent. The doors were probably constructed in the classical fashion – a frame fitted with recessed panels – but they may have been made using solid panels of secondary wood, which were then completely veneered. Their sobriety, in any case, was not the result of restrictive economic measures, but constituted a voluntary aesthetic choice, reflecting a return to the severe *goût à l'antique*, even in the furnishings of the royal apartments.

Prior to the institution of the Consular government, the services of the *Garde-Meuble* has been temporarily dissolved and its stocks of furniture and fittings were freely disposed of. During these years there were virtually no significant official commissions for furniture. The Revolution accelerated the renewal of a generation of craftsmen at the zenith of their art. The oldest-established practitioners lost their working capital and were forced into liquidation, while others retired or changed their profession leaving the way clear for younger workers.[88]

The Château de
Saint-Cloud

Following the decision by the First Consul to renovate the Château de Saint-Cloud, Citoyen Pfister, *Intendant de la maison du Consul*, began to commission various pieces of furniture, bronzes and other decorative objects in the years X and XI (1801–3). After serving as a dance hall during the Revolution, the Château was restored and refurnished by the Consul for the sum of 1,347,567 *francs*. An inspection of the list of craftsmen participating attests to the limited number of Parisian workshops then capable of undertaking the necessary high quality of work that was demanded. Among the craftsmen appointed, Molitor figured as the only great *ébéniste* who had been active before 1789, and whose workshop had survived the Revolution. It was only after 1802 that the growing importance of state commissions was capable of challenging the talents of a new generation of craftsmen.[89] It is generally considered that the two *guéridons* by Molitor, 23 and 44, were part of the shipment to the Château de Saint-Cloud, as both carry the castle's cipher of a fire-brand.

Napoleonic patronage
1804–14

Under Napoleon I, the administration of the *Garde-Meuble* adopted a non-commital attitude towards Molitor's workshop. There seems to be no satisfactory reason to explain this short coming. Molitor's manifest royalism should no longer be entertained as the sole reason for the *ébéniste's* paucity of official commissions. The disdainful attitude of the *Garde-Meuble*, was especially harsh if we consider that Molitor's works, and all the extant documents, testify to the brilliant productions and sales that the *ébéniste* realized for other patrons during the Empire.

Other questions should also be raised. The Royal Châteaux, emptied of their furniture by the sales held during the Revolution, were refurnished with great magnificence by Napoleon, but it is probable that the government, in its efforts to industrialize and promote factories, had a policy of favouring and appointing certain workshops which would then serve as model enterprises, at the expense of others. This state of affairs was manifest until the economic crisis of 1806, following the continental blockade. The

43
Gerard, portrait of Napoleon as Consul, dated 1803. After the sale of all its furnishings, the Château de Saint-Cloud became a public dance hall. Napoleon decided to refurnish it in 1802–3 as his personal country residence.
Private collection

NAPOLÉON

44
(opposite) *Guéridon* in mahogany veneer with ormolu mounts. It bears the mark of the Château de Saint-Cloud where it was delivered by Molitor in 1803 (cat. 97). Château de Versailles, Petit Trianon

development of the Jacob-Desmalter factory is a good illustration of the effects of these factors.[90]

It should also be noted that Molitor never participated in the industrial fairs, annual events since 1801, which awarded prizes to the best craftsmen.

An examination of his *oeuvre* shows that Molitor preferred to carry on the tradition of small workshops, executing a limited production of the highest quality, rather than evolving towards a larger factory, turning out mass-

produced items, with the inevitable loss of quality. During the economic crisis, after 1807, the State began to invest in various French workshops and industries. Besides looking for the best possible return on its investments, an assessment of the political convictions of individual Masters played a direct role in determining who was eligible for this aid. The appraisal of the Jacob-Desmalter factory, quoted in the *Avis de Préfet* is a case in point: 'The Prefect of the Department and the Prefect of the Police join together to give the most favourable information concerning this factory and particularly on the morality of the individual who directs it'.[91] Other workshops, beside Molitor's, were overlooked and only received commissions after the return to power of the Bourbons. Molitor's only documented State commission from this period concerns a dozen chairs for the offices of the administrators of the *Garde-Meuble* which were ordered in 1809. On 5 January 1810, he delivered twelve chairs to the *Guarde-Meuble* for which he received the sum of 433.20 *francs* (*doc 7*).[92] A description furnishes us with details of their design: 12 chairs, with walnut *dossiérs à planche*, covered in yellow leather with gilt nails *leur galon faux*'. The next day, the concierge of the Palais des Tuileries, Mogé, went to claim them for the employees working in the offices of the Ministry of Finance.

These chairs correspond to a sober model featuring a spade back and sabre legs (as illustrated in the catalogue, 167). Subsequently, in 1811, Molitor was awarded other commissions within a specific programme of economic support.[93]

After the Revolution, the loss of earnings in the various sectors of the luxury goods industry, and particularly that of the *ébénistes*, was a constant problem. Foreign commerce was especially disrupted since France was at war with virtually all of Europe. Moreover, the European markets were overrun with a glut of old-fashioned French furniture which had been dispersed during the Revolutionary sales. The renewed demand for luxury items after 1795 was still completely insufficient to provide a livelihood for the numerous Parisian *ébénistes* and their suppliers. One solution was to furnish French ministries and the official residences of the Empire with furniture produced in France. This alternative was widely employed, and during the Napoleonic occupation, French Empire furniture was imported to numerous European countries. In year VII (1798) the Ministry of the Interior contemplated exporting Parisian furniture to Egypt. The project was abandoned and instead a lottery was organized in Paris.[94]

The agitations of April 1789, including the pillaging of the Reveillon wallpaper factory, and the events leading up to 14 July, had their roots in the artisans' quarter – the Faubourg Saint-Antoine. Hard times in the Faubourg had previously led to explosive unrest, and had even triggered the Revolution, mindful of this, Napoleon announced an important decree on 9 May 1811, increasing the annual budget allowance for Imperial furnishings by

350,000 *francs*.[95] This had the dual aim of both refurbishing the ministeries and the Château de Versailles and forestalling further tumultuous events in the Faubourg. Commissions were addressed to 120 underworked Parisian *ébénistes* and joiners. *Marchands-merciers* were excluded from the measures. Marked by a sense of rationalism and the desire for economic rehabilitation, the scheme aimed to employ between 1,600 and 2,000 craftsmen and their respective suppliers (locksmiths, carvers, polishers and dealers in marble) for forty-five days. A first series of commissions was launched and work was completed some 65,342 *francs* under budget, due to the withdrawal of several workshops, and to tight price negotiations. With the excess, a second series could be considered.[96] Before assigning these latest commissions to particular workshops, a list was drawn up by the Ministry which was divided into two categories. One applied to *ébénisterie* in mahogany, or other con-

tinental veneers for the official reception rooms in ministerial buildings, the other concerned furniture '*pour domestiques*' made in solid local timber. Given that these commissions were particularly destined for those workshops with financial difficulties, or even facing bankruptcy, the inclusion in the list of Molitor and other renowned *ébénistes* demonstrates the complete extent of the crisis experienced by the trade.[97]

A first order reached Molitor on 20 May 1811. The Master committed himself to execute the pieces after a design furnished by the *Garde-Meuble*, to

45
In 1810 Molitor supplied a dozen chairs to the *Garde-Meuble*. From descriptions in the buying order and the delivery receipt we know that they were stylistically based on the Antique *Klismos* chair (cat. 170A–F).
Private Collection

complete, and to mark them with his *estampille* within two to three months. An inspector from the *Garde-Meuble* passed by the workshop daily to ensure the faithful execution of the pieces as dictated in the contract. Molitor's commission consisted of twenty-two items in mahogany. The most important part of the commission concerned the manufacture of ten console tables, all of the same design but of varying lengths: '*consoles en acajou à dessus de marbre de 4 pieds ½ de devant à double balustre, pieds de derrière à pilastres profilé de moulures, tablettes d'entrejambe en acajou massif, le marbre petit granit*'. The commission also included six oval *tables à manger* with folding leaves and six *tables à jeux*. A note dated 2 June 1811, confirmed that the order had been executed and delivered according to instructions. There is no trace today of either the tables or the consoles in the *Mobilier National*.[98]

A second commission stipulated a deadline of 31 May 1811, for two *secrétaires* and two commodes. Both models exceeded the estimated price by more than 450 *francs* each. The general estimate had listed the price of a *secrétaire* at 300 francs, and a *commode* at 250 *francs*.[99] The *Garde-Meuble* delivery form carried the date 7 June 1811. The entire commission totalled 7,460

46
*Secrétaire abattant* in burr elm veneer executed as part of Napoleon's special commission of 1811 to support Parisian *ébénistes*, hard pressed by the Continental Blockade. Delivered in 1814 from the *Garde-Meuble*, the *secrétaire*, remains in the Ministère de la Marine (M531) (cat. 63B).

47
Mahogany console with ormolu mounts (see also 98), one of four identical pieces commissioned from Paris by Napoleon's brother Jérôme, King of Westphalia, for his Kassel residence (cat. 93A). Schloss Wilhelmshöhe, Kassel

*francs*, an average amount in comparison with the others.[100] The prices announced in the estimates were probably imprecise and exploratory, with the intention of reaching an acceptable agreement with the *ébénistes*, who usually executed more costly commissions. One of the two aforementioned *secrétaires* is now in the Ministère de la Marine in Paris, 46. The other *secrétaire*, as well as the commode, are listed in the inventory of the *Mobilier National*, although their exact location is not known.[101]

A commode almost identical to the two supplied to the *Garde-Meuble* is now in a private collection 50. This piece was not part of the commission manufactured for Napoleon, but helps us, nonetheless, to evaluate the furniture commissioned by the *Garde-Meuble*. Molitor probably had in stock some of the pieces ordered in a semi-finished state and found himself obliged to deliver them, considering the imposed prices, in a simplified form. The very few days which elapsed between the commission of the four pieces and the delivery date seems to support this idea. The furniture delivered by Molitor was registered in the great ledger and stored in the *Garde-Meuble* warehouses on 8 August 1811.[102] Three years later, after the fall of Napoleon and

the return of the Bourbons in the spring of 1814, they reappeared in the furnishing of the ministries and châteaux. The destruction caused by the troops occupying Paris, in addition to the demands of the restored princes to refurbish their palaces, suddenly kindled an important demand for luxury furnishings, which the impoverished Bourbon government was able to meet due to the valuable reserves of the *Garde-Meuble*. On 7 August 1814, one of Molitor's console tables was delivered to the concierge of the Tuileries, Monsieur Mogé, for the Royal Family.[103] Three other consoles were intended for the prince de Condé and the duc de Bourbon at the Palais Bourbon.[104] The destinies of the tables are, however, more difficult to follow. One was sent at the end of May 1814 to the Palais Royal, while another was dispatched to the Tuileries on 7 June 1814.[105] On 28 June 1814, a *secrétaire* and a commode were delivered to the Ministère de la Marine. As we have seen, the *secrétaire* is still to be found in its original place, but all trace has been lost of the commode.[106] The second *secrétaire* and its commode were delivered to the Château de Saint-Cloud in 1824 and were installed four years later in 1828 in the chamber of the duchesse de Reggio, the duchesse de Berry's first lady-in-waiting. Later, in the nineteenth century, these two pieces were returned to the *Mobilier National*.[107]

## Commissions from Jérôme, King of Westphalia: 1808–13

Other European monarchs commissioned pieces from Molitor, notably Jérôme, Napoleon's youngest brother and King of Westphalia, who bought furnishings for his Kassel residence, as well as for the Palais Napoleonshöhe (now called Wilhelmshöhe).[108] When, in the latter months of 1807, the King and his wife Katharina von Württemberg, decided to take up residence there, the premises were practically empty. Jérôme sent for the architect Grandjean de Montigny, entrusting him with the completion of the interior decoration. The architect was assisted in his task by the elector architect Jussov.[109] The renovation and refurbishing of Kassel and Napleonshöhe took place between 1808 and 1813, and the spending was lavish. Known for his extravagant tastes, and grand lifestyle, Jérôme's reputation followed him from Paris to Hesse. His furnishings were only partially supplied from the existing stocks of the *Garde-Meuble* in Paris. Exports to the Empire from Paris were usually limited to bronzes, clocks and porcelain, and by order of the *Garde-Meuble*, all other items of furniture had generally to be manufactured more cheaply on the spot. But an examination of the projects carried out by Jérôme, during his brief stay in Kassel, and of contemporary commentaries, reveals the significant extent of his spending.[110] Several commissions were accorded to local cabinet-makers, as stipulated by the *Garde-Meuble*, but all of the most important works were ordered from Paris through the administration of the Kassel palace and were later delivered to Westphalia.

Although few of the pieces bear the manufacturer's label, many of the items of Parisian provenance are identifiable as the products of Molitor's

48
Unsigned bust of Katharina von Wurtemberg, wife of Jérome and Queen of Westphalia
Formerly collection G. David

49
Jérôme, Napoleon's brother,
crowned King of Westphalia
in 1807.
Private collection

50
Commode in burr elm veneer.
Of the four pieces in burr elm
veneer which Molitor
delivered to the *Garde-Meuble*
in 1811, only a *secrétaire*
remains, in the Ministère de la
Marine. We have an
approximate idea of the lost
commode *en suite* from a
similar example shown here
(cat. 24).
Formerly collection Roger
Imbert

workshop, due to the exceptional quality of their execution and the variety
of timbers employed. For some pieces, only the gilt bronzes were imported;
these were then mounted by local cabinet-makers on then finished pieces. A
Parisian intermediary, the furniture merchant Isaac Mausbach, is mentioned several times in the Kassel ledgers, as is the transporter Wengeroth,
who received large sums on several occasions for *'transports de meubles'*.[111]

51
One of a pair of mahogony
consoles with ormolu
mounts, part of the
Westphalian furniture
commissioned by Jérôme
(cat. 92).
Schloss Wilhelmshöhe, Kassel

Mausbach was responsible for the Westphalian King's acquisitions in Paris. In addition to six console tables bearing his label, Molitor probably supplied other pieces for Kassel between 1809 and 1812.[112] Certain other pieces displaying stylistic similarities and identical technical details in the workmanship and the choice of bronze mounts could also be attributed to him.[113]

The entire group of Parisian-manufactured furniture which Jérôme succeeded in amassing displays an exceptional coherence: the epitome of the excellence of Empire style. Two evident factors are at play here – the furniture was produced over a very limited period – five years – and it was made by a few exceptionally talented craftsmen. Still more importantly, as 'ambassadors' of the French Empire style, which was highly reputed in Germany, the pieces also influenced aspects of German Empire style, and were a source of inspiration to the Kassel as well as the central German cabinet-makers.

The Bourbon acquisitions 1818–20

Documents now preserved in the National Archives, allow us to reconstruct exactly the negotiations which led to the purchase of two Japanese-style

52
Engraving by Le Barbier depicting Louis XVIII as the protector of the Arts and the Muses. The Bourbon King's purchase of two Japanese lacquer and ebony cabinets in 1820 brought Molitor's long career to a close.
Private collection

53
*Bonheur-du-jour* in ebony and Japanese lacquer, sold in 1820. In the accompanying explanatory note to the *Garde-Meuble*, Molitor claims that this furniture was commissioned by Marie-Antoinette and executed prior to 1792 (cat. 67A).
Musée du Louvre, Paris

lacquer and ebony cabinets, 53 and 54 (now in the collection of the Musée du Louvre). With the return of the Bourbons to power in 1814, Molitor attempted to recreate his pre-revolutionary success and to resume his contacts with survivors of the *ancien régime*. In the letters which punctuated his negotiations, the hopes that the *ébéniste* had entertained concerning the restoration of the monarchy are fervently expressed.[114] The negotiations were laborious and dragged out over a period of two years, through a lack of funding. The Bourbons were giving priority to other matters, which checked spending on luxury furnishings.

After a series of persuasive discussions and the intervention of former aristocratic clients, Molitor succeeded in selling some pieces to the *Garde-Meuble*, although well below their original price. At the request of mesdames de Kersalaim and de Villeneuve, the baron Bourlet de Saint-Aubin wrote a letter of introduction on behalf of Molitor on 28 February 1818, to his relative, baron de Ville d'Avray, the *Intendant de la Garde-Meuble* (*doc* 9).[115] Upon receipt of this letter, Ville d'Avray delegated the inspector Veytard to visit the *ébéniste's* workshop to inspect his production. His report details pieces with a total value of 14,300 *francs*, notably four cabinets, (or *bonheurs-du-jour*), consoles, and *jardinières*.

Although in his appraisal Veytard remarked upon the exceptional quality and beauty of the pieces, the *Garde-Meuble* had no intention of purchasing the *ébéniste's* work due to its financial limitations.[116]

The attempts to conclude a sale only resumed in December of the same year, when the comtesse de Clarac, wife of the *Conservateur au Musée des Antiques au Louvre* addressed a letter to Monsieur de Ville d'Avray in which she wrote '. . . they are very beautiful, and he [Molitor] has sold the same to the King of Prussia and the Duke of Wellington . . . He will not be in a hurry for the money but would like to take his furniture out of the warehouse, where he has placed them for he fears that the merchant will soon go bankrupt . . . I pray Monsieur Ville d'Avray to pardon my importunity, but it is to oblige a good man who worked for the Queen before and to reaffirm to him all the old feelings that unite us . . .' (*doc* 11).[117]

The comte de Forbin, *Directeur Général des Musée Royaux*, addressed another recommendation to Ville d'Avray on 21 December 1818 in which he insisted on Molitor's exceptional workmanship and intimated that the *ébéniste* might consider reducing his prices. A note in the margin explains that once again the request was rejected due to lack of funds (*doc* 12). Another year passed before Molitor himself wrote to the comte de Clarac on 27 December 1819 asking him to intervene. This missive testified to the *ébéniste's* eternal devotion to the Crown. Molitor refers to his Royalist stance during the hundred days of Napoleon's reign after his return from Elba in the spring of 1815. During this period the *ébéniste* had hidden chests and trunks full of valuable objects and personal effects belonging to aristocrats who had fled Paris. He also points out services rendered by him during the Revolution to *l'ancienne Cour'* which led him to be judged by the Revolutionary Tribunal and from which he escaped only by *'un miracle de la providence'*. A small note accompanies the letter, as if there were nothing to add; the comte de Clarac forwarded Molitor's letter to Ville d'Avray praying him 'to be of service to this able and honest *ébéniste* who merits it in any case. It would be excellent to employ him for the *Garde-Meuble* as much for his taste, his love of work well done as for his integrity . . .' (*doc* 13). This time Molitor's avowal and Clarac's note were effective and on 31 December 1819, the buying order was released. Several months passed, however, before Veytard transferred the estimate to Ville d'Avray.

54
*Bonheur-du-jour en suite* with 53. They were delivered to the Château de Saint-Cloud where they remained until 1870 when they were transferred to the Louvre (cat. 67B).
Musée du Louvre, Paris

In this estimate, for the first time, the Japanese-style cabinets were designated as having been commissioned by Marie-Antoinette: 'Sieur Molitor, one of the most distinguished *ébénistes* in Paris executed, according to the orders of the late Marie-Antoinette who honoured him with her benevolence, six pieces of furniture, of the greatest beauty, in marquetry, old lacquer work and mahogany, with ornaments in matt bronze gilt … these pieces, for which he was commissioned in 1790 could only be completed before 1793 and the grievous events of this period prevented Sieur Molitor from delivering them: they remained in his store, too beautiful to be sold in commerce or to individuals: these works could only be suitable for the King.

Sieur Molitor asks now that the *Garde-Meuble*, with consideration for the august person for which they were intended, be well-disposed to acquire them.' Meanwhile, the adjoined list had been slightly modified and contained fewer pieces. Clearly the sale of precious pieces featuring lacquer work was problematic since Molitor consented to lower his prices, from 18,000 *francs* for the whole collection, reaching a compromise at 10,000 *francs* (*doc* 14).[118]

On 25 May 1820, the baron de Ville d'Avray accepted definitively the purchase of Molitor's works, payable in two drafts of 5,000 *francs* each. The cabinets comprised the first shipment and the other pieces were to be transferred at the end of the year. The comte de Pradel, *Directeur Général du Ministère de la Maison du Roi* consented to accord the necessary funds, and on 30 June 1820, Molitor delivered the two cabinets to the *Garde-Meuble* whence they were dispatched, shortly afterwards, to Saint-Cloud.[119] Neither the existing documents nor the reserves of the *Mobilier National* provide us with clues in tracing the second shipment. It probably never took place – the lengthy negotiations attested to financial difficulties which held up the acquisition of the works, and the *Garde-Meuble* balked at purchasing completed works for which it had no formal buying order.

At this time the *Garde-Meuble* received, on several occasions, proposals to buy furniture and art objects which were supposedly the property of the Royal Family. Even if, in certain cases, their authenticity was dubious, the commercial value, under the new monarchy, of any item which was supposedly manufactured for the Crown prior to the Revolution, should not be underestimated. Possibly Molitor did receive a commission for the furniture before the fall of Louis XVI. He was certainly commissioned to make the mahogany doors for the Tuileries, but no trace can be found in the pre-Revolutionary ledgers of the *Garde-Meuble*, of a possible commission for the six cabinets for Marie-Antoinette. The only existing records, as we have seen, are various fragments of registers concerning the *Garde-Meuble de la Reine*, which provide no information on the subject.

Molitor's assertion that the Japanese-style cabinets were unsaleable due to their overtly lavish nature lacks credibility; we need only compare them with cabinets executed for the duc de Choiseul-Praslin between 1797 and 1802, or with his production during the Empire, which found a large number of solvent buyers. The cabinets are neither mentioned in the 1796 inventory nor figure on the list of unexecuted pre-Revolutionary Royal commissions. The Tuileries doors delivered in 1795 on the orders of the Crown are recorded, however. Given Molitor's acute business sense, it also seems unlikely that he should withold from sale such a number of finished works, for more than twenty years. Molitor would have had to settle with subcontractors before he himself received payment and this could have led to financial ruin for the *ébéniste* in the case of the apparently unhonoured commission for the Queen's lacquer cabinets. No doubt, under the Empire, he could have sold them elsewhere.

After the Bourbon restoration, the *ancien régime* came to be seen as a 'paradise lost' and Molitor was clearly participating in this nostalgia. The grand, now elderly *ébéniste*, was regarded as the living representative of a legendary period; one of the last great surviving craftsmen who had served

55
Small *bureau plat*. The front part of the frieze drawer can be folded down to form a writing surface. This bureau is probably identical to one mentioned in Molitor's sale offer to the Crown in 1818 (cat. 133).
Formerly in the Hagenauer Collection

56
After a portrait by Elisabeth
Vigée-Lebrun, the duchesse
de Polignac, intimate friend of
Marie-Antoinette and client
of Molitor.
Bibliotheque Nationale

57
(opposite) Drawing by
Carmontelle of the duchesse
de Fitzjames, another client of
Molitor, surrounded by her
friends the duchesse de
Bourbon, the marquise de
Barbantane, and her two
daughters.
Archives Didier Aaron

the pre-Revolutionary monarchy. We can perhaps imagine Molitor in these last years as an ageing man who looked back to the period of his greatest success and for whom a final sale to the restored monarchy represented an affirmation of the loyalties he had for so long held dear.

## Molitor's private patrons: 1785–1820

The clientèle of an *ébéniste's* workshop is a clear indication to the modern observer of that craftsman's social rank. In Molitor's case, over a period of thirty-five years, it is possible to follow the fluctuations among the 'great and powerful' which paralleled France's successive political turnabouts. Before 1792, the names are those of the nobility of the *ancien régime*, demonstrating the extent of Molitor's relations with the aristocracy. In his early years these were the people who formed his reputation, and with it, created all his aforementioned difficulties during the Terror.

58
Portraits by Girodet, *c.*1803, of
Thomas Merlin and his wife.
From 1796–1803 the couple
furnished their *hôtel* on rue
Louis Le Grand with the most
fashionable pieces. Now in the
Château Grand Maison, they
represent a unique example
of a complete suite of Parisian
furniture from the Directoire
period.

Molitor's career can be divided into distinct phases, the direct result of
the changes in France's dominant political and social class. The first, during
which taste in furniture was dictated by the Court, covers seven years from
1785 to 1792. The interval between the summer of 1793 and the winter of
1795 must be left in parenthesis; Paris was plunged into dark years of trouble
and distress until the institution of the *Directoire* in November 1795 and the
renewal of society life. The period from 1794 to 1814, saw a revival of Molitor's fortunes and the final phase in his career commences with the return
of the Bourbons in 1814. Here, as we have seen, information abounds in the
correspondence concerning the sale of the lacquer cabinets to the *Garde-
Meuble*.

The names cited between 1785 and 1793 are important in that they dis-
close the active relations which Molitor entertained with the aristocracy up
until the fall of the monarch and the abolition of the privileges in August
1792. The exceptional reputation of his works dates from this period. Even if
the four account books which are itemized in the 1796 inventory have disappeared, an excerpt from the inventory itself tell us the names of a large
number of Molitor's patrons. Of the four ledgers listed, three were of

59
S.C. Miger, portrait of the
marquis de La Fayette. Upon
his return from America, La
Fayette decorated his *hôtel* in
the Faubourg Saint-Germain,
which became known for its
*avant-garde* furniture.
Private collection

60
Engraving by Ambroise
Tardieu of General Baron Paul
Grenier, (married in the first
years of the nineteenth
century) who subsequently
commissioned furniture from
Molitor.
Private collection

61
Engraving by Fauchery of
Madame de Staël, the wife of
Baron de Holstein Staël,
Swedish ambassador to
France, who was a client of
Molitor before the
Revolution.
Private collection

medium size, while the fourth was larger. All were bound in light red leather. The first enumerated Molitor's completed orders including a description of the works. The entire volume was filled to the last page and two additional booklets, also completed, were attached.

The second listed the workshop employees. The third, two-thirds full, comprised complementary information about the *ébéniste's* works.

Suplementary details can also be gleaned from receipts which turned up among papers requisitioned from those who had fled Paris during the Revolution.[120] Documents concerning the claims filed by creditors against these 'emigrés' constitute another valuable source. Creditors were authorized from 1792, and appointed to recover the debts. For this reason on 20 November 1792, Molitor appointed Citoyen Joseph Guillou as the authorized representative to deal with debts he had incurred from 'emigré' patrons.

After the Assembly encouraged the creation of creditors' unions on 31 July 1793, numerous organizations for this purpose came into existence between September 1793 and February 1794. It is known that Guillou defended Molitor's interests on four occasions.[121]

A number of prominent clients of the *ancien régime* had held an official function at Court. A select few formed the immediate entourage of Louis

GRENIER.

Fauchery del.

M^me DE STAËL.

XVI, Marie-Antoinette and the Royal Family. The comte de la Charte, the prince de Vaudemont, the duc de Fitz James and the marquis de la Suze all held various posts for the King, and the duchesse de Fitz James was Marie-Antoinette's lady-in-waiting.

Since 1785 the role of *gouvernante des enfants de France* was undertaken by the duchesse de Polignac. The duc de Polignac, the comte de Tessé and the prince de Carament were also members of the Queen's household. The comtesse de Margueritte and the comtesse de Boisgelin were the ladies-in-waiting to the King's sister and aunt, mesdames Elisabeth and Victoire.

Occasionally, the family provenance of some of Molitor's existing works leads directly back to some members of the King's household. Others who bought his works moved in fashionable Parisian circles, residing for the most part in the Faubourg Saint-Germain and engaged in diplomatic or military activities at Court. Typical of these are the comte de Jaucourt, La Vieuville, and the comtesse de La Marck (*doc* 3),[122] the Swedish Ambassador the Baron Staël-Holstein, husband of Germaine de Staël; the Ambassador to the King of Spain, the Comte Fernand de Nunèz;[123] the comte de Médavy and Monsieur Bonnecarère.[124] Members of the National Assembly – The marquis de La Fayette and the duc de Mirepoix – participated actively in events during the first years of the Revolution.[125] Madame de Mirepoix was a key figure

63
Ebony veneer and Japanese
lacquer commode (see also
66). The remarkable work
constitutes part of the
furniture supplied to Antoine-
César de Choiseul-Praslin
between 1797 and 1802
(cat. 5).
Private collection

and a trendsetter in contemporary Parisian society. The name M. Crosbie also appears, but nothing is known of him.[126]

From the period 1795 to 1820, the names of several private patrons are known. Some are documented in various archives; others have been discovered due to works which have remained to this day within the same family. Among the names from the post-Revolutionary period, we find notable personalities from the new bourgeoisie, and later, under Napoleon, from the military nobility. With the return of the Bourbon princes under the Empire, Molitor was reunited with some of his patrons of the *ancien régime*. There is documented proof that *l'agent de change*, Monsieur Merlin bought certain pieces with the intention of furnishing his *hôtel* on the rue Louis-le-

64
Engraving by Texier of duc
Antoine César de Choiseul-
Praslin.
Bibliotheque Nationale

Grand.[127] The comte Nicolas-Antoine-Xavier Castella de Berlens, General under the orders of Napoleon, purchased furniture for his Parisian hôtel which was later shipped to the castle of Wallenried in Switzerland.[128]

In the year X (1801), *Citoyen* Claude-Louis Saisseval commissioned two *armoires* in mahogany, *'ouvrages de fantaisie'*. In the end the works were ultimately considered unsatisfactory by the former marquis; one was sold to a Monsieur Fachet and the unconcluded sale of the other resulted in litigation between Molitor and Saisseval (*doc* 5).[129] In September 1803, upon the death of Madame de Jaucourt, Molitor asserted his rights on unpaid commissions. The exact amount of the debt is not known, but the settlement of this litigation continued until 1808, and Molitor was nonsuited of his demands in a judgement handed down on 26 Nivôse year XIII (16 January 1805).[130] The descendants of the de Gèze family still have a Molitor tea caddy in their possession acquired during the Empire.

## The Commission of Antoine-César de Choiseul, fourth duc de Praslin

The discovery of documents concerning this great commission obtained by Molitor deserves separate treatment. Through various divisions of the duc's inheritance, we are able to trace the destiny of each of the pieces commissioned, in a record unbroken until 1861.

Upon the death of his father in 1791, Antoine-César de Choiseul Praslin became the fourth duc de Praslin. In pre-Revolutionary Paris, the third duc's collections were famous – his gallery contained the works of Wouwermann, Teniers, Rembrandt and Van Loo. The furniture was of the same outstanding quality: pieces by André-Charles Boulle; a clock by Ferdinand Berthoud and several clocks by Breguet.

Antoine-César and his wife Charlotte-Antoinette-Marie O'Brian de Thomond belonged to the progressive aristocratic circles of Paris prior to the Revolution. Like many other key figures of the period, they were members of the Parisian masonic lodge. The duchesse herself had founded the first masonic lodge for women in Paris. During the first years of the Revolution, her husband actively participated as a member of the National Assembly, but this did not protect the family from serious difficulties with the Convention after the fall of Louis XVI. After 1792, the family often stayed in their Auteuil estate, in the countryside outside Paris. The duc had bought and refurnished it around 1787, and the family took refuge there as soon as the first Revolutionary riots broke out. Although they had never left France, and testified to their attachment to the new government, their names were to be found on the list of those who had fled, their property was confiscated and the duc and the duchesse were arrested. They barely escaped being condemned by the Revolutionary Tribunal and ending their days at the guillotine, but with the help of friends and of their faithful servants, who cared for their three children Alphonse, Félix and the new-born Lucie-Virginie, they were freed just after the fall of the Convention. Between 1796 and 1797 the duc

65
Pair of one-door commodes *en suite* with commode 63. The ormolu mounts on the pilasters can be attributed to Thomire. The interior and drawers are lined with aromatic sandalwood (cat. 41A and B).
Private collection

succeeded in having his name removed from the emigrés' lists and in recovering his personal property. The Choiseul-Praslin family had probably commissioned work from Molitor prior to 1792; their family *hôtel* in rue de Lille was conveniently situated in the vicinity of his Saint-Germain workshop.[131] Having recovered his possessions, the duc bought the former d'Harcourt *hôtel* on the rue de Grenelle in 1803. This newly-acquired residence needed refurbishing and Choiseul called upon Molitor as well as other Parisian craftsmen for the important commissions. The duc and duchesse spared no expense on furnishing and decoration. Of the 200,00 *francs* spent, the mirrors, already in *situ*, alone cost 50,000 *francs*. When their son Félix married, his parents fitted out a private suite in the *hôtel* as was the tradition in prestigious Parisian families.

Most of the furniture made by Molitor for the family was in lacquer and ebony. At the death of the third duc, the inventory established for inheritance purposes in 1791, mentioned several screens in Japanese lacquer; it is supposed that Antoine-César left the dismounted lacquer panels, which the duc had inherited, at Molitor's disposal. A large *commode* 63 and two smaller ones 65, a cabinet and a bookcase as well as a console table (*91*) have been located. Another work, a large *secrétaire abattant* with inlays of *pietra dura* was sold in a public auction in 1808 (*55*). Molitor also executed a large commode 18 and a *secrétaire* in mahogany 17 as well as *a bureau de dame* and a *coiffeuse* with remarkable marquetry imitations of oriental lacquer work 22 and 42. All these pieces were inscribed in the ducal inventory and can be traced through various notarial acts until the second half of the nineteenth-century.[132]

66
Detail of commode 63 with
the doors open. The three
doors are lined with
polychromatic lacquer panels.
The front of the solid
mahogany drawers *à l'anglaise*
are veneered in burr elm
(cat. 5).
Private collection

# Work

Before embarking upon a detailed, formal description of each of Molitor's creations, it is well worth studying his materials and techniques – factors essential to an understanding of the form, and more importantly, the character of the furniture. The specific workmanship and materials of individual pieces can also help us with dating. Molitor's works are constructed around a basic carcass, veneered with precious timbers or lacquer. A few pieces are decorated with marquetry, and we know that inlays of brass and pewter are also used. We will begin with an examination of these 'surface' embellishments, followed by a look at the construction of the carcass itself.

## Marquetry

In Molitor's *oeuvre* we know of six pieces for which marquetry was used (for example 22, 42 and 152). His personal style in the medium is derivative of Riesener or Weisweiler: a ground of diamond-shaped marquetry covers the entire surface, with a prominent central motif. In the projections of the top rail, the *ébéniste* employed a motif similar to the needlework stitch called *point d'Hongrie*, which was probably imitating a type of straw marquetry, much in vogue in the second half of the eighteenth century 42. Here, the central motif of the tabletop consists of two superimposed ovals inlaid with a rosette and a shell motif. The latter would seem to indicate that Molitor was aware of contemporary English cabinet-making: similar motifs often decorate Hepplewhite models. Molitor adapts the popular English motif to his own uses, and in this he is unique among the Parisian *ébénistes* of his day.

67
(top and bottom) The importation of English designs considerably influenced furniture produced in Paris at the end of the *ancien régime*.

68
(opposite) Detail of the *lits de repos* supplied to General Castella de Berlens. The feet and the reliefs on the sides are patinated *à l'antique* to contrast with the mahogany (cat. 156B and 158A). Collection B.B. Steinitz

## Veneered furniture

Most of Molitor's production is covered with veneers of exotic timbers, principally mahogany. To qualify as *ébénisterie*, this veneer had to display the natural characteristics of the wood type, the grain and structure; it had also to be distinctively figured. The massive, costly planks favoured by Molitor allowed him to obtain veneers of the highest quality and value. Mahogany veneers are to be found throughout Molitor's *oeuvre* and his originality in the medium is evident even from his very earliest works. Only very much later, during the Consulate, was his style generally adopted by other *ébénistes*.

The vogue for mahogany reached its zenith around 1805. The Empress Josephine, cautioned by Napoleon to spend wisely and well, instigated a highly fashionable economy drive in the first years of the new century; the widespread use of mahogany veneers in furniture constituted one of the period's, arguably rather false, economies. One contemporary commentator

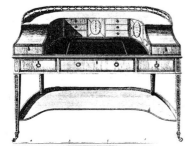

notes that 'we are beginning to employ less gold in the pieces which must be ornamented accordingly to suit fashion. We are seeing less gilt griffins, lions' heads, and arabesques. The most attractive wooden furniture is that to which the *ébéniste* applies the most simple decoration. For this reason only the closest-grained mahogany is used, either marbled or speckled.' However, the considerable cost of imported timbers meant that simplicity was not synonymous with lower prices. Because of their high price, exotic timbers were often sold by weight. The only solution, according to the *Journal des dames*, was to cut the planks into even thinner sheets.[133]

With a true *ébéniste's* sensitivity to his materials, Molitor invariably respects the natural composition of his wood veneers. Some sheets, such as the fall-front of 133, present unusual markings. The juxtaposition of matched veneer panels is another favourite technique. Placed perpendicularly, side-by-side, the sheets create a decorative design which enhances and accentuates their natural grain. The markings on the central panel of commode 137 are identical to those on four other catalogued pieces – a clear indication of the number of sheets that could be cut from one solid plank. A visually unified effect, giving the impression of a solid wood construction, was rarely sought in pre-Revolutionary veneered furniture. It was only later, with the advent of new forms of furniture, that pieces wholly covered with veneer began to present an overall, supposedly monumented, appearance. The pattern formed by speckled mahogany veneers covering the doors of the commode 18 give the appearance of being diamond-shaped. The full sheets of veneer used on the doors of the pre-Revolutionary *secrétaires* 133 and 138, display unusually decorative figuring. The grains of the doors and the upper part of the drop-front *secrétaires abattants* offset one against another, being

69
*Desserte*. The use of mahogany veneer, as well as the reduction of ormolu ornamentation clearly illustrates the English influence on Parisian furniture (cat. 38).
Private collection

70
*Secrétaire à abattant*. The
*ébéniste* enhances the patterns
formed by the grain in the
wood by the careful
positioning of the sheets of
veneer on the fall front and
the doors (cat. 58).
Private collection

positioned vertically on the former and horizontally on the latter (138, 133 and (56)). On the later, more monumented Empire forms, continuous sheets are applied vertically over the whole structure, emphasizing the imposing character of the pieces. Through the use of different grains and mark-

71
Fashion engraving from *Le costume parisien*, published in 1798. The chair has armrests in the form of griffins, carved *en ronde de bosse*, comparable to those on Molitor's chairs. Bibliothèque Nationale

ings on the principal panels and cross-banded edges, Molitor displays a number of different woods to their best advantage 17. The *ébéniste* also makes use of the naturally striped patterns to accent the panels of the carcass, setting them off from the more discreetly figured cross-banding. His late works include pieces wholly covered with close-grained veneer, accentuating their volume and unified structure 46.

## Lacquer

Molitor seems to have had an especial fondness for black lacquer, employing it throughout his career, and showing a decided preference for Japanese varieties. Certain of his pieces feature Oriental lacquer panels, prominently positioned on the front, while the side panels are of European production, easily distinguishable since they lack finesse and their surfaces craze easily.

The interiors of the pieces, as well as the supports for the ormolu friezes, could also be decorated with aventurine. These priceless lacquer pieces replaced the vogue for inset, painted porcelain plaques, which had enjoyed great favour during the 1770s.

**72**
*Fauteuils* derived from the classical *Klismos* design. The curves of the back uprights and legs are designed to be seen from all angles. Molitor collaborated with J.B. Demay and Brion for the carved wooden elements of his furniture (cat. 164).
Musée Mamottan, Paris

**73**
(below) Chair belonging to Thomas Merlin, with the Merlin cypher inlaid in brass on the back (cat. 171).
Private collection

## Inlays

Inlays generally take the form of fine strips, no more than several millimetres wide, in contrasting colours which accentuate the contours, or frame the surface of a piece of furniture 177 and (*126*). On certain models, inlaid bands constitute the sole decorative motif 73. Citronwood, ebony and amaranth were used as inlays by Molitor, as were brass, pewter and whalebone.

## Mahogany

Among the timbers used for veneering, mahogany held an honoured status. From the 1750s onwards, its use was widespread in French furniture. Following the trend begun in England, the following decade saw the adoption of mahogany for *ébénisterie*. The costliness of the wood, imported from San Domingo and Cuba, made it something of a status symbol, and it was soon essential for a Parisian *ébéniste* to be adept in its use. Molitor was the first to begin gradually abandoning ornamental bronze mounts in favour of richly decorative veneers. He carefully selected sheets with varying designs – patterned with cloud-shaped, flame-shaped, hazy, speckled, curled, striped or moiré figuring – and used a broad palette of the available colours, from dark brown through several hues of red to light orange and even paler shades. Numerous varieties of mahogany have, alas, disappeared since Molitor's

time. Solid, carved mahogany was also used, for detached columns or caryatids – proof that Molitor's clients were able to choose the most costly materials.

Lacquer and ebony

According to the *menuisier* and writer André-Jacob Roubo, lacquer furniture was on an equal footing in the hierarchy of *ébénisterie* with pieces inlaid with copper, pewter, tortoiseshell or *pietra dura*, following the famous technique developed by André-Charles Boulle. Hence pieces veneered with lacquer were among the most prestigious items an *ébéniste* could produce.

Lacquer, imported for the most part from Japan, was very much in demand in the mid-1780s. The *marchand-mercier* Daguerre must have promoted the fashion, since important pieces in lacquer by Riesener were delivered to the *Garde-Meuble* from the former's showroom during this period. The use of Oriental motifs and materials was prompted less by a desire simply to copy Japanese and Chinese art, than by a wish to recreate 'the exotic character and mysterious attraction' exerted by the items then being exported to Europe from the East. Certainly it is not difficult to imagine the allure of gleaming, black lacquer panels, often gilded, in the candlelit interiors of the time.[134]

Of the sixteen pieces veneered in lacquer, known to be by Molitor, seven are pre-Revolutionary. With these and other pieces mentioned in the documents, we can see how important this technique was in Molitor's *oeuvre* as a whole.[135]

The lacquer panels imported from Japan often depicted landscapes enlivened by figures, plants and animals. The compositions did not obey Western laws of perspective, and had therefore, to be carefully selected and deployed within the architectural context of Western furniture. On commodes fitted with double doors and on *bonheurs-du-jour*, individual lacquer panels would be 'paired' to form compositions with symmetrical axes. By far the greater number of panels were also 'doctored' on arrival in the West. Expert craftsmen would add elements to the design, with the aim of

74
Designs for commodes published in *La Mésangère*, plate 10, *c*.1800. Bibliothèque des Arts Dècoratifs

counter-balancing composition, or filling awkward empty spaces. In this way, Molitor often sought to create more harmonious views, adapted to a European eye. Large birds, trees, bamboo, branches, butterflies and insects

75
Commode in Japanese lacquer and ebony veneer with ormolu mounts. Of an extremely unusual design, the commode has detached columns on the corners and the lacquer panels are decorated with additional designs. The commode was acquired for the future George IV of England (cat. 7). Royal Collection, Windsor Castle, by kind permission of H.M. The Queen.

were his preferred motifs for the additions. Such panels are easily discernible from authentic, un-doctored examples. European lacquer designers often filled blank areas in the original design with trees on hills, or birds in the sky.

Plaques destined for a specific piece of furniture were often retouched to create a central axis, with the addition of a stalk of bamboo. Often the additions are faithful recreations of Oriental models, their presence is betrayed

by a certain confusion which they introduce into the original design. A pair of one-door commodes by Molitor, 65, demonstrates this perfectly: during restoration, some extraneous Western birds and plants have been removed from one of the two commodes, leaving four other birds in a circular arc in the sky, not realising that these, too, were painted in Paris.

Satinwood

'In England, mahogany has been dethroned by a novelty, which charms us by its lemon-yellow colour. Because of its satin brilliance, we commonly called it *bois des îles* or Satin Wood', commented the *Journal des Luxus* in April 1794.[136] Commissions for furniture in *bois des îles* were executed in Paris, in 1786 and 1790, for the château of Fontainebleau and Saint-Cloud respectively. Elegant interiors contrasted pale yellow satinwood furniture with tones of bottle green for the silk wall coverings and window drapes.

Several pieces in satinwood by Molitor are mentioned in documents. With typical inventiveness, the *ébéniste* uses an overall surface finish '*en pointe de diamant*' whenever he has covered a carcass entirely in satinwood veneer, thus accentuating the magical play of light over its surfaces. In the 1796 inventory, we note '*... un secrétaire de trois pieds en bois jaune, avec feuille* *de chêne, . . . deux armoires en bois jaune . . . une table à manger en bois jaune, . . . une table creuse en boise jaune.'* Only the commode 77 and the *secrétaire* 76 have been positively identified, but these few pieces are of outstanding quality and among the most modern of their day.

Sandalwood and exotic timbers

Once again the *Journal des Luxus* is sensitive to contemporary trends: 'the most recent novelty in the domain of futility', says the June 1789 issue, 'is the discovery of sandalwood with which the *ébénistes* have made a multitude of ravishing and precious frivolities which have reaped in several months a great success with the public'.

Molitor used sandalwood for the linings of his pieces. This extremely precious, orange-honey coloured wood possesses a smooth, satin finish as well as a very agreeable perfume, with insecticidal properties, and was therefore ideal for the linings of commodes or *armoires* used for the storage of clothing or furs. The commodes 65 are lined with sandalwood. A receipt for the comtesse de La Marck dated 1792, tells us that Molitor *'a . . . pour elle . . . fait et fournit deux coffres en bois de santal plaqués en bois jaune, ornés de fils blancs et noirs . . .'* The comtesse de La Marck bequeathed to her daughter Augusta in 1793 a *secrétaire '. . . de bois jaune encadre dans un bois de'acajou et double d'un bois odoriférant . . .'* From this description we can suppose a very recently-made piece, perhaps of Molitor's creation.[137]

In *Les petites annonces* of 1796, a *boudoir-bibliothèque* is advertised with shelves in sandalwood. Moreover, the *Journal des Luxus* recommended cedarwood for the lining of the drawers 'a fin qu'il s'exhale du meuble une odeur agréable et durable . . .'[138] The use of fragrant wood was, then, a sign of refinement. The same is true of exotic woods in general, and inlays and marquetry were often executed in amaranth, palissander, tulipwood, rosewood, kingwood, sycamore, yew and amboyna. Only one large piece by Molitor in palissander veneer has been itemized (*40*). Ebony, a costly, hard and unyielding wood, occupies a special place among the exotic timbers, and Molitor used it in some twenty pieces. During the pre-Revolutionary period and in his later works, he combined it with Oriental lacquer panels, fitted into an ebony structure. These pieces constitute the most precious elements of the *ébénistes* entire production.

After 1806 the continental blockade, and a dictat issued by Napoleon, forced *ébénistes* to use local timbers, even for luxury items. Far from discouraged, the craftsmen began to work enthusiastically in elm, Sycamore and ash. The resulting predominance of light hues in French furniture was not without influence in other European countries. A commode and a *secrétaire abattant* by Molitor 46 and 50 are veneered with elm burr; the 1833 inventory lists pieces in yew and ash.

78
A rare example of steel decoration used on this toilette table by François Rémond. Given in 1806 to Empress Josephine by the City of Paris. The steel mounts are signed by Schey who is known to have worked with Molitor.
Musée National, Château La Malmaison

Base metals

At the end of the eighteenth-century, brass, pewter or steel inlays on furniture became increasingly popular. Bronze mounts, bases and capitals, were frequently replaced by bands in polished steel or brass – materials whose cold, hard brilliance corresponded more closely to the sober Republican spirit than did the warmth of ormolu. The abandonment of ormulo was not due to restrictive, cost-cutting measures, but reflected a deliberate choice. At the end of the 1780s, the use of brass inlays in particular developed as Parisian *ébénistes* began to reflect the dual influences of England, where they were in widespread use, and of Antiquity. Brass inlays often constituted the only ornament on a piece, and Molitor used them in this way to create geometrical motifs, monograms, Antique craters, ciphers or shields. In their earliest forms, these inlays were polished and finely chiselled. Molitor also employed lozenge-shaped inlays on the backs of chairs. The same motifs appeared on bookcase door grilles, and were reproduced by Sheraton in 1790 in the *Cabinet-Maker and Upholsterer's Drawing Book*.

The use of polished steel inlays was a new technique immediately adopted by *ébénistes*. Riesener's furniture for the *cabinet de retraite* at Fontainbleau executed in 1787, featured steel inlays. Orders for steel bedframes delivered by Courbin in 1785 for Marie-Antoinette's children are also known.[139] Molitor used steel for decoration; the 1796 inventory lists a *guéridon* with polished steel mounts. The raw material was supplied by *Citoyen Chaille, fournisseur en acier poli, Faubourg Saint Denis'*, but to this day these works have not been found.

Varnish

Most of Molitor's furniture was varnished *au tampon*. The varnish was applied in a circular movement with a pad which gave a shiny film, the durability of which depended upon the number of coats applied. This technique, obtaining optimum results, was introduced in the 1780s from England. Before this, the most widespread technique used in France was *le ciré rempli*, in which wax permeated into the wood before being polished with brushes and skins. Lower-grade solid wood furniture was either waxed, covered with linseed oil or painted. The superior copal-based varnish was reserved for the Royal furniture. Both this, and *le ciré rempli*, cast a discreet lustre which perfectly enhances the natural sheen of the wood,

79
Engraving from Sheraton's *The Cabinet-Maker and Upholsterer's Drawing Book*. The English taste for geometrical designs inspired Parisian *ébénistes*.

80
Engraving by Prieur depicting a pair of doves is very similar to the motif decorating the escutcheon of the *bureau à cylindre* 8.
Private collection

81
Detail of the escutcheon from the *bureau à cylindre* 8. A written description allows us to date it to *c*.1788 (cat. 70).
J. Paul Getty Museum, Malibu, California

while *vernis au tampon*, applied today when furniture is restored, has a more aggressive effect. In an advertisement in June of 1790, the *merchand-tapisseur* Boucher extolled the virtues of the latter, however, and announced it as '*un poli anglais susceptible d'être lavé.*'

In the Germanic countries, *vernis au tampon* was in use in the Mainz and Leipzig region from 1792. The technique spread very quickly, and is still practiced today.[140]

Ormolu mounts

Before the Revolution, *ébénistes* were obliged to buy ormolu mounts from a *fondeur* belonging to the Guild of *Maîtres Fondeurs*, all of whose models were registered designs. Several privileged *ébénistes*, such as Oeben or Riesener, were, however, authorized by Royal licence to create original designs for ormolu mounts in their own foundry workshops.

Until the abolition of the guilds, it was customary to buy ormolu mounts either direct from the *fondeur* or from the *marchands-merciers*. In the latter category, Dominique Daguerre was a leading supplier of mounts, who worked with several *ébénistes* in the 1780s. No documents exist confirming a link between Molitor and the *marchand-mercier* Daguerre, but we can suppose that it was from them that he acquired his mounts. The ormolu mounts on the *secrétaire à cylindre* 8 are models which we know to have been available from Daguerre. The latter also furnished identical mounts for the interior of the Château de Saint-Cloud. Molitor seems to have had exclusive rights to certain models, such as the large escutcheon with chimera which was only found on pieces signed by Molitor.

It is very difficult to establish definite links between the working drawings in a *fondeur*'s catalogue, and the finished mouldings in a given piece of furniture. The pattern books of the designers Jean-Demosthène Dugourc, Henri Salembier, Thomire, Cauvet, Forty and Le Normand include Ancient Egyptian-style elements intertwined with arabesques, comparable to mounts found on furniture by Molitor, but in certain cases it is possible to suggest a direct connection between a sketchbook design and an extant model. Ormolu mounts used by Molitor featuring animals or human figures interlaced with flowers and fruits are identical to designs by Dugourc. In the ledgers of the *fondeur* François Rémond, a model '*de frise à nid d'oiseaux pour*

82
Applied ormolu decoration from the *bureau à cylindre* 8. The motifs are characteristic of the enthusiasm for the *goût etrusque* motifs before the Revolution (cat. 70).
J. Paul Getty Museum, Malibu, California

*entrée de serrure'* designed by Gambier, is registered on 1 October 1787. This piece is reminiscent of a mount used by Molitor 8.[141]

In relation to the furniture supplied by Molitor to the Imperial *Garde-Meuble* for king Jérôme we could cite the fondeur Pierre-Philippe Thomire, who designed the capital mounts 96 and Claude Galle, who created the mounts of fantastical animals seen on 115 and (74). The sacrificial bull motif on console table 47 and 161 is comparable to a similar one from Delafontaine's workshop.[142] Existing documents afford only imprecise descriptions of the models, however, and it is often difficult to attribute particular designs

83
Escutcheon from *secrétaire à abattant* 76 and commode *en suite* 77. The extraordinarily fine chiselling is characteristic of Directoire pieces (cats. 18 and 57).

84
Engraving for a frieze from the *Cahier d'arabesques* by the designer Henri Salembier. Such source books were vitally important in the elaboration of ormolu elements.
Private collection

to individual *fondeurs* with any degree of certainty. The frequency with which designs are used by the various *ébénistes* underlines the close connections that existed between their Parisian workshops. Carlin, Avril, Beneman, Levasseur, Riesener, Roentgen, Saunier and Weisweiler all used the same, more current models as Molitor at one time or another.

The plastic quality and the fine detailing of the ormolu pieces used by Molitor and his contemporaries are remarkable. This finesse is heightened by the meticulous character of their chiselling which often gave them a jewel-like character. The metal could be covered either with burnished, or with matt gilding; alternatively, the two different finishes could be employed simultaneously, creating a contrast between different parts of the mount. Large ornaments, friezes and borders were fixed to the wood by rivets attached behind the mounts, while smaller elements were held in place by small nails integrated into the design. The quality of craftsmanship tended to vary according to the particular pieces of furniture for which the mounts were destined. It was this that determined the standards of the chiselling and gilding, the finesse of which declined in exact proportion to the falling furniture prices after the Revolution. The price of an item was determined by the amount of decoration, and by the quality of its finish. Strangely, some *ébénistes'* later works often combine mounts of differing craftsmanship with uneven results. With the advent of semi-industrial production during the Empire, the aesthetic qualities of the mounts were increasingly dependent on the supplier with whom an *ébéniste* had decided to collaborate.

Compared with other craftsmen, the mounts which Molitor employed, even in his late works, were always of excellent quality. The rich variety of

designs and decorative motifs to be found on his pieces and the inventive ways in which they are used, merit a close examination.

Friezes

Inspired by Etruscan art, Molitor's palmette friezes can be divided into three variants, all of which were frequently used between 1787 and 1818. With the exception of one other isolated example, Etruscan palmette friezes of this type are unique to Molitor. *Palmette frieze 1* decorates commodes 10 and 18, made between 1788 and 1793, and is striking for its exceptionally finely-rendered detail. *Palmette frieze 2* is a later elaboration, punctuated by palmettes and curnucopiae. Rather stylized, it is more architectural than *frieze 1*, giving an impression of greater relief. This model appears on three pieces –

85
Palmette frieze 1, which is on commode 18 as well as two other pieces (cat. 27).

17, 53 and 54. A *secrétaire* in the Rijksmuseum in Amsterdam attests to Weisweiler's use of the same frieze. *Palmette frieze 3* is the best known and can be seen on four works by Molitor – 34, 35, 137 and 138. This frieze probably also existed in carved wood and gilt in which form it adorns two consoles belonging to Madame Mère Marie-Laetitia Ramolino, the mother of Napoleon I, at the Hôtel de Brienne (GME 6477 and 7477), and it is possible that Molitor collaborated on the design for the pieces.

*The interlacing frieze* has affinities with the Louis XVI style, and the quality of execution is exceptional. Examples exist on four works 5, 7, 34, 35, as well as an unstamped commode, 6, in the Wallace Collection, London, which has been attributed to Molitor as an early work. Riesener and Roentgen both used their own variants of the interlacing frieze motif. Festoon friezes, composed of garlands of vine leaves intertwined with pomegranates and other fruits, adorn four pieces by Molitor 14, 53 and 54, and 152. In strongly contrasting style, the frieze on (66) is composed of flat bands and beads occasionally punctuated by floral motifs. A *table à ouvrage* executed by Riesener in 1787 for Marie-Antoinette bears this same frieze.

The *lambrequin* frieze, used by Molitor to edge *guéridon* or console table

trays, is inspired by the Orientalizing tendencies of *le goût turc*. Four known works bear a lambrequin frieze – 23, 44, 172 and (91).

The most naturalistic of Molitor's friezes takes the form of ivy sprays, following the natural habit of the creeping foliage, which seems to clamber around the columns of the furniture. The meticulous, naturalistic execution of each and every ivy leaf is quite remarkable. Seven pieces by Molitor, all pre-Revolutionary, feature detached, tapered columns, decorated with ivy sprays. One other piece, *bonheur-du-jour*, 152, shows that Molitor renewed his use of this ornamentation between 1810 and 1816. We know that Dugourc also sketched furniture adorned with ivy around 1789. The motif, often cited as typical of the *goût étrusque*, is among the most exemplary of Molitor's preferred designs.

86
A preparatory design by Dugourc dated 1789, illustrating a console with garland-entwined columns, a motif found throughout Molitor's *oeuvre*.
Formerly Collection Tassinari-Châtel

87
Chimera frieze from commode 18 (cat. 27).

Escutcheons

Prior to the Revolution, Molitor used a model in the form of two winged lions flanking an oval wreath of flowers. The wreath is attached to a bow and inside is the keyhole. Later, other models are employed, such as the shield motif found on 51 and (*56*). The former features three intertwined arabesques 55 cm in length, behind the chimera, and is found on commodes 18, 75 and 137. The latter has only one arabesque of 29 cm in length; it was used very frequently between 1790 and 1810 (*20B, 36, 51, 52, 56, 60, 91, 92* and *133*).

Three pieces by Molitor 17, 138, and 140 feature an escutcheon with two swans holding a circular floral wreath in their beaks; with the keyhole

88
Chimera frieze from *secrétaire abattant* 17 (cat. 52).

placed at the centre of the wreath. The tail feathers of the swans are transformed into palmettes composed of pods, flowers and interlacements. At the crest, a lion's head unfolds from the final whorl.

89
Design by Dugourc for an Allegory of the Earth in the form of a sphinx wearing an Egyptian royal headdress and supporting in the scrolls below two wild cats.
Private collection

90
Detail of the escutcheon from commode 18, apparently inspired by Dugourc's design for the Allegory of the Earth. The motif is only found on Molitor's work (cat. 27).

Molitor's use of Ancient Egyptian-style motifs has already been mentioned. Indeed, he was a precursor of the style later called '*retour d'Egypte*' in reference to Napoleon's military campaign. A few pieces feature Egyptian-inspired escutcheons 14, 18 and (56). Their designs seem to have been directly derived from Dugourc's engravings.

Medallions and reliefs

The *secrétaire, à abattant*, 5, is the earliest piece by Molitor to be decorated with a central ormolu medallion on the fall front. The medallion depicts a pastoral scene with a shepherdess listening to a flute-playing shepherd. An identical model is also to be found in the work of Carlin and Weisweiler. Only three catalogued works by Molitor feature bas-relief friezes – 146, 147 and (84). *Amours* and mythological scenes were the preferred subjects for this type of ornamentation; and the bas-relief used by Molitor, the mouldings for which were executed by the *Manufacture Royale de Sèvres*, depicts the Sacrifice to Ceres. It can be dated to *c.*1791, and was employed on a *bonheur-du-jour* 147 and a small *bas d'armoire. Amoire* (84) is decorated with a bas-relief of putti. To the left of the keyhole one putto is depicted in the act of

91
Design by the architect Le Normand depicting chimeras which relate to those appearing on mounts used by Molitor.
Bibliothèque Nationale

92
Drawing of caryatids on the façade of a building in the Faubourg Poissonnière in Paris, by Le Normand and reproduced by Krafft and Ransonette. They are reminiscent of mounts used on Molitor's *bonheurs-du-jour* 34, 35, 53, 54 and 152 (cats. 67–9).
Bibliothèque Nationale

sculpting and to the right, another is sketching the *Torso Belvedere*. The complete frieze is an allegory of the seven arts. Another version exists on a *serre-bijou* by Riesener now in Windsor Castle. Here, a group of putti play around a centrally positioned telescope.

Caryatids

Sculpted female figures appear on the front two corners of three *secretaires en cabinet* 34, 53 and 152. This Classicizing motif was inspired by the caryatids supporting the entablature on the south portico of the Erechtheum in Athens. The robes of the figures are artfully draped to imitate the folds of wet material. Two different models are catalogued, the first on cabinet 53, being 40 cm in height. She unfurls the pleats of her *peplos*, with her arms, while above her head, a delightfully shaped basket, overflowing with fruit,

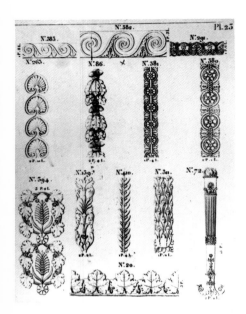

93
Ormolu ornaments with *flambeaux* and *rinceaux* motifs published by A.P. Giraud and Beunat in 1813, plate 23. The flambeaux are identical to decorative elements employed by Molitor on commode (33A).
Private collection

94
Design for a *bonheur-du-jour* by Dugourc in 1770, intended for the then Dauphine, Marie-Antoinette.
Formerly collection Tassinari-Châtel

is balanced on an Ionic capital. The caryatids on 34 are 26 cm tall. Obliquely draped, their robes are more closely fitted. Stylistically, all these figures are reminiscent of Empire *surtout de tables* figures. They are also surprisingly similar to figures in a drawing attributed to Thomire, now in the Berlin Kunstbibliothek.[143] However, with their aloof, distant air, they are quite far removed from the figures employed by Weisweiler or Riesener,

95
The caryatids on this console
are notable for their rams'
hooves (cat. 88).
Archives Galerie Mancel-Coti

whose grace emanated from the erotically executed drapery of their robes
and the frivolity of their smiles.

Capitals

Seventeen different models of busts or heads have been catalogued adorning
the terms of Molitor's furniture. At the base they repose on bare or cloven
feet or simply *tori* and *scotia*. Four terms are Egyptian in inspiration and bear
the royal headdress known as the *klaft* or *Pschent*. The latter are characterized
by a charming detail: two or three locks of hair are free and hang over the
ear. In this they are distinct from terms appearing later in Molitor's *oeuvre*,
which are more heiratic and severe in their expression.

Molitor's early works are decorated with capitals in the form of husks.
The first design used recalls Egyptian lotus capitals, and features leaves ending in whorls, surrounded by flowers. Acanthus leaves intersperse the
volutes and the large leaves are separated by *thyrsi*. Commode 137 features
rare spool capitals, whilst console table 7 is decorated with simplified

96
Design for square section
capital ornamented with
stylized acanthus leaves,
flowers and a smiling female
mask on a console table
delivered to the Grand
Trianon in 1809, and
employed as a decorative
motif on *bonheurs-du-jour* (cat.
66A and B). The capitals can
be attributed to Thomire.

97
Pilasters and pillars published
in various source books
represented a popular form of
architectural decoration in the
1790s. The Théatre du Marais,
built in 1791, as well as the
tribune built for the Assembly
in the Tuileries designed in
1792 by Percier and Fontaine,
were both decorated with
pilasters. Engravings by
Duplessis-Bertaux.
Private collection

98
Square section capitals used
by Molitor to decorate
consoles and *bonheurs-du-jour*.
Two different sizes were
employed (cat. 93A and B).

variants of the same design. Similar capitals were utilized by Weisweiler.
Thanks to the discovery of an etching in the Metropolitan Museum, New
York, by Philippe Cauvet, we are able to identify the designs which may have
inspired this unusual model.[144] Eight other types of round capitals have been
identified, 32, 46, 50, 55, (*33*), (*36*), (*95*), (*112*), (*172*), each slightly different.
Some are simple, flat rings (*85*) while most are encircled by small, stylized
leaves (*50*). Richly decorated with palmettes and acanthus leaves, the capitals on commode (*33*) are, however, an exception. Models of square capitals
exist, the most frequently-used of which appears on nine pieces, in two different sizes: 4.5 cm high (53 and 35), and 6.5 cm ((*91*) and 47). Here, the corners are covered with large, stylized acanthus leaves, and the facets with
palmettes, cotyledons and flowers. Two other models are visible on 96 and
37. Stylized acanthus, flowers and foliage are the dominant features of the
former, surrounding a central female mask. A console currently at the
Grand Trianon at Versailles (part of the furniture which comprised the '*con-
signation*' in 1812) features capitals identical to those executed by Thomire
(96). The richly decorated capitals on 37 comprise finely sculpted acanthus
leaves at the corners, surmounted by eagle heads. The similarity of these
pieces suggests that all four came from Thomire's workshop.

99
Three door designs by the
Parisian architect Mandar,
published in 1796. The centre
door is designed to be flanked
by pilasters. The capitals are
shown in detail; acanthus
leaves are similar to those
found on Molitor's furniture.
From *Les plus belles maisons de
Paris* ..., Krafft and
Ransonette, 1800.
Bibliothèque Nationale

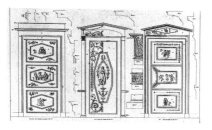

## Baguettes and mouldings

Straight mouldings are used to structure and encase corners and surfaces on many of Molitor's pieces. Ormolu mouldings performed this function on furniture of the Louis XVI period, but with the development of new forms, and the post-Revolutionary trend towards less ornamentation, veneers increasingly constituted the principal decoration and mounts lost favour, taking the form of simple baguettes or elaborately-carved wooden lengths applied to the surface of the carcass, 133. Only later, during the Empire, with the advent of more architectural furniture do carved ormolu mounts reappear; typically, Molitor now reused models which had been popular before the Revolution.

Whenever a marble slab reposed directly on the top of a carcass, the edges were framed by mouldings in the form of a large *ovoli* freize. Different types of ornamentation decorated the surface. Delicately carved mouldings, beading, fluted or foliage friezes, large fretted or striped bands, *baguettes* or *tori* were the most commonly used.

100
The Manufacture Royale de
Sèvres produced this
porcelain medallion from
1788 representing *La punition
de l'Amour*. Sèvres medallions
adorn three works by Molitor,
(see for example 13).
Private collection

Porcelain medallions

In February 1787, the *Journal des Luxus* published the following commentary: 'In his boutique, *Au petit Dunkerque*, it seems that the famous *marchand-mercier* Monsieur Granchet had launched the fashion of those pretty cameos with white figures on a blue ground imported from Wedgwood, to be worn as bracelets or brooches ...' Two years later the fashion had spread and the *Journal* was able to announce that 'Wedgwood cameos have been favourably received by the well-to-do'. They are to be found on all the refined home accessories such as teapots, cups and small dishes in pale blue with white relief'. Wedgwood plaques were also used to decorate furniture, as witnessed by Molitor's pre-Revolutionary production. In Paris Wedgwood bisque plaques even replaced the highly-favoured polychrome porcelain plaques manufactured at Sèvres. Not to be outdone, the *Manufacture Royale* soon began to produce perfect imitations of its competitor's wares. The *marchands-merciers* exercised a monopoly on the distribution of these costly items and Daguerre was soon offering furniture decorated with the plaques. From the 1770s onwards, the *ébénistes* Carlin and Weisweiler used them on many of their pieces. In dazzling white, the delicate plaques were adorned with floral design, garlands or lively genre scenes.

The *Secrétaire en cabinet* in the Huntington Collection, San Marino, 152 is mounted with pre-Revolutionary painted porcelain plaques, although the piece itself dates from the Restoration. Archive documents allow us to date the Huntington plaques, since the central image, of Armida seducing Renaldo, was executed by Dodin, an artist who worked at Sèvres in 1783. This was, in fact, the largest decorative plaque ever produced at Sèvres at this date, with the significant subject of the *pièce de réception* by Dodin after François Boucher. Smaller plaques on the sides of the *secrétaire à cabinet* were also painted by Dodin after works by Fragonard, and date from 1772 and 1778. After 1785, the production of important commissions combining ebony and lacquer work initiated a move away from the use of polychrome porcelain plaques in furniture. In bisque porcelain, (bisque, meaning biscuit due to their being unglazed) the white figures on a duck-egg blue (or more rarely green) ground, found great favour with the *ébénistes*, however, as they proved to be the perfect foil for the rich, dark tones of mahogany surfaces. In Molitor's *oeuvre*, two *secrétaires* are catalogued: pre-Revolutionary in production, they feature cameo medallions on the fall fronts, the subjects of which are '*La Punition de l'Amour*' and '*la Leçon de l'Amour*'. Mythological subjects were a frequent source of inspiration from 1789–90, and plaques were produced and issued in series.[145]

Marble

Molitor used a wide variety of marbles – Languedoc white-veined, '*chipolin*', white, *griotte*, *vert de mer*, *petit bleu turquin*, and Saint Anne – to name but a few. The colours ranged from yellow and red to bluish tones and, of course, white, grey and black in differing intensities. For prestigious works, the *ébéniste* preferred yellow Italian marble or porphyry 66 and 146. Molitor often made skilful use of the veins of his numerous marbles. A tabletop in *pietra dura* is itemized in the 1796 inventory, and a *secrétaire* included in the Revolutionary auction of the belongings of the duc de Choiseul-Praslin, also in 1796, featured lacquer panels framed by stone mosaic. For the tops of his commodes, Molitor ordered thick slabs with straight or projecting edges. The edges of important works from the Consular period are treated in *doucine allongée*. The tops affixed on smaller pieces are often quite thin and protected by bronze frames. The marble surfaces are invariably polished. In 1796, Molitor was probably supplied with marble by Berder, on rue de Sèvres.

## Carcass construction

The carcasses of Molitor's commodes and other large pieces were most often executed in solid oak. Beech was also used, less frequently, for rails and supporting pillars and frames, but oak was always preferred for panels and joints. If a large area of timber was required either poplar or pine was used, which was then veneered. The same exacting workmanship prevails at all stages of construction; even those parts which remain invisible to the eye are beautifully finished and treated.

The mortice-and-tenon joints used for the carcass may seem simple, but they are in fact, highly complex. Examination of the joints carried out by restorers reveals that for larger pieces, Molitor invariably employed complicated double mortice-and-tenon joints. Inner oak panels were joined to the carcass mountings and solid wood elements and drawer backs were chamfered to allow for expansion and contraction due to climatic variations. The drawers are of oak, with sides varying in thickness from a surprising 7 mm to 15 mm, enabling them to be used with ease despite their great width. The

101
Detail of a drawer showing Molitor's exemplary craftsmanship.

drawers of commodes 137 and (40) also feature a technical detail more often found on English models: the wood forming the bottom of the drawer is extended to jut out as an outstanding ridge along the sides of the drawer. This then slots into a purposely carved groove in the carcass of the commode and guides its smooth, gliding movement.

Many of Molitor's works are remarkable for their exacting, internal finish. This, in the context of eighteenth-century Parisian *ébénisterie*, was rare – the external refinements often masked a rough interior. David Roentgen was one other exception, whose pre-Revolutionary production set high standards. The care he took in elaborating internal mechanisms was probably one of the reasons for his prestige at Court. Molitor paid special attention to the smallest detail of the interior fittings of his *secrétaires*. Internal elements were often made separately. The *ébéniste* subdivided receptacles into several compartments of varying dimensions, including both apparent and secret drawers as well as pigeon-holes. This entire element was then inserted into the *secrétaire* from the front, and fastened with screws passing through the carcass.

Most of Molitor's commodes fitted with doors have English-style drawers 18, 66, 137 and (40). The upper edges of the borders of the drawers on

102
View of commode 12 shown open. The ten, small, inner drawers are a typical example of features favoured by Molitor's sophisticated clientèle. These were taken from a Japanese cabinet which Molitor modified for his own use (cat. 28A). Private collection

commode 18 are decorated with brass. The matching pair of commodes, 10 and 12, are an exception, with ten small inner drawers behind double doors 102. These originally came from an Oriental lacquer cabinet and Molitor re-used them. Other lacquer pieces were similarly re-cycled, as drawers for a number of *bonheurs-du-jour*. Molitor's internal compartments are veneered in exactly the same way as the outer surfaces of his furniture. Some have matt ormolu mounts, (*54, 56* and *66*) and some pieces are lined with cedar or sandalwood. The tops of the *bureaux plats* are covered with leather and are framed by ormolu mounts.

103
View of *secrètaire à abattant* 76 shown open. The *ébéniste's* internal fittings were treated with the same care and artistry as the exterior. The drawers and other small compartments were designed to be convenient for the user (cat. 57).
Private collection

## Metal components for assembly

The iron or steel components that were used by Molitor for assembling his pieces were developed for specific functions, and remind us of high precision pieces. The choice of nuts, bearings and sockets, as well as screws and other supporting elements, was crucial for the assembly of the vertical axes. The detached columns ornamenting 17, 18, 137 and 138 are secured by a metal rod with a diameter of 3–4 mm, which pierces the plinth, the base and the capitals before screwing into a recessed bolt, concealed in the upper part of the carcass.

The technically simple, even fragile assembly of Molitor's corners indicates that his conception of corners often went against the basic dynamic laws of the material he was using. Terms are also affixed by nuts and sockets. On certain *guéridons* the extravagant forms precluded a solid, traditional method of assembly, so the *ébéniste* improvised by using hardware to join and stabilize the delicate side limbs 62. The caryatids on the *guéridon* 44 are pierced vertically by a metal rod fixed in the top rail by an embedded nut, and at the bottom, by another encased in the tapering leg. For lock mechanisms, Aubert is listed as Molitor's supplier in the *Garde-Meuble* registers of 1795, recording the delivery of the Tuileries doors. In the 1796 inventory the name of another locksmith, Virieux, is mentioned, to whom Molitor owed 29 *livres*.

Through his innovative use of hardware Molitor could conceive furniture whose shapes and tectonic parts were not dependent on a traditional plan of construction defined by the established rules of cabinet-making. With the complete range of hardware which he employed, he developed a range of new techniques which were to influence the whole of the nineteenth-century furniture industry.

## Glass and mirror glass

Molitor used glass fittings on various pieces 95, 105, 119, 147 and (*91*). Whether on furniture or as part of an overall scheme of interior decoration, looking-glasses were very fashionable after the Revolution, to the extent that certain pre-Revolutionary pieces were later fitted with mirrors 7. During the *ancien régime*, furniture '*ornés de glaces*' was reserved for a select and aristocratic wealthy few. The temporary closure of the *Garde-Meuble* and the liquidation of existing stocks allowed Parisian *ébénistes* to purchase mirrors of all dimensions, at advantageous prices, and to use them, following the *Directoire* period, more widely in their production.

The *secrétaire en cabinet* 105 can be taken as a representative *Directoire* piece; the top element is recessed and supports a mirror. A '*secrétaire orné de glaces*' executed for the duc de Choiseul-Praslin, known through documents only, has not been traced since the middle of the nineteenth century.[146] Dur-

104
Reproduction of a small *bureau de dame*, plate 11 from *La Mésangère*, published in 1801. The upper part is fitted with mirror glass. Bibliothèque des Arts Décoratifs

105
*Secrétaire en cabinet* which is typical of *Diretoire* furniture and features mirror glass (cat. 64).
Private collection

ing the Consular period, the interiors of console tables were often lined with mirrors, as were entire rooms. Such fashionable bathrooms as in the Hôtels de Beauharnais and Bourienne, which still exist, were described in 1805 by a contemporary in the *Zeitung für die elegante Welt*: 'There are not only salons covered with looking-glasses . . . but even those areas where, in the most elegant homes, the walls are normally not even covered, are now decorated with looking-glasses . . . and where the German, at least, would not consider his position so aesthetic as to be worthy of reflection in a looking-glass . . . a room must be of very reduced proportions, or the glass-maker's bill goes beyond several thousand florins.'

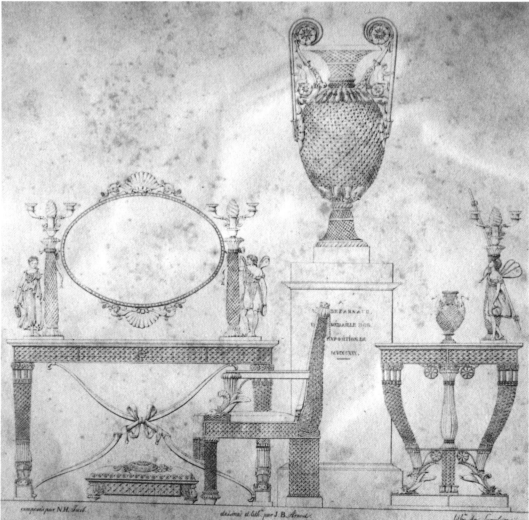

106
Cut glass *guéridon* with
decorative ormolu additions.
Collection Aveline

107
Designs for crystal furniture
after pieces sold in Veuve
Desarnaud's shop 'l'escalier
de cristal' and exhibited at the
Louvre in 1819 during the
industrial exhibition.
Bibliothèque des Arts
Décoratifs

The cut glass baluster of the *guéridon* (*144*) demonstrates the Parisian interest in glass furniture during the Restoration.

Technically, such pieces were made possible through the use of metal enforcements; for the *guéridon*, a tube was passed through the centre of the baluster. On Garnerey's watercolour of the duchesse de Berry in one of her *salons* in the Pavillon Marsan, a glass *guéridon* is prominently placed in the middle of the room.[147] Perhaps not surprisingly, only a few pieces of glass furniture are known, the Louvre has in its collections a glass *table de toilette* and a chair entirely executed in crystal. Nicolas-Henri Jacob presented them in 1819 at an industrial exhibition; later, they belonged to the duchesse de Berry 107.

### Legs

Cabriole legs are an integral feature of Louis XV furniture, emerging from and continuing its curvaceous forms. During the Neo-classical period a more architectural style was adopted, with round legs fitted under the carcass. An affinity with Antique models is evident in the frequent use of a turned, spindle-shaped leg with ormolu decoration, resting on an ormolu hoof. On the best examples of his work, Molitor invariably integrated the legs with the front corners of his pieces, aligning them with the vertical axes of the carcass, 17, 18, 137 and 138.

After the Revolution, naturalistic styles predominated, with legs either carved or cast in ormolu, in the form of animal limbs. These rest directly on the floor or are placed on a plinth 63, 119. The feet can also take the form of a claw or talon grasping a ball 133, (*19*), (*56*) and 174.

Furniture bases followed this general stylistic evolution. In Molitor's earlier pieces, when the base rested on fluted legs or claw feet, the base consisted of a plinth of varying heights 66, 95 and 145. With the progression towards more monumental architectural carcass forms, we see a high base acting as a support for columns and other decorative elements. This base, projecting beyond the corners of a piece, together with the use of a recessed marble top, diminishes the potentially heavy, massive appearance of such pieces. During the Empire, the upper corners of the base overhang even more 32 and 122 and are often framed by wooden or ormolu mouldings.

Furniture constructed around a carcass invariably comprises the fundamental architectural elements of the base, façade, and cornice, allowing the *ébéniste* to arrange the volumes of the piece to achieve a monumental effect. Various solutions presented themselves for the articulation of corners. Molitor's first works feature rounded corners with fluted legs, cone-shaped columns and husk or spool capitals 18, 137, and (*40*). Before the Revolution, Molitor combined round and square elements on the various levels of an individual work, to emphasize large surfaces framed by thin mouldings; the

108
Fashion plate of the year X (1802) showing a console table resting on animal feet. Bibliothèque Nationale

result giving an impression of lightness and finesse 14 and 138. From 1800, square corners were preferred, to which vertical axes were added 77, 145 and (*19*).

The relinquishment of the tripartite front was a decisive stage in the evolution of new forms for commodes. Where the horizontal orientation of the carcass parts had previously been defined by clear vertical axes, the base and entablature now ran along three sides, slightly projecting. After 1805, the role of the square-section angle was clearly defined: the base and the entablature were now distinctly projecting. The central part was generally supported by a pillar or column 32, 50, (*33*) and (*34*) but in certain cases, the *ébéniste* opted for simple square corners without ornamentation 151, (*20*) and (*56*).

The estampille

Molitor applied the *estampille* either by branding or by stamping without heat. The position of his mark 'B. Molitor' varies according to the type of furniture. Few pieces carry the Guild monogram JME (*Jurande des Maîtres Ebénistes*), as Molitor was only accepted as a maître in October 1788, three years before it was abolished in 1791. Certain works have been marked with the *estampille* in several places. The carcass is usually stamped on the border of the top surface under the marble slab, however, *armoires* and *secrétaires* are stamped on the back upper corners, and tables and *guéridons* are stamped on or under the top rail. There are specific locations for the *estampille* on seat furniture. The *lit de repos*, (*156A*) is stamped very visibly on the upper part of the frame. Chairs are usually signed underneath the seat with the exception of the armchairs 183, where the estampille is placed inside the groove which receives the seat chassis. This very specific positioning of the *estampille* is peculiar to Molitor. Many of his pieces are also stamped on the edge of fall fronts, doors or drawers 34, 35, 53, 54, 138, 152, 154. After the abolition of

109
Molitor's estampille.

the Guild, the *estampille* became, following the English example, the mark of an individual workshop. In this role, as an advertisement or trademark, it is most often found on Molitor's later works. Pieces produced during the Empire carry a label on which the name and address of the workshop are listed, together with an advertisement 47, 51, 161.

Styles, fashions and tastes

'Furniture must be Greek, Roman, Etruscan, Turkish, Arab, Chinese, Persian, Egyptian, English, Gothic, in fact of all nations as long as it is not French. The workers of the nation apply themselves to imitating all that is worth knowing in all styles, borrowed from all peoples'. August von Kotzebue reported in his *Souvenirs de Paris* in 1804.

Through contemporary documents and engravings, we can see that the period 1785–1820 was one of cultural pluralism, when a great number of styles and artistic movements enjoyed parallel existences.[148] Besides the well-known variations of neo-classicism on the themes of Ancient Greece, Rome, Egypt and Etruria, Republican furniture or successive waves of anglomania, other notable trends include Turkish, Chinese, Gothic or Moorish elements, all pre-1789. For each of these new styles, a precise repertoire of forms and decorative elements existed. Most important was undoubtedly the *goût à l'antique*, which often served as the basis for an overall scheme of interior decoration, into which other styles could then be introduced: a room decorated *à l'antique* could be furnished with Ancient-Greek inspired pieces as well as a Gothic clock. Commenting in 1783 on Parisian society's apparent thirst for novelty, Sébastien Mercier found that 'Their installations are like ephemeral scenic décors'.[149] Epicureanism, with its devotion to the pursuit of increasingly refined pleasures and sensory experiences was the basis of this constant desire for decorative renewal.

Through numerous travel journals, reports and books telling of ancient or extra-European cultures, the second half of the eighteenth century was well supplied with details of far-flung countries and cultures. A willing acceptance of new, exotic influences in the applied arts went hand-in-hand with a general open-mindedness, and the popularity of geographically and historically eclectic styles. The passport to these decorative voyages of discovery was, of course, money. Hence, they remained the preserve of a wealthy few – noblemen, diplomats, foreign princes and rich travellers. An army of highly qualified, Parisian craftsmen ensured the prompt satisfaction of their extravagant demands. Those who could, changed their furniture, even their wall coverings, with each new season and kept themselves abreast of the very latest fashions, quickly relegating the vestiges of past fancies to the attic. Molitor, not surprisingly, was attracted by these new tendencies. He was particularly inspired by Turkish and Egyptian motifs, for the decorative elements of his furniture, and excelled in his interpretation of the Republican style. Other styles, notably Antique, Roman Etruscan and

English were also embraced, and played their parts in engendering new forms.

The pluralism of styles and the waning interest in excessively rich, ostentatious furniture prepared the way for the creation of new, more functional forms in furniture in Paris well before 1789. By the beginning of the nineteenth century, this trend had led, throughout Europe, to the evolution of bourgeoise furniture – a period style known now widely as *Biedermeier*.

Molitor's first works are broadly Louis XVI in style, and can thus be compared to those of other *ébénistes*, yet his careful use of the finest woods, and the purity of his forms, enhanced by comparatively modest ormolu mounts, set his works apart from those of his contemporaries. With hindsight, the *ébéniste* is clearly in the vanguard of future development. These pieces served as prototypes for his more directly architectural, post-Revolutionary output. His later use of materials and bronze ornamentation during the Restoration, can be directly compared to his earliest styles.

Molitor's long career, spanning a period of thirty years, allows us uniquely, to trace a vital development in the history of European furniture through one master's work. In Molitor's *oeuvre* we see a move away from the courtly forms of the eighteenth century towards a new type of functionalism which seems equally modern today.

Classicism

The most important trend affecting furniture forms was undoubtedly the neo-classical revival, inspired by archaeological excavations at Naples and Herculaneum during the 1750s. By the middle of the 1760s, the *goût grec* was

110
Engraving by Nicolas Xavier Willemin depicting Antique vase paintings. Reproductions such as this often provided *ébénistes* with new decorative ideas.
Bibliothèque des Arts Décoratifs

111
(previous page) Painting by
Girouste, *Princesse Adélaïde
d'Orléans during her harp
lesson.* Clearly Etruscan chairs
*à l'antique* existed before the
Revolution. The duc
d'Orléans was well known for
his *avant-garde* tastes as
displayed in his Parisian
interiors, the furniture for
which was often supplied by
the *ébéniste* Georges Jacob.
Private collection

well established, and antique motifs were being widely used. Among the
first examples of the new style in furniture were the pieces created by Le
Lorrain in 1756 for the collector Lalive de Jully. Montfauçon's *Recueil
d'Antiquités*, issued by Caylus between 1752 and 1754 and the *Diverse maniere d'adornare i cammini* by Piranese, published in Rome in 1769, introduced
craftsmen and designers to the precepts of Ancient forms.[150] In the early
1780s, such artists and designers as Dugourc, Belanger and Jacques-Louis
David developed a new antique Roman variation of the style, the latter
reached its high point of expression, however, in the works of Percier. The
'austere' character of the chariots designed by Dugourc is proof that such
interpretations of Roman forms and uses do pre-date the Revolution. The
furniture unearthed by the archaeologists was limited to basic tables, chairs
and beds. Larger carcass furniture was unknown.

Prototypes for the adoption of the Antique motifs newly-discovered on
monuments and in excavations can be found in a number of chairs designed
by David and executed by George Jacob.[151] The Greek-inspired *Klismos* chair
is one of the earliest examples of the assimilation of Antique designs in furniture. Molitor's chair, 45, features sabre legs and a concave back-rest like

112
Chair inspired by Etruscan
design. Molitor used brass
motifs, inspired by Antique
kraters, which he inlaid in the
back of the chair (cat.
169I–J).
Private collection

those found in engravings by Willemin.[152] This form was soon widely in use
in fashionable salons, and a 1787–89 painting depicts Princesse Adélaïde
d'Orleans seated on just such a *klismos* chair. The *marchand-tapissier* Boucher's advertisement in 1789 for the *klismos* chairs provides us with a detailed
description: 'Etruscan chairs in mahogany with concave backs, ornamented

with cameos, the feet are à l'antique . . .'. Several variations of the *klismos* chair exist, with differing backs and front legs. While remaining faithful to the Antique models, three different types of chair leg were developed. Slender, sabre shapes corresponded to Greek styles, while baluster legs were inspired by Roman bronzes and naturalistic lions' feet by Ancient Egyptian motifs.

Discovered during archaeological excavations in Italy, Antique monopodia were carved in marble. The most luxurious Parisian versions were made of hard wood – highly polished mahogany which was reserved for the most precious pieces 44, 171, 172, 187. For less exclusive, more widely available pieces, walnut or beech was used, applied with a patina in imitation of Antique bronzes 68. Later, during the Empire, some models were gilded 51. In addition to their extraordinarily functional nature, tables 62, 118 and 171 are eloquent examples of Molitor's desire to capture the essence of

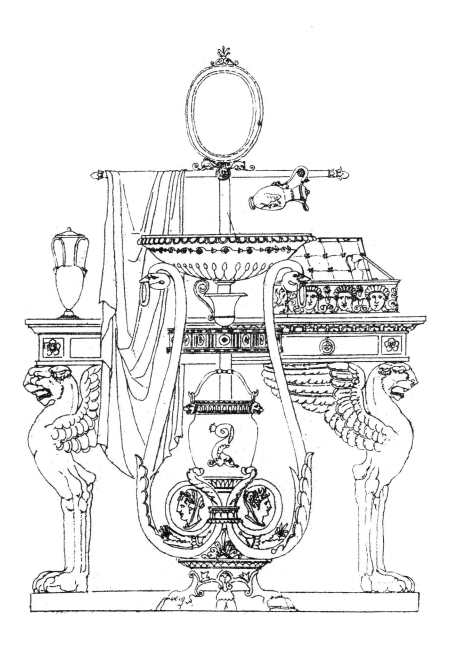

113
Reproduction of a mural in which a table rests on monopodia, created before 1800 for 'Citoyenne V' from *Recueil de Décorations Intérieures*, Percier and Fontaine, 1801–12, plate 17. Private collection

Antique bronze furniture, copying its basic design and reworking the models in wood. For Molitor, the implementation of new techniques went hand-in-hand with this quest.

The creation of new forms of carcass furniture began in the 1790s. Inspired by various architectonic forms such as altar tables and pedestals, larger models were created, complementing the developments in smaller pieces, which had taken place earlier. Monumental and massive in its conception, this new kind of furniture was not without its problems, as described by the *Journal des Dames* in year XII (1805). 'We so admired the forms of Antique furniture, originally destined to adorn immense spaces that we hurried to imitate them and to place them in small rooms for the use of small women who, for the sake of fashion, bruised their delicate limbs on angular

**114**
Unsigned fashion engraving of 1800 illustrating the general evolution towards architecturally inspired furniture and the increasing adoption of the *goût antique*.
Bibliothèque Nationale

**115**
*Table de chevet* resting on a high base, ornamented with ormolu mounts on the top rail, and with terms on the corners. It illustrates the effect of new, formal designs on Molitor's works (cat. 46).
Private collection

**116**
Engraving by Nicolas Xavier Willemin of a decorative ram's head from an Etruscan *rhyton*. The head probably inspired decorative mounts used by Molitor such as that on *guéridon* 106.
Bibliothéque Nationale

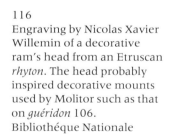

forms, and are scarcely able even to move an arm-chair'. The new style for commodes is also mentioned by the *Journal des Dames* of the same year: 'Commodes are flat, without any visible drawers, two pilasters are placed at each end. The top rail is decorated by a frieze of lyres and Greek vases, and medallions frame Ancient figures, distributed at equal distance along its whole length'.

French furniture was now known throughout Europe as a result of Napoleon's political expansionism and as such it determined the subsequent evolution of bourgeois furniture on the Continent as a whole. Supplied to Napoleon in 1811, Molitor's commodes and *secrétaires* flanked by detached columns are the quintessence of the architectonic, classically-inspired models that were to endure even into the twentieth century.

117
Fashion engraving of 1798, showing a *guéridon*, the construction of which is apparently dependent upon the use of bronze or steel assembly hardware.
Bibliothèque Nationale

118
*Guéridon* designed by Molitor which displays his characteristically innovative approach to construction (cat. 106).
Formerly collection Roger Imbert

119
Console table ornamented with Egyptian terms bearing the royal headdress. It was probably part of the furniture originally belonging to Madame Mére at the Hôtel de Brienne (cat. 87).
Château la Malmaison

120
Design for an Egyptian style clock by de Verberis. Dating from the year VII (1798), it combines many characteristic Egyptian motifs: a figure wearing a royal headdress, *thrysi*, palmettes and snakes. Molitor employed all of these in his Egyptian style ornamentation.
Bibliothèque Nationale, Cabinet des Estampes

The Egyptian inspired décor had been a feature of European interiors since the Renaissance, and long before then sculptures and *objets d'art* exported from Egypt by the Romans awoke interest in the mysterious culture that had flourished along the banks of the River Nile. Temples dedicated to Isis – even pyramids – were erected in parks, and this early adoption of Egyptian forms was entirely unconnected to interest in archaeological findings; scientific research had not yet begun, but the ancient civilization was already exerting its exotic charm. The sculptures and *objets d'art* reproduced in contemporary engravings were from collections in Rome and Torino, or from the editions of the sixteenth-century German Athanasius Kircher.

'Egyptomania' took on other aspects such as the spiritualistic *'soirées egyptiennes'* with their *'thier magnetisme'* or *'somnambulisme* organized by such personalities as the Vienese doctor, Franz Anton Mesmer or the comte Cagliostro.[153] Sketches and plans bear witness to the marked taste for all things Egyptian, well before Napoleon launched his military campaign there. One catalogued drawing represents an Egyptian room for the Escorial, Madrid, designed by Dugourc in 1786. In the *cabinet de retrait* at Fontainebleau, redecorated for Marie-Antoinette between 1785 and 1787, sphinxes decorated the *boiserie* above the doors. Egyptian-inspired escutcheons, chimeras, lotus-shaped capitals and most particularly caryatids bearing the Egyptian royal headdress or *Klaft* on Molitor's works are evidence of his pre-Revolutionary adherence to this trend. In March 1802, the chronicler of the *Journal des Luxus*, reported that Paris was still very much in the grips of Egyptomania.

In 1798 Napoleon embarked on his military conquest of Egypt, accompanied by scientists and draughtsmen whose mission was to amass documentation on the culture and existing lifestyle of the country. This new confrontation with Egypt revived general interest and influenced the Parisian decorative arts in numerous ways. Molitor very simply copied the ornamental motifs which were introduced as a result of the campaign. Influenced by the archaeological findings, the forms espoused by the Consular

121
Portrait by C. Pallissat showing an unknown 'man of science', 1798. The attitude, clothes, historical references and modern furniture are clearly intended to reveal the sitter as a man following the ideals of his time.
Private collection

122
Mahogany veneer *secrétaire à abattant* decorated with ormolu mounts. The stars are references to the *goût turc*. Some of the other motifs were later additions (cat. 62). Private collection

123
Reading table intended for a library (cat. 148). Private collection

style are more severe than those pre-1792. The Egyptian busts bear the royal headdress and are remarkable for their aloof facial expressions. Other decorative elements are also known, such as various sculpted paw feet and friezes featuring palmettes, lotus flowers or snakes.

The influence and symbolism of the masonic lodges, then at the height of their powers in Paris, should also not be underestimated. Many of Molitor's patrons were masons.

Le goût Turc

Oriental motifs have always been highly favoured in Europe and Turkish styles in particular enjoyed a revival in the 1780s. Mozart's *Abduction from the Seraglio* is one notable manifestation of this vogue, which also embraced fashion and interior design.[154] Since 1776, the comte d'Artois had been commissioning cabinets in the refined *goût turc* style for the Temple in Paris and for Versailles. His taste was soon copied by Marie-Antoinette and other personalities.[155]

The most easily identifiable elements of *le goût turc* are its decorative motifs – stars, crescent moons, pods, cloves, husks and various different trimmings – jumbled together with other popular styles of the period. Cabinets or alcoves were fitted with mirrors and their interiors were covered

124
Two designs for marquetry work by Thomas Sheraton, 1787, which seem to have directly influenced marquetry motifs used by Molitor. Private collection

with luxurious silks. The backs of chairs were richly carved to form scroll-backs and upholstered in costly fabrics. Larger pieces were characterized by finely sculpted ormolu mounts. *Le goût turc* was particularly influential in interior decoration, where it remained highly fashionable until the nineteenth-century. Molitor's *guéridons* 172, 177 as well as his chimera escutcheon are fine examples of the pre-Revolutionary *goût turc*. Probably Molitor had this period in mind when he ornamented his later Empire furniture with stars and drapery 51, 122 and (*91*).

Anglomania

The lifestyle *à l'anglaise* of certain noted French aristocrats such as the comte d'Artois, in spite of a long-standing French disdain for their near neighbours, could be seen as a deliberately provocative stance against contemporary tastes. Gardens *à l'anglaise*, private gentlemens' clubs, fox hunting and taking tea were stylish places and activities for the socialites of the day. After the Anglo-French commercial treaty signed in 1786, steel, textiles and stoneware imported from England seriously rivalled French production.[156] The English products were noted for the high quality of their workmanship and

**125**
Tea caddy decorated with a seashell motif. The striking resemblance to contemporary English examples is understandable since Molitor was familiar with English furniture which was imported to Paris. The *ébéniste* is also known to have enriched English furniture with Parisian ormolu mounts (cat. 155).
Private collection

for their reasonable prices. French businesses promoting English style could therefore hope for bigger profits and greater prestige.

Mahogany imported to Europe on a massive scale was highly fashionable and widely used by English cabinet-makers. English furniture was greatly respected for its functionality, solidity and uncomplicated elegance. Its restrained, rectilinear forms, devoid of excess ornament, were quite the opposite of their French counterparts, as noted by the *Journal des Luxus*, in 1789. 'Overly worked wood carving is still rampant in French furnishing, which is far from attaining the handsome English restraint.' Edited in England in 1777 and 1778, *The Cabinet-Maker and Upholsterers' Guide*, published furniture designs by Robert Adam and George Hepplewhite and was instrumental in disseminating their ideas widely on the continent. Adam's distinctive architectural style introduced neo-classical forms to England some time before their adoption in France. Later, in 1793, projects and designs published by Thomas Sheraton in the *Cabinet-Maker and Upholsterers' Drawing Book* presented to a large public designs of furniture selected for their functionality and beauty. These English publications were partially accompanied by French translations and were, in fact, destined for

**126**
*Tables à dejeuner* or *en cas* with two drop leaves. The designs for these gate-leg tables arrived from England and were enthusiastically acquired by Parisians. Small pieces were especially favoured since they took up little space and were often produced in series (cat. 119).
Private collection

**127**
(opposite) Small *guéridon* featuring unusual, carved mahogany columns. It is a replica of an English piece, but the refinement of its forms distinguishes it from the original (cat. 140).
Private collection

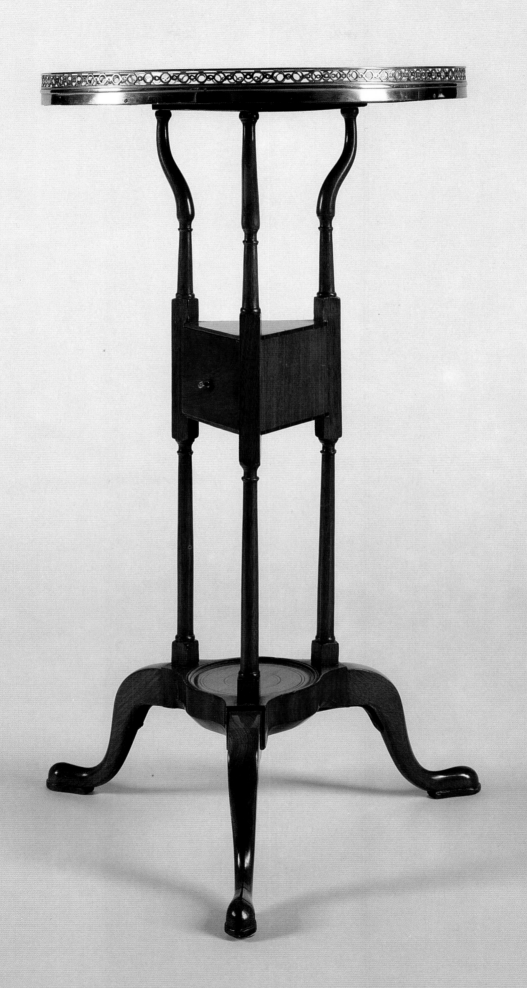

128
Pair of chairs similar in style
to the work of Robert Adam.
The Parisian element lies in
the quality of the carving (cat.
172A–F).
Private collection

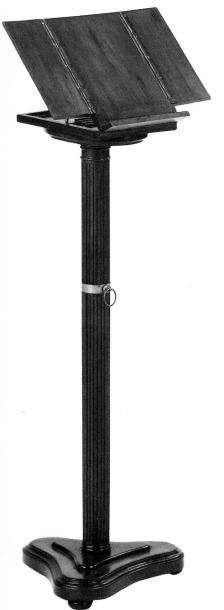

an overseas market. Cross-channel contacts and collaborations between French and English architects and decorators were numerous. The marquis de Marigny, *Surintendant des Bâtiments de France*, commissioned the cabinet-maker Cremer of London, as well as the Parisian *ébénistes* Louis Moreau and Pierre Garnier, to make furniture in mahogany after English designs for his Parisian residence.[157] Similarly the artist-decorator L.A. Delabrière and *ébéniste* François Hervé went to England and obtained the commission for the interior decoration of Carlton House in 1786.[158] Engravings of English furniture designs in Paris became indispensable guides for *ébénistes* seeking to imitate their general style, or particular technical details of their construction. Commodes made by Robert Adam between 1774 and 1778 were decorated with prominent central medallions, constituting their sole ornament in an otherwise very sober setting. This same decorative device was adopted by Molitor 5, 13 and (*50*). The flat front of commode (*20A*) is fitted with three full-length drawers framed by thin wooden moulding. Molitor's commodes with exterior doors, enclosing sets of drawers, and the luxurious, detailed finishing of inner compartments of his large pieces are indicative of his adoption of English techniques 29, 66. Anglomania introduced other radical new forms of furniture: In the large newly-industrialized English cities, small multi-functional pieces equipped with castors were developed which were better suited to life in a small apartment.

English decorative motifs were widely adopted, for example the shell marquetry and delicate inlays on table 42. The contemporary English

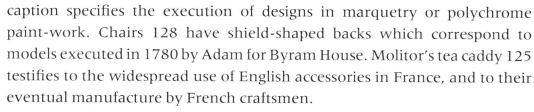

**129**
(below and far left) *Pupitre à lecture* or *à musique*. This small piece of furniture with a number of uses is typical of the furniture created to simplify the lives of people living in small apartments. Prototypes were developed in England and rapidly reached the continent in response to increasingly cramped living conditions in the large urban areas (cat. 142A and B). Private collection

caption specifies the execution of designs in marquetry or polychrome paint-work. Chairs 128 have shield-shaped backs which correspond to models executed in 1780 by Adam for Byram House. Molitor's tea caddy 125 testifies to the widespread use of English accessories in France, and to their eventual manufacture by French craftsmen.

The influence of anglomania on Molitor was undeniable. He was inspired by English style, but not indiscriminately so. Preferring to adopt just those elements that would sufficiently anglicize the shapes and proportions of his furniture, for Parisian tastes, he succeeded in uniting the best of both styles and in bringing an elegance and perfection to his creations that distinguishes them from their English counterparts 123, 126, 127, 129, 162.

Republican furniture

In 1795, the *Journal des Luxus* commented that 'The Revolution has harmed so slightly the fine arts, that it has, on the contrary contributed to their ennoblement, refinement and generalization.' As we have seen in the years prior to 1789, and particularly under the influence of the English and Classical styles, a new type of furniture came into being that reflected the prevailing Republican attitude and constituted a deliberate denial of the pomp and richness of the existing Court style.[159]

Various contemporary advocates of the new rationalism stressed that the ideal of the 'natural' was to be found in sobriety and severity. In *Belisaire*, written by Marmontel, first published in 1767, the protagonist proclaims that '. . . the tastes for noble simplicity and wise economy will soon be the Court's . . . pure and austere morals will replace licentious and frivolous ones.' As the architects Ledoux and Boullée often stated in their writings, the principles of necessity and functionalism must dominate creativity. The latter must not be allowed to submit further still to the passing fancies of a frivolous society. For the architect, as for the *ébéniste*, this thirst for restraint manifested itself in the suppression of costly, superfluous ornamentation. Such writings were clearly an open critique of the pompous, expensive art forms sanctioned by the court. The *Journal des Luxus* chronicled in 1787 that 'the spirit of a true furniture, comfortable and in good taste, is in convenience simplicity and pure lines. This fundamental character can be found in a precious piece as well as in an inexpensive one, for this pure form costs no more than a stupid form in bad taste'. A price hierarchy was thus established depending on the origin of the timber employed, imported or local.

The vanguard of the aristocracy as well as some rich bourgeois who espoused liberal ideas and wanted to demonstrate this *largesse d'esprit* in their choice of furnishings were among the first to commission furniture in this new style.[160] With the spurning of all superfluous ornamentation, the study of a legitimate treatment of materials and the quest for elegance and restraint became essential for the modern *ébéniste*: 'Honour to the distinguished artists who, carried by the love of beauty and guided by the study of Antiquity, render a domestic use to these elegant forms, these severe contours, the beautiful proportions which we continue to admire in the works of Antiquity'.[161]

130
*Armoire* from the post-Revolutionary period. Furniture forms began to display new trends around 1795. The bases of large pieces became higher and the volumes were simplified through the almost exclusive use of continuous sheets of mahogany veneer. The frieze is replaced by an architrave supporting the marble top (cat. 83).
Private collection

131
*Guéridon* from the *Directoire*.
The geometrical elements and
pure lines are typical of the
Republican period (cat.
103A).
Private collection

132
*Table de travail*. Its form is
reminiscent of models by
Thomas Sheraton. Molitor has
replaced the folding rest by a
rail drawer as well as a small
pivoting drawer which is
hidden in each rounded table
end (cat. 131).
Private collection

The quality of execution and the use, for the most part, of extremely costly veneers translated, however, into prices every bit as expensive as those previously commanded by Court furniture, with all its pomp and abundance of bronze. Molitor was quickly won over to the new trend for large, unornamented surfaces of expensive veneers. He reduced or even abandoned the use of elaborately decorative ormolu mouldings – a move that marked his *oeuvre* as nothing had heretofore – and concentrated instead on simple, clear-cut shapes with sharp outlines and meticulously-placed sheets of veneer. Besides indispensable functional hardware, embellishments were now limited to thin ormolu mouldings or beading. Mere finishing touches in the context of the pieces as a whole. The *ébéniste's* basic structures remained faithful to the forms of late Louis XVI furniture, but a deliberate restraint recalls the Republican convictions of his patrons. They reveal Molitor's efforts to modify traditional models through the innovative treatment of surfaces. The subsequent fame of his work attests to his success; the perfect quality of execution, and of the materials employed, are proof of the great worth of his pieces. A commode by Molitor, fitted with a door said to come from the Marquis de La Fayette's office, is veneered with palissander, one of the most costly timbers known to *ébénistes* (40).

The Republicans sought to distance themselves from the splendours of the Court by favouring functionalism and restraint, and by working towards a reduction of forms. Georges Jacob made mahogany work-tables for Lavoisier's laboratory, (now conserved in the Musée National des Techniques in Paris) which were completely devoid of ornamentation. This systematic paring down of furniture forms and styles, from the end of the 1790s onwards, marks the severing of all links with the lavish furnishings of the *ancien régime*.

The mahogany veneer doors supplied for the Tuileries in 1792 bear little embellishment: the few, plain, yet handsome *baguettes* and bronze rosettes indicate that Republican principles at this time had also influenced the Court's taste. The ideals and conditions of the new epoch, which had burst forth with the taking of the Bastille, manifested themselves everywhere in Parisian daily life. New motifs began to appear in the applied arts: military emblems, Phrygian caps, bundles of lances, sabres, arrows, fasces and axes decorated bed-heads and other items of furniture, and the *Journal des Luxus* of January 1791 found that: 'Until recently our little masters and our elegants distinguished by rich, silky clothings, covered in gold frivilities and painstakingly coiffured sometimes even in a grotesque manner, now exhibit themselves in quite the reverse, extreme simplicity, combined with a strong dose of Anglomania, bordering on boorish rusticity . . . '.

The military character of Parisian apartments during the first years of the Revolution corresponded to the new combative attitude of the Parisians. According to one contemporary: 'In the houses there are rifles, sabres and cartridge belts amidst the mirrors and paintings, it's like entering Ancient Rome, or the castle of a valiant knight from the twelfth century'.[162] And even in 1804, the German composer J.F. Reichardt tells us that 'One of my friends . . . won . . . magnificent rifles during Republican festivities in the past . . . and used them to decorate his bedroom.[163]

The decorations which initially embellished the furniture forms *à l'antique* no longer satisfied the Republicans after the fall of the Monarchy, however, and the new creations were only part of a process which was to overtake every aspect of the applied arts.[164] Craftsmen with Republican sympathies who had begun working in the new, austere style before the Revolution were now able to produce their severe, sober-looking wares with official blessing. Through crosschecking various documents, and by the dating of certain pieces, we see that the transformation first took place on small works; changes on the larger models followed later (see 62, 123, 127 (*139*), (*141*). For example, chairs with concave backs can be dated prior to 1787.

133
*Secrétaire à abattant* displaying pre-Revolutionary elements combined with revolutionary features such as claw feet and a marble slab resting directly on the top. This work has an unusual and monumental aspect. The veneer is of the highest quality, suggesting the piece was destined for the luxury market (cat. 54).
Collection Daxer and Marshall Gallery, Munich

134
*Secrétaire à cylindre* in
mahogany veneer. This sober-
looking piece with few, purely
functional ormolu mounts,
dates from the Revolutionary
period (cat. 71B).
Collection B.B. Steinitz

The evolution of the *guéridon* is a perfect illustration of these various trends. The formal evolution of the carcass came about in the first years of the Revolution. In comparing the few sketches and the pieces which date from the period 1792–1800, it is possible to trace parallels between works in the Louis XVI style and the more *avant-garde* form, with shapes that were to become standard after 1803. Drawings by Biennais of a commode and a *secrétaire en suite* in the Musée des Arts Décoratifs in Paris are an excellent case in point. The design of the pieces illustrated in the Biennais album is generally attributed to Percier, and their eventual execution (the pieces are now in the Château de Fontainebleau) is attributed to the *ébéniste* Beneman. The sketches of alternate corner legs demonstrate how new-style elements could be introduced to complement traditional forms.

Within Molitor's *oeuvre*, the lacquer panel commodes supplied to the duc de Choiseul-Praslin offer a perfect example of the metamorphosis in furniture which evolved with the coming of the new century 63. The carcass is

135
Fashion engraving from 1799.
Motifs taken from Antique
architecture such as the
stylobate, or altar, played an
important role in the
evolution of large-scale
furniture.
Bibliothèque Nationale

136
(below and far left)
Anonymous designs for a
commode and *secrétaire*. The
various solutions proposed for
the corners and feet illustrate
the confrontation of various
stylistic trends at the end of
the eighteenth century.
Musée des Arts Decoratifs,
Cabinet des Dessins

decidedly more massive. The ormolu mouldings and sharp angles give articulation to its surfaces and contribute to its monumentality. The evolution of
new forms can also be seen in the *secrétaire en armoire* 140, reminiscent of a
pedestal with caryatids standing at the four corners. A contemporary fashion
plate depicts a young woman leaning on a *stylobat de forme ''antique'''*, the
surfaces of which are painted to imitate marble.[165] In the application of
architectural forms to furniture, continuous sheets of veneer replaced the
marble elements 114, 115, 136.

'Same noise, same movement, same madness and same security as in
the good old times when we didn't even dream of the Revolution', remarked
the yeoman traveller Heinrich Meister upon his arrival in Paris in 1795. The
*Journal des Luxus* for June of the same year is in agreement: 'The false idea
that the reign of the *sans-culottes* would have destroyed the Parisian art of
luxury . . . is contradicted by eyewitness reports which have reached us. The
Old Parisian takes on new airs and never before has the contrast been greater
between life refined by luxury and a desolating poverty than in the last three
months.' Society life recommenced for a few wealthy bourgeois after the
years of the Terror, during which time the *salons* had ceased to exist. Those
whom the Revolution had made rich longed for comfort and luxury, signifi-
cantly boosting the market for luxury goods. Harlequin, an anonymous
journalist writing under this pseudonym, remarks during a walk along the
Parisian boulevards in 1799: 'The taste for Antiquity presides over the works
of our modern *ébénistes* and opulence takes pleasure in crowning their
efforts. The arts are improving because of it, industry is bustling, taste is
refining, commerce is developing, and fashion extends its empire'. This
rapid expansion was to last until the Napoleonic wars and the *Journal des
Luxus* could report in 1804 that: 'the daily changes in the previous fashions
in furnishings and clothes goes beyond all imagining . . . such opulence
reigns in furnishings that a grand bed for a lady of fashion now costs more
than the entire contents of an elegant apartment in the past. All these considerable sums spent on interior splendour, and with the sole aim of satisfying a thousand small fancies varying each month, each week and which
sustain the industries of luxury.' Eminent government functionaries now
demanded privileges which had been reserved during the *ancien régime* for
nobility who were attached to the Court. This necessitated the use of the furniture in the reserves of the *Garde-Meuble*. Lacking the necessary finances to
replenish stocks with new, high-quality works, the government distributed
the pieces that had been held in storage until the *Garde-Meuble* was closed in
June 1797[166]. The closure of the *Garde-Meuble* was due to the fact that it had
been drained of furniture over the years without the resources to commission replacement pieces. Some Royal pieces which had not been sold during
the Revolution, but which had been reserved for the museums, thus passed
into private hands. Later, during the Consular period, the decision to

137 and 138
Commode *en suite* with
*secrétaire à abattant* (opposite).
The pieces form an
unparalleled ensemble of
furniture in mahogany veneer
with high quality ormolu
mounts from before the
abolition of the monarchy
(cats. 1 and 51).
Formerly Villefranche
collection

refurnish various châteaux brought about the re-opening of the *Garde-Meuble* and the authorizing of the first new commissions.

Still another new society, and new forms of furniture were once again required. Percier and Fontaine's *Recueil de décorations intérieures*, which appeared from 1801, was the first to illustrate them.[167] This publication fostered the triumph of new forms throughout Europe, many of which predominated well into the century. The style, which during the revolution and the post-Revolutionary years had been the exclusive property of a select *avant-garde* became, after 1804, the official style of the young Imperial society. The rather severe forms and lighter structures of the *Directoire* gave over in time to monumental, luxuriously ornamented pieces – the style which was officially to represent the Napoleonic Empire. This metamorphosis and its contrast with functional Republican furniture, was criticized by the *Journal des Dames* in 1805: 'Furniture that was made only a few years ago, so light and so fragile that we were afraid to touch it, is today so massive and so heavy with smooth surfaces and bronze accessories that we can scarcely move it. When a lady enters a modern salon, it takes two gentlemen to bring her an antique chair.'

Molitor seems to have had some difficulty in adhering to the Empire style under the official dictates of Percier and Fontain. With the advent of

massive, monumental styles, he was far better able to adapt however. His pre-Revolutionary production had already embodied certain precepts which were not part of the standard design vocabulary. The *ébéniste* developed his own idiom directly inspired by Neo-classical architecture and as always he chose only the finest veneers and most impeccable ormolu mounts.

## Series and suites

139
Fashion engraving from *Costumes Parisiens* from the year VIII (1799). Fashion publications focussed on the latest creations in every sphere of Parisian society life. Models were depicted alongside the latest pieces of furniture.
Bibliothèque Nationale

The existence of several cabinets, tables or items of seat furniture of the same model is proof that Molitor produced works in small series. Besides several commodes which have companion *secrétaires*, 76, 77, 137 and 138 for example, no large suites of furniture have been catalogued.

The furniture produced was intended more as a complement to an existing scheme of interior decoration. Several pieces have been catalogued which together form suites of furniture showing similarities of construction, motif and usage. Six Kassel consoles (for example 47, 51 and 161) and six

lacquer works which belonged to the duc de Choiseul-Praslin (for example 63, 65, (66) and (91)) constitute the best known examples. Other works are complementary and can, due to their stylistic similarities, be considered *en suite:* 10 and 12, 17 and 18, 34 and 35, 137 and 138. After two politically

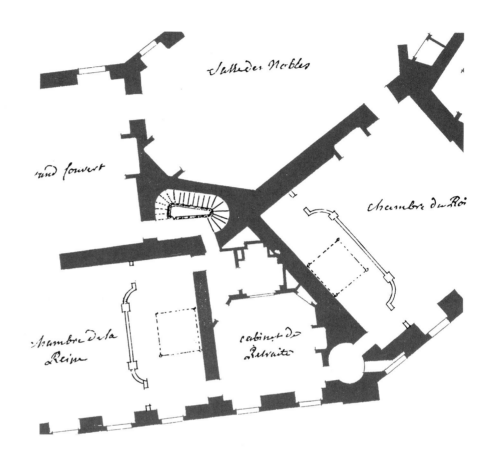

unsettled centuries, certain groupings, now dispersed, can only be reconstructed photographically.

The organization of the Guilds and the specific 'trades descriptions', clearly defined in the statutes, bear witness to the professional confines within which the pre-Revolutionary *maître ébénistes* had to produce his range of works. According to contemporary reports and documents of schemes, interior decoration often encompassed case and seat furniture, bronzes and textiles – a broad range of craftsmanship. The repetition of similar forms and motifs created a unity among the various decorative elements of the room. Textiles would harmonize with other colours in the scheme, to create a visual ensemble. This concept of an overall design was confined, before the Revolution, to the Royal Court and to a few select connoisseurs. Only after the Revolution, with the abolition of the Guilds, and of the rigid guidelines governing the practise of each, individual craft, were such integrated decorative schemes generally possible. The increasing industrialisation of the means of production also played an significant role in this.

140
(opposite) *Secrétaire* veneered in speckled and Cuban mahogany is similar to the one depicted in *Costumes Parisien* and is therefore dated *c.*1799 (cat. 56).
Private collection

141
Plan showing the *cabinet de retraite* at the Château de Fontainebleau. Molitor executed the parquet floor, incorporating the Queen's cipher as the central motif.
Archives Nationales

Ebénisterie and
interior decoration

We have knowledge of two commissions that Molitor executed in the field of interior design, and documents exist which would seem to imply his col-

laboration on other projects. In addition to the Fontainebleau parquet floor, the *ébéniste*, working with the joiner Trompette, constructed the Tuileries doors which had been commissioned by Auguste Renard, the *Inspecteur des Bâtiments du Roi*, in the spring of 1792. The ornamentation of interiors and the harmonizing of the various elements in a decorative scheme were standard tasks for the eighteenth-century Parisian *ébéniste*; in 1788 Jean-François Leleu completed a parquet for the Palais Bourbon, and we know that the Spindler brothers carried out important marquetry panelling at the castles of Bayreuth and Potsdam. Now conserved in the Vienna Decorative Arts Museum, a series of large panels were supplied by David Roentgen for the magistrate's court in Brussels.

The increasingly widespread demand for comfortable, luxurious domestic interiors brought with it the concept of an overall decorative scheme, embracing everything from a room's panelling or *boiseries*, to its doors and furnishings. The English precedent of conceiving complete suites of furniture, as an integral element of a particular interior, certainly contributed to this trend.

In 1787 Bernard Molitor is mentioned in the registers of the *Bâtiments du Roi* with regard to a mahogany parquet floor, along with other work, completed at the Château de Fontainebleau. Still intact today, 142, the parquet

142
The parquet floor executed by Molitor in different varieties of mahogany for Marie-Antoinette's *Cabinet de retraite* at the Château de Fontainebleau.

143
(opposite) Pre-Revolutionary commode displaying characteristic restraint combined with excellent craftmanship (cat. 15). Private collection

floor is composed of several different varieties of mahogany. A compass card intertwined with the Queen's cipher constitutes the central motif. This represents only a part of the original commission, but is all that has survived. The remodelling of interiors at the Château, coordinated by the architect Rousseau, commenced in 1786 and was finished at the end of July 1787.[168] Situated in the inner chambers, the *cabinet de retraite* was a small room with three exits connecting the King and Queen's bedchambers 141. Two windows opened from the *cabinet* on to the *Jardin de Diane*. The floor plan shows a square room with oblique angles opposite the windows. The parquet floor was only one element of the luxurious interior design: the walls were covered with coloured and silver arabesques by Michel Hubert; the fireplace, the window casements and *espagnolettes* were embellished with ormolu ornamentation by Pithoin. Pierre-Joseph Laplace carved the *boiseries* and the furniture, inlaid with mother-of-pearl, pewter and steel, is from the workshop of J.-H. Riesener. The *cabinet* is a masterpiece of Etruscan Classicism, appearing on the eve of the Revolution. After 1786 the Royal Family and the Court were no longer to sojourn at the Château as had been their custom every autumn for the hunting. Marie-Antoinette was never to see her *cabinet*, after the abolition of the monarchy, the Château remained vacant for several years. The *Commission temporaire des arts* included the contents in the planned sales of Royal furnishings, and there were even plans to

demolish the Château itself and sell the building materials. In anticipation of the sales an inventory was drawn up on 5 June 1794, in which it was decided that the '*boudoir de la ci-devant Reine*' was to be dismantled and sold abroad because '... *il nous apparut dans son ensemble trop riche et trop fastueux pour des Républicains*'. A detailed plan of dismantling was drawn up which would facilitate its reconstruction elsewhere. After a period of abandonment and delapidation the Château was saved, however, and remained intact. Fortunately the *boiseries* and the parquet were preserved, and now figure in the restored *cabinet de retraite*.

Furniture forms and their stylistic evolution

## Commodes

The basic model for a commode is a rectangular body resting on tapering legs. Before 1800 the front is generally subdivided into three vertical panels, according to the model in the late 1760s. The most prestigious pre-Revolutionary works have a three-door front concealing interior drawers 137. The innovative two-door model *en armoire* was an enormous success: several variations, all perfectly executed, are to be found among Molitor's works. The majority of his commodes, however, are fitted with exterior drawers. Sideboards, or four-door *dessertes*, are a distinctive element of his production. The unstamped Wallace Collection commode 6 (inv. no. *F249*), is the prototype for 137. Reminiscent of works by Riesener of *c.* 1785, it is traditionally attributed to either one of the two *ébénistes*. Certain stylistic parallels tend to corroborate Molitor's participation in Riesener's workshop prior to his acceptance into the Guild as *Maître*. The proportions of this piece seem rather heavy in comparison with Molitor's stamped works, however. A tripartite front also appears on commodes with exterior drawers, 75 and (9). Here, the slightly projecting middle section is larger than the two flanking it. The ormolu mouldings and strips on the sides seem to run under the middle section, thus accentuating its projection. The frieze is fitted with drawers and is distinctly separated from the doors by a *torus*, a strip or a fillet. On 15 and 137 the bronze escutcheon is symmetrical in form and centered around the keyhole.

Detached columns announced the revival of Louis XIV style; several models by Molitor testify to the renewed popularity of the furniture of the Sun King, on the eve of the Revolution 18, 137 and 144. Husk or spool capitals crown the vertical axes of the columns. Other examples show engaged, fluted columns (2), (8), (9), (10), (12), but only a few present canted corners (15), (25A). Early works are characterized by fluted columns; but in later pieces these columns are undecorated or treated as pilasters 15 and 145. On the far side corners, pilasters complete the articulation of the surface of the piece, these are straight, fluted or of a differing width at the top and bottom.

The bases of Molitor's first commodes are narrow and of limited height. The central front panel is wider at the bottom by one or two centimetres, and attention is focused on this central section by the insetting of a superb lacquer panel, or a distinctly figured veneer. The side panels are symmetrically veneered with matched sheets. Nonetheless some early pieces have large veneered surfaces which are unadorned. The interlocking points of doors and fall fronts are accentuated by fine bronze *baguettes*. The tectonic parts of the structure as well as the friezes serve to frame the veneer panels. The fact that Molitor reduced mouldings to thin framing elements proves that even before the Revolution, he favoured large, unencumbered veneer surfaces. The particularly large sheets of veneer, showing an assymmetrical figuring, employed for the front panels of commodes 137, (3) and 15, are from the most precious varieties of mahogany. In similar works executed by other *ébénistes*, an impression of symmetry is created by similarly coloured and figured veneer pieces, rather than matched panels cut from the same plank. His employment of ormolu mounts to define the separating elements of a piece's ornamentation, follows the example set by Neo-classical architecture. The skilfully carved and chiselled friezes and mouldings are concentrated on certain well-defined areas and serve as visual accents to the whole.

At the bottom of the structure ormolu hooves or paws and rings enrich the feet. Bronze mouldings and strips create a horizontal focus point at the base; on intermediary elements any ornamentation is generally subdued, the large areas of the front being accented by thin mouldings at the most. Small *baguettes* enrich the bases of detached columns, which sometimes have inlaid copper fluting. Some of the most precious pieces have columns entwined with trails of ivy 18 and 137. The ormolu mounts are concentrated on the architectural 'capital' of a piece, where the three drawers are surmounted by a frieze and escutcheon, a moulding or an *ovoli* frieze directly below the marble top. The capitals of the columns are the crowning ornamental features. As a general rule there is always an ormolu ornament on the frieze. During the Revolution, in the 1790s, there was a general trend towards reducing ormolu mounts. Commode 15 has rosettes and acanthus leaves on the canted corners. Shield escutcheons, lion masks on the side drawers and a laurel wreath on the centre drawer constitute the only ornament, perfectly off set by the dark mahogany. For the rest, the *ébéniste* relies on the rich veneer figurings. Other examples of this type include commode (3), *armoire* (82) and *secrétaire* 133.

After the Revolution, Molitor returned to the use of mounts as compositional elements punctuating the furniture body. Commode 63, executed between 1797 and 1803 and which belonged to the duc de Choiseul-Praslin, announced this return. The use of the three-door commode is reminiscent of the *ancien régime*. Its appearance is determined by ornaments accentuating the heavy, monumental, linear and sober forms. If the forms of *ancien régime* pieces often gave the impression that the structure was 'suspended' between two separate columns, the *ébéniste* henceforth applied flat pilasters as vertical components to the sharp corners. The weight of the monumental carcass rests on paw feet. The detached columns of commodes 18 and 137 are functional supports while the applied pilasters of 15, 63, 144, 145 are purely decorative elements.

Weight is distributed differently and the trend is towards massiveness. Costly pieces made of ebony and lacquer were a speciality of Molitor's workshop. Some of the lacquer and ebony pieces 10, 12 and 75 and (*2*) must be considered as part of the pre-Revolutionary production. Commodes 75 and (*2*) have identical elevations. The central area of the base or *cul de lampe* carries over on to the side panels and is inlaid with diamond-shaped pewter stringing. On one hand, the structure of (*2*) with fluted elements is still typical of late Louis XVI style; on the other hand, it is a precursor announcing a design which Molitor later elaborated with detached columns. The two-door commode 12 and 102 is an extremely simplified variation: a nest of ten small interior drawers is an unexpected addition and shows that the *ébéniste* was constantly attempting to anticipate the demands of his whimsical clientèle. Technically, the ormolu framing and mouldings held in position and protected the delicate lacquer panels, and were in this sense indispensable, leaving Molitor with rather less scope for stylistic and formal experimentation than did veneered furniture. For this reason one supposes that he abandoned the use of lacquer for several years during the Empire. The important commission for the duc de Choiseul-Praslin, at the same time as 151, could seem slightly dated in style when compared with other contemporary veneered pieces. At the end of his career Molitor reintroduced the production of ebony and lacquer pieces. *Bonheurs-du-jour* 34, 35 and 53, 54 as well as 174 and (*135*) attest to his use of these materials *c.* 1810.

144
*Commode*, the front is punctuated by three fluted, tapering pilasters. The frieze is built into the doors. Since it is stamped with the Guild mark, *J.M.E.*, it was probably produced before 1791 (cat. 29A).
Collection Galerie Perrin

On commodes fitted with drawers, 75, 77 and (*8*), (*9*), (*12*), (*18*), superimposed drawers without separating rails are characteristic of Molitor's superior craftsmanship and his desire for a unified effect. The middle section of all these pieces is slightly projecting and framed by ormolu mounts. The central panel of commode (*8*) projects from the flanked sections which are divided by uprights fluted *à chandelles*.

On other examples the division into three parts is either reduced to an entablature, fitted with three graduated drawers (*12*), or is simply abandoned. The slow evolution towards new forms for larger pieces began during the mid-1790s. Few stamped commodes have been found. In addition to those which were damaged, this could be due to the abolition of laws concerning the *estampille* in 1791; authenticity is hence difficult to establish. An overview of stylistic evolution is only possible if we take into account other types of furniture. Even within Molitor's *oeuvre*, progressive structural changes tend toward heaviness. The tripartite model was discarded later. Precursors of things to come, commodes 15, 63, 151, (*3*), and (*40*) display sober forms and ornamentation. Through an almost complete absence of gilt-bronze mounts, commodes 15 and (*3*) still espouse the Louis XVI concept of tripartition. The assymmetrical, opposing figuring of the veneer panels accentuates the sober quality of the large surfaces. In comparison with the contemporary production of other *ébénistes*, the radical character of Molitor's works is manifest. Later on, by abandoning the frieze

145
Two-door commode from the Consular period. A vestige of the conventional division into three parts is reflected in the three terms resting on unusual, carved and gilded hooves (cat. 30).
Private collection

drawer, the monumental aspect of the body is reinforced as the pursuit of new shapes continues.

Commode 63 bridges the gap between old and new forms: the front is tripartite and hence pre-Revolutionary in spirit, but its decorative austerity and monumentality are harbingers of modernity. The basic structure is maintained, although the proportions are slightly modified. The base of the rectangular carcass is slightly projecting and rests on paw feet. We can also see a tripartite front on commode 151, attributed to Molitor, but the former shape is nonetheless subdued. The massive carcass rests on a solid base. The frieze has been modified and now forms a narrow architrave. To appreciate the transformation, we can compare this element on commodes 63 and 151 with the version used on console table (*91*). On the latter, the frieze design respects tripartition, which has been reduced to an applied element on the architrave. The base of commode 151 is particularly high; the architrave, narrow. Molitor has totally abandoned richly decorated corners and now they are treated as simple, sharp edges 96 and (*20*). The use of large veneered surfaces presented in an architectural context, free of ornament, was part of Molitor's design vocabulary during the Louis XVI period 15, 137 and (*3*). Pillars and columns constitute the main vertical components on the front 37, 47, 145 and (*66*). Flanking the façade and resting on the base, the isolated columns are treated *en rond de bosse*, complementing the solid nature of the components 32, 50. Equally, we notice the vertical axes, directly continued by the legs crossing the slightly recessed base 66, 145 and (*21*). The two-door commode 28 has been dated to the Consular period. Its massive structure rests on gilded bronze feet; the doors are completely veneered and only framed by the base and the architrave, which is supported by caryatids. The use of ormolu mounts is restrained, limited to escutcheons and Egyptian term capitals. Commodes 28, 77 and (*19*) all have a large projecting base and architrave. The caryatids, with their feet resting on the base, appear to be supporting the weight of the architrave, following the architectural example. On other models, Molitor has abandoned the architrave in favour of a hood crowned by a talon or *cyma recta* under the marble top 145 and 151. The façade is decorated by flanking term capitals of Egyptian 28 and (*21*) or Greek 77 and (*19*) inspiration in matt ormolu.

After 1800, most commodes are fitted with three superimposed drawers, often separated by rails. The front and side panels are wholly veneered and decorative ormolu mounts are limited to escutcheons and ring handles which form the vertical components on the front 77 and (*19*). (*20*) and (*21*) follow English designs inasmuch as the drawers of each are framed by a fine wood moulding. The next stages in this stylistic evolution can be seen in the works supplied as the result of Napoleon's commission of 1811. *Secrétaire* 46, as well as commodes 18 and 32 exemplify the characteristic shapes of the period. The monumental structure rests on square feet or directly on the base (33) and (39). The carcass is held between the base and the entablature; the corners are framed by detached columns. The fine markings of the panels of elm burr serve to unify the different components of the structure 46. Veneering, however, can be used to other ends: the base, the entablature and the columns form the outlines of the front panel; the vein and colour of the wood catch the eye and rather than unifying, they can accentuate the various different elements (33). Molitor employs a variety of veneering techniques with the sole aim of obtaining the most refined architectural effect while reducing the use of ormolu mounts to the strict minimum. These pieces are designed to be viewed frontally. Ormolu is employed in a totally functional role: for the capitals, bases of columns, small escutcheons and drawer-pulls. Another group of furniture, however, supports the notion that Molitor could equally employ ormolu to enhance decoration or highlight his surface designs 146, 147, 148, 149 and (84). In this group a wide range of ormolu elements are used which draw on the entire Neo-classical repertory: stylized palmettes, diamonds, flower palmettes, stars, *thyrsi, flambeaux*, wreaths, interlacements, poppy flowers, rosettes and imbricated discs. A disparity in the quality of ormolu mounts on the same piece could lead us to conclude that certain components were added at a later date. The doors on *desserte* (39) are decorated with Sèvres medallions. Two *genies* surround the keyhole which ornaments the drawer of *pupitre* 33. These essentially decorative elements can on occasion take on a narrative aspect – as in the case of commode (33) where the mounts allude to the story of Cupid and Psyché – or have allegorical connotations 115 and 146–47. The employment of allegorical elements remains rather vague, however; they serve a solely decorative role. A work in which all the decorative components relate to the same subject is exceptional, but this is the case on commode (33).

Parallel to later Empire forms, a revival of pre-Revolutionary stylistic motifs and elements came into being. The ormolu mounts which ornament the doors and vertical components on commode 148; the small bas-relief of the drawers centred on the entablature of 146 and (84), already familiar from Riesener and Beneman; the large medallions on the doors of (39) – all are reminiscent of pre-Revolutionary motifs and techniques.

## Secrétaires à abattants

This type of furniture combines an upper portion made up of a fall front and drawer in the frieze, and a lower supporting element fitted with drawers or two doors. The general concept of the *secrétaire* is very similar to that of the commode, which is understandable since the two were often made *en suite*, 76, 77, 137 and 138. *Secrétaire* 14 is one of the earliest pieces in Molitor's *oeuvre*. The carcass consists of a drawer in the frieze, a fall front and two doors. The cornice is recessed as well as the double ormolu frame running round the structure; these two components characterize the elevation. *Bureau à cylindre* 8, which can be dated prior to 1789, also has a double ormolu frame. The ormolu imitation bamboo columns which flank the upper portion on 14 are reminiscent of models found in Weisweiler's work. The very narrow base has been conceived as a plinthe following the shape of the piece, and upon which the bureau rests. A dialogue is instituted between the visible forms which make up the elevation and the ornamentation; we would consider it elegantly simple. To lighten the fundamental concept of these pieces, and as a precursor of the monumental Empire forms, Molitor applies a whole range of small ormolu ornaments in the Etruscan style. *Secrétaire* 5 is fitted with tapering legs, canted, fluted corners and a drawer in the frieze; it corresponds with typical Louis XVI models. The ormolu ornaments are familiar – identical ones are used by Riesener. The new element here is provided by two superimposed panels which subdivide the front. In addition to an ormolu moulding, the panels fit into a narrow frame which is

146
Single-door commode adorned with a bas-relief identical to that on the *secrétaire en cabinet* 147 (cat. 42).
Private collection

veneered in dark and light woods. The horizontal vein of the mahogany defines the surface of the upper and lower central panels. As the only ornament, Molitor employs a circular medallion on the upper portion and escutcheons on the doors. *Secrétaires* 13 and (*50*) represent examples of a model unique to the *ébéniste* – the corners are decorated with fluted columns. Molitor shows his interest in accentuating the monumental aspect of the structure by rounding out corners in 13. A fifth foot placed in the middle of the front serves the same purpose, augmenting the impression of monumentality. The central part of the slightly projecting fall front recreates a type of tripartition. Similar projecting elements can also be found in David Roentgen's *oeuvre*. The Sèvres bisque porcelain medallions which ornament the *secrétaires* are the keys to dating them. Their motifs – *La leçon de l'Amour* and *La punition de l'Amour* – situate them within the period 1789–92.

*Secrétaire* 138 is *en suite* with commode 137 and both must have been produced between 1790 and 1798. Their form, the quality of the ormolu

147
*Bonheur-du-jour*, 1803–06.
The rail drawer can only be
opened by pressing a button
hidden inside the cabinet
(cat. 65A).
Private collection

148
*Chiffonière* featuring terms
identical to those
ornamenting the *secrétaire en
cabinet* 147 (cat. 44B).
Private collection

mounts and the fine execution of detail are the epitome of refined *ébénisterie*. The sober-looking shapes and the large front panels are indicative of the Republican influence. The detached conic columns, the capitals and the friezes form the tectonic framework of the panels. A thin, finely chiselled ormolu frame outlines the fall front and the doors. The vein of the Cuban mahogany figuring unfurls marvellously over the large surfaces, banishing any suggestion of heaviness. The palmette frieze, the husk capitals and the band of diamond motifs on the drawer of the entablature all serve as part of a stylistic return to the Egyptian-inspired pieces created at the end of the 1790s. *Secrétaire* 17, with its superimposed terms on the lower columns, remind us of two pieces designed by Percier. The two different types of corners and the presence of sphinxes allows us to date this *secrétaire* – which belonged to the duc de Choiseul-Praslin – between 1795 and 1800.

A comparison of *secrétaires* 17 and 133 is a good point of departure for a discussion of the evolution of new forms. The carcasses are identical and correspond to a design in use at the end of the Louis XVI period. But the lack of ormolu mounts, the fine wooden mouldings used as framing devices, and

149
*Secrétaire à abattant* from the
Consular period. Richly
decorated with ormolu
mounts probably added
towards the end of the
Empire, the piece illustrates
the later tendency towards
increased ornamentation
(cat. 60).
Private collection

the small, slender columns, suggest these pieces are post 1790 creations. Stylistically, very little separates 17 and the more evolved 70, 76 and 133.

In some cases sheets of veneer cut from the same plank and used on several different works lead us to believe that they were produced successively
within the same period of time. This is the case for commodes 137 and (3),
where the veneer is used vertically; and for *secrétaires* 133, 138 and (53)
where the panels are used horizontally. *Secrétaire* (56) exemplifies the next
steps in the evolution of new forms. Although the proportions and arrangement of the piece still adhere to those dictated by traditional designs, it rests
on paw feet and the canted corners display Egyptian terms and Molitor has
completely abandoned ormolu mouldings. The writing slide is a simple
'shelf', devoid of framing, but the doors are surrounded by fine wooden
bands. The visual harmony is counterbalanced by the play on the figuring of
the veneer: the horizontal vein on the fall front is opposed to the vertical
vein on the two doors. An almost identical piece illustrated in a contemporary fashion plate allows us to date the piece to 1799.

*Secrétaire* 76 and commode 77 were created *en suite*. The projecting architectural elements, the base, the terms and the entablature constitute the architectonic framing of the front. The veneer is applied *en pointe de diamant* on the central panel. *Secrétaire* 70 illustrates another stylistic advance – Molitor has created distinct separations between the upper and lower portions of the work. The sides are flanked by pillars surmounted by terms. This distinction is even more marked by the various directions given to the vein on the doors and fall front. The lower part shares stylistic traits with the one-door commodes 65. Similar recessed marble slabs are also found on others pieces constructed around the same time 146.

An antique pedestal seems to be the architectural inspiration for (59). The fall front, the doors, even the ornaments are all subordinate to the architectural forms of the whole. The most accomplished testimony to architecturally inspired models is most assuredly *secrétaire* 46, fitted with detached columns, *en suite* with the model for commode 50 and 25.

*Bonheurs-du-jour*

The small *bonheur-du-jour* 105 is the first known example by Molitor of this type of lady's writing desk. Fashion plates from *La Mésangère* illustrating

150
Sketch of a clock by Sigisberg-François Michel, 1810. Associated with the *ancien régime*, the enduring fashion for things Etruscan persisted until the late Empire period, as evidenced in the finely chiselled ormolu mounts applied to the base of this piece.
Bibliothèque Nationale, Cabinet des Estampes

151
Three-door commode in Japanese lacquer and ebony. The meander frieze ornamenting the base was probably added at a later date. The doors enclose three drawers veneered in satinwood (cat. 6).
Private collection

similar pieces justify a date of *c.* 1796–98. Undoubtedly produced in the first years of the new century, the *bonheur-du-jour* 147 rests on pillars which are similar to those on console 47. The fall front is flanked by Greek terms and the frieze is fitted with a drawer. Stylistically it serves as the link between the pre-Revolutionary *bonheur-du-jour* executed by other *ébénistes* and the series of works, all exemplifying the same spirit, produced for the duchesse de Choiseul-Praslin – *66A and B*, a *bibliothèque* and a small *secrétaire* – all stylistic prototypes in Molitor's *oeuvre*.

The known models of *bonheurs-du-jour*, 34, 53, 152, and four others which are mentioned in various documents, can be considered as a series of similar designs which evolved around 1797 (66) and were reused between 1810–16. The later examples, those which are now in the Louvre and

152
*Secrétaire en Cabinet* decorated with marquetry and displaying an eclectic mixture of pre-Revolutionary and Empire elements. From various accounts we know that Molitor reinstated the use of marquetry in his furniture around 1810. The Sèvres plaques were only added at the end of the last century (cat. 69).
Huntington Art Collection, San Marino, California

in the English Royal Collection at Buckingham Palace, London, were produced during Restoration.

Information gathered from irrefutable documents justifies dating cabinets (*66A and B*) between 1797 and 1803. First mentioned in the duchesse's will in 1805, they were part of the Choiseul-Praslin commission and were probably among the furnishings for the family's *hôtel* on rue de Grenelle in 1803. A stylistic comparison with 34, 53 and 152 permits us to date these three pieces to between 1812 and 1816. Molitor's cabinets all follow the same design. The lower part consists of a table, either flanked by square pillars corresponding to an Empire console table, or resting on tapering legs after a model of a small *bureau de dame*, 42, now in the Wallace Collection, London, which has been dated until now to the Louis XVI period. Fitted with a fall front to use for writing or with two doors as a book case, the upper part is always fashioned after the same model. The surfaces are either veneered with lacquer or marquetry. Elements such as bun feet, the plinth flush with the floor, and drawers occupying the whole length of the entablature are characteristic of the Empire period. This holds true equally for ormolu mounts such as caryatids or palmettes ornamenting pillars. The lacquer panels on the front of cabinets 34 and 53 are framed by stylized leaf moulding. An identical frame surrounds the central panel of a commode executed by Beneman in 1787 for the King's bedchamber at the Château de Saint-Cloud 153. This piece underwent modification during the Restoration and is now in the J. Paul Getty Museum in California.[169] The common element supports the suggestion that Molitor might have modified the commode.

The capitals of the columns on cabinet (*66*) are identical to those on a console that Thomire supplied to the *Garde-Meuble* in 1812, 96. Most of the ormolu mounts figure in Molitor's pre-Revolutionary repertory. 137 and 138 both feature a palmette frieze. The interlacing frieze decorating 34 is also to be found on *secrétaire* 5. The terms which support the *guéridon* 23 rest on a shaft with a polygonal base encircled by garlands of flowers which recall similar examples found on tables by Martin Carlin and used again on 152. The garlands of flowers on the rail of 96 are reminiscent of those used on Riesener's furniture and also of ormolu mounts executed by Thomire in the 1780s. Since the old ormolu mounts were still in circulation in Paris and were not difficult to obtain, their use should not be surprising. Mounts of differing quality do appear on the same piece, and might be due to recasting from old models.

The elevation of the *bonheur-du-jour* 152 is almost identical to the others. However, we have already encountered the lower table, the marquetry and the mounts on Molitor's earliest works and this could lead us to place it among his pieces produced in the last years of the monarchy. The porcelain plaques were added much later, at the end of the nineteenth century. (This information was kindly supplied by Michael Hall.) Originally destined to decorate the central part of the Teschen table, the composition depicted a scene from the story of Rinaldo and Armida. The plaque had been manufactured at Sèvres in 1785 under the direction of the *marchand-mercier* Daguerre. During the later nineteenth century the damaged table was dismantled and the plaques were re-employed on other pieces of furniture.[170] The cabinet stand is in the same style as the small *bureau de dame* 21. In joining various components in a new manner, the *ébéniste* could create different designs. His use of unfluted, tapering columns as table legs can seem surprising; when columns are used on pre-Revolutionary furniture, they are most often in flanking corner recesses. Here they have been isolated from any architectural context and the relationship between the column as a component and the whole structure is absent. The execution of the stretcher lacks the precision and the dynamic line which we so admire on earlier works 172. The rail conforms to the one used on 21.

As a result of Molitor's exploitation of the highest quality timbers and old ormolu mounts, all the cabinets present a veiled impression of modernity corresponding to the prestigious creations of the 1780s. The lacquer, ebony and diamond-shaped marquetry pattern reinforce this impression. Prior to 1789 the great Parisian *ébénistes* had supplied the Crown with *bonheurs-du-jour* and highly ornate cabinets – those of Weisweiler, Riesener and Schwerdfeger are good examples. But in comparison with his eighteenth-century colleagues, Molitor displays an innovative use of materials and motifs. Three different types of diamond shaped marquetry grace the rail, the front and the sides of cabinet 152: this would have been unthinkable on a pre-Revolutionary work. This cabinet, and other pieces described in

153
Detail of the *pietra dura* work on a commode supplied by Beneman for Louis XVI at the Château de Saint-Cloud and placed in the Royal bedchamber. During the Restoration it underwent various modifications: the mounts with motifs of stylized leaves round the central panel are identical to mouldings that Molitor employed on his *bonheurs-du-jour* (cat. 67–9). J. Paul Getty Museum, Malibu, California

various documents, attest to the fact that Molitor was advanced in restoring the use of marquetry in his furniture during the Empire. Already in 1810, in the inventory drawn up after Michel Molitor's death, there is mention of marquetry commodes that had been left on consignment with the renowned *marchand-mercier* Baudouin on rue Grange-Batelière (*doc 6*). Among the pieces that Molitor proposed to the *Garde-Meuble*, several lacquer cabinets and another standing on columns and ornamented with three oval marquetry medallions are noted. It is probable that Molitor dismantled certain old pieces he had previously acquired in sales in order to reuse some of the decorative elements on new creations. This reuse of decorative motifs goes back to the years following 1810. The cabinet series, and other pieces, lend credence to the contention that Molitor, with the return of the Bourbons and the Restoration, espoused a restoration of former fashions. At the end of the Empire, other *ébénistes* likewise appeared to share an interest in *ancien régime* forms. Both the series of *secrétaires en cabinet* executed by A.-Louis Bellangé and a *bureau de dame* produced by Levasseur Jeune took their inspiration from Louis XVI models. It is surprising to note that this new generation of young *ébénistes*, who had not practised their profession prior to

154
Roll-top *bureau à cylindre* 8, shown open (cat. 70). J. Paul Getty Museum, Malibu, California

the Revolution, experienced difficulties in marrying the forms and applied decorative elements of the *ancien régime* period.

## Bureaux à cylindres

Initially developed for a piece destined for Louis XV, this new type of furniture had been created by Jean-François Œben, and was then refined by Riesener. They rapidly became a standard item for all Parisian *ébénistes*. In form, Molitor's models correspond to one employed at the end of the Louis XVI period. The rolltop was formed from a single piece of curved wood completely covered by veneer. We have catalogued six *bureaux à cylindres*. 8, remarkably luxurious, and now in the J. Paul Getty Museum is very similar to those delivered by Daguerre to the Château de Saint-Cloud between 1787 and 1789. Here Molitor puts into play the same principles found on commodes 18, 15 and 137: the sides of the rolltop are veneered and ormolu mounts are concentrated around the rail and the drawers surmounting the rolltop. The wealth of ornamentation lavished on 8 by Molitor, with bronze models directly comparable to those used by other *ébénistes* who worked for the Crown, suggests that the piece has a prestigious provenance.

Although the maker of a *bureau plat* in the Gulbenkian Collection, Lisbon, is unknown 155, parts of it correspond very closely to the lower part of this *bureau à cylindre*, 154, and it is conceivable that it was made by Molitor. The description of a very similar *bureau plat* is included in the Revolutionary Inventories of the Château at Saint-Cloud.

134 and (*71A*) exemplify more restrained variations from the Republican period. Limited frame mouldings and exclusively functional ormolu mounts serve as the only accents on the body of the work. The supporting structure of the rolltop is inlaid with copper and yew stringing. The domi-

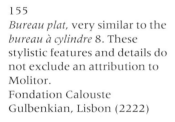

155
*Bureau plat*, very similar to the *bureau à cylindre* 8. These stylistic features and details do not exclude an attribution to Molitor.
Fondation Calouste Gulbenkian, Lisbon (2222)

nant decorative effect is achieved by the flame motif created by the figuring of the mahogany veneer.

Bureau (*74*) has been attributed to Molitor on the strength of the ormolu mounts employed. By its design, it is an Empire model; the straight, rectangular forms and the limited use of framing elements underscore the monumentality of the body. Towards the end of the Empire period, the *ébéniste* returns to a more widespread use of ormolu mounts.

### Bureaux plats

Molitor's *bureaux plats* correspond to a known model from the late Louis XVI period. No known examples from the post-Revolutionary period are stamped. Those that appear in the catalogue are fitted with three drawers and have fluted, tapering legs. The middle drawer on 157 is not as deep as the two flanking ones, allowing for added leg room. *Bureau plat* (*77*) has three graduated drawers of the same depth, a unifying aspect of the top rail; it is equally supported by fluted, tapering legs. All the pieces are clearly designed to be freestanding.

### Pupitres

*Pupitre* 33, which bears Molitor's stamp, is the only known one of its kind. Its heavy forms allow us to place it in the late Empire period. *Pupitre* 156 can be attributed to Molitor on the strength of certain components which appear elsewhere in his *œuvre*: the pillars, the tall base and motifs in bronze are comparable to those found on the *bonheur-du-jour* 147. It can be given an approximate date of between 1807 and 1811.

### Armoires

Five *armoires* appear in the catalogue: all conform to our analysis of Molitor's construction methods with regard to case furniture. Large, glazed doors dominate bookcase (*80*); its tectonic forms are limited to thin elements which give an impression of elegance and lightness. The proportions of bookcase (*81*), the high base and the narrow width, support the idea that it is the only surviving free-standing piece, possibly placed between two windows, in a room entirely fitted with bookcases which followed the same design. The narrow cornice and flanking consoles on the lower portion are better appreciated when seen in relation to contemporary architecture. The writing slide can be drawn forward from its hidden place behind the entablature; this type of detail was a speciality of Molitor's workshop. *Armoire* (*82*) was also conceived as a free-standing piece. The carcass and doors of (*81*) and (*82*) were made using the groove-and-rebate technique. The generous edges

156
*Pupitre de voyage* resting on a pillared stand (cat. 79). Private collection

157
*Bureau plat*, one of the few known examples by Molitor (cat. 76).
Pels Leusden Gallery, Berlin

158
Design by P.L. Fontaine, around 1800, of a *bureau plat* resting on pillars and a solid base. Such a base was often used by Molitor for commodes and *bonheurs-du-jour*.
Private collection

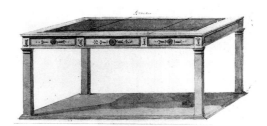

159
Design sketched by P.L. Fontaine illustrating a grouping of articles imagined by the architect, among them, a console resting on terms.
Private collection

of the solid mahogany structure dominate here. *Armoires* 130 and (*84*) are excellent examples of post-Revolutionary furniture. Large, unadorned veneered surfaces and sharp edges predominate; symmetrically matched mahogany veneers draw together the doors of 130 in a visually unified whole. Intentional restraint is the rule for the Republican style, expressed in the complete absence of ormolu mounts: furniture in this context depends for its effect on well-balanced proportions and on the play of opposingly applied grains of the veneer.

The small *armoire* (*84*) can be dated to between 1805 and 1810. Its elevation resembles that of a pedestal, with a rather high base and a projecting entablature. The ormolu decoration is limited to the terms, while bas-relief on the entablature masks a drawer.

Console tables

Only one stamped console, (*85*), figures in the catalogue among the pre-Revolutionary works. The design is austere and the console was probably created between 1788 and 1795. Framed by a moulding and fitted with a drawer, the top rail rests on fluted columns terminating in tapering legs. A rectangular bronze plaque *à strilles* decorates the corners above the columns. The lower shelf is placed sufficiently high to assume the role of the base; it is inset with marble. Attributed to Molitor, console 7 corresponds to a model from the last years of the *ancien régime*. It is distinguished by its large size and its shaped concave sides. A similar piece is illustrated in engravings and also in a project which appeared in the *Journal des Luxus* in 1792, 160. Detached, fluted columns support the top; the console terminates on tapering legs. Fitted with a drawer, the top rail is decorated with an elaborate interlacing frieze. Here also, the lower shelf is inset with marble and can be used to display *objets d'art*. The back of the shelf holds a large single sheet of mirror glass. Several other consoles have a back mirror although these were very costly; here however, it appears to have been a later addition. On this work, richly ornamented in ormolu, wood has a limited, functional role: a support on which to apply the decorative elements. The architect Henry Holland had supplied a console of similar design to the Duke of Bedford for the library at Woburn Abbey around 1787. The console that Molitor supplied to the comtesse de La Marck in 1792 might have been comparable (*doc 3*). Console 119 displays a stylistic advance, adhering to the principles of construction elaborated by Percier and Fontaine between 1798 and 1800. The console rests on paw feet, and Egyptianized terms have replaced the fluted columns. The entablature has sharp edges and is completely veneered; the marble lies above a rail which terminates in a *cyma recta* moulding. The lower shelf is distinctive but cannot be considered as a base.

The shapes of consoles 95, (*89*) and (*90*) evolve with the continuing changes in design and meet the massive, architectural character of the Empire style. Here a low base rests directly on the floor. The entablature has been raised and the height of the console rests on terms, thus avoiding an impression of undue heaviness. The terms rest on the base, on hooves or

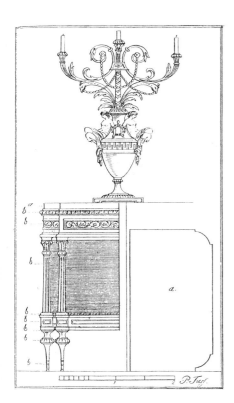

160
Design for a console published in the *Journal des Luxus* in 1792, related to 7.
Private collection

161
Console, part of the Parisian furniture acquired by King Jérôme of Westphalia (cat. 93C).
Schloss Bad Homburg v.d. Höhe

162
Gate-leg mahogany table with an oval top. The table reflects Molitor's gradual adoption of English designs in the years prior to the Revolution (cat. 144B).
Private collection

human feet. The busts are remarkable for the exceptional quality of their execution, the chiselling and the subtle use of matt and burnished gilding. The top rail rests either directly on the heads of the busts, as in 119 or on a double console, as in 95. Console (*91*) was part of the furniture supplied to the duc de Choiseul-Praslin. The arrangement of the ormolu mouldings recreates a semblance of tripartition, a re-emergence from pre-Revolutionary times (see commode 63). The use of lacquer panels on the shelves and the large back mirror show the importance that the work held for Molitor, and his desire to attain perfection in its execution. Unfortunately the complete reflection in the large area of mirror glass is obscured by the shelves. The ormolu ornaments combine pre-Revolutionary and Empire motifs. The lambrequin frieze which decorates the shelf edges and the gallery, decorated with diamond-shaped motifs, surrounding the marble top illustrate the revival of oriental motifs in a post-Revolutionary context. The capitals are identical to those gracing furniture delivered to Kassel 161. Molitor's success in creating a stylistic continuum with the past is only evident at first glance, however. Closer inspection betrays a certain dissonance between Molitor's

163
Fashion engraving from the
year VIII (1798–99). A lady is
seated in front of a small
bureau supported by caryatids
which are related to those on
*guéridon* 23 and on other
pieces from the same period.
Bibliothèque Nationale

memories of the past and the advent of new forms and techniques, resulting in the rather eclectic character of works of this period. The evolution of form is evident with consoles 47 and 51. The latter corresponds to an engraving, signed by Percier and Fontaine, representing an identical monopodia console 113. (The engraving shows a design for a mural, executed before 1800.) Documents dating from 1801 inform us that Brion executed carving for Molitor. The monopodia on console 51 do indeed resemble Brion's work. In the stylistic evolution towards greater monumentality terms are often replaced by monopodia executed *en rond de bosse*. A rather narrow base rests directly on the floor while the top rail has increased in thickness, being now twice the height of the base. Despite the ponderous character of the piece, Molitor succeeds in establishing a well-balanced relationship between the various components by putting a recessed marble slab on top. Conserved in Hôtel de Brienne in Paris, two other mahogany and carved wood consoles, which belonged to Napoleon's mother, Madame Mère, are comparable to the Kassel pieces. Here faun heads grace the monopodia and it should be noted that in these elaborately carved and gilded examples only the base is veneered in mahogany.

## Tables

The great diversity of table types necessitates an analysis of their function, before assessing Molitor's forms. The *ébéniste* created a large number of tables – as early as 1796 the prominence of various models in the inventory of that year is striking. In 1811, Molitor's delivery to the *Garde-Meuble* included sixteen tables as well as other large pieces. Inventiveness here was a necessity and the *ébéniste* succeeded in continually evolving his aesthetic, stylistic ideas. The use of small occasional tables set about as needed, had been commonplace in *ancien régime* society, and such courtly traditions were now filtering down to the bourgeoisie. Molitor enjoyed an excellent reputation for his round *guéridons* and this was also true for his tables. His variations on certain models illustrate his consistent ability to innovate. Most of Molitor's *guéridons* and small tables were originally fitted with castors under their bronze feet, to facilitate their movement.

A study of table forms leads us to the obvious conclusion that Molitor was preoccupied with the elaboration of new furniture shapes. Literature from the period explains and comments on this pursuit, expressing the demands of restraint *à l'antique* in the formulation of new designs. Various contemporary accounts relate the important role accorded to tables during the 1780s. Conversation around a table in the *salon* was a fashionable new activity inspired by the infatuation with English *moeurs*. Large tables were placed in different areas of the *salon*, following the example set by gentlemen's clubs, serving as focal points around which groups were seated.

In Paris it was not enough for tables merely to be serviceable and *ébé-nistes* were quick to test their craftsmanship with their own interpretations. We can judge the response of the public from contemporary chronicles; in 1797 *Le tableau général du goût* reported: 'Since good taste has been restored through the study of the beauties of Antiquity, the objects which have best shown the effects of its perfection are pieces of furniture such as beds, chairs, armchairs and tables; several *ébénistes* have been occupied with copying the antique style with care and intelligence.' Inspired by the examples drawn from Antiquity, the *ébénistes* created masterpieces of craftsmanship and

164
In 1797 the *Tableau général des Modes* published designs similar to those which would have been known by Molitor. The precise outline is evocative, however, of metal furniture.
Bibliothèque Nationale

165
Painting by Louis-Leopold Boilly featuring a *table à thé*, visible behind the young woman. Each tier has a specific function; the tea urn rests on the upper tier.
Formerly collection René Fribourg

functionality. In order to preserve the lightness and the linear design of the Antique bronze prototypes, Molitor abandoned traditional techniques and conceived new forms which anticipate the first move towards the develop-ment of some very *avant garde* ideas. Some of Molitor's models were adopted and transformed by other craftsmen, and various examples exist, represent-ing adaptations from Molitor's production.

It would seem that the Empire put an end to this frenetic evolution of tables, although certain models were still produced for a number of years. New designs for *guéridons* were evolved along formal lines by Percier and Fontaine. Various models by Molitor were adopted and developed in Ger-many. Several years later, the large circular table came into use, a form which was to become the focal point in the *salon* during the Biedermeier period.

*Tables à manger* were mentioned in the 1796 inventory; which pre-sented a comparatively new challenge for the *ébénistes* in the 1780s. It was fashionable to dine in small groups seated around separate tables rather than

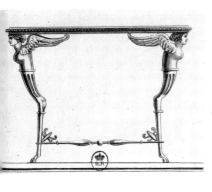

166
(above) A *guéridon* from early in Molitor's career which prefigures *guéridon* 167 (cat. 101). Private collection

167
(above right) Characterized by the sinuous and elegant outline of the base, this particular *guéridon* was elaborated during the Revolution and was produced in many variations (cat. 103B). Private collection

along the more traditional banqueting table – a custom described by Baroness von Oberkirch after her reception at the Château de Chantilly by the prince de Condé. Previously, tables were installed for the occasion, and consisted of simple boards on trestles covered with large tablecloths. The same inventory also listed *tables de jeu* of varying qualities of execution. The *table à thé* appeared as, influenced by English custom, Parisian high society adopted this noble pastime. A new type of table model was invented in response to demand, and enjoyed success. Placed in the *salon*, the *table à thé* was used only for the preparation of tea. Cups and other accessories were set out on the table top; the *fontaine à thé* was placed on a smaller raised tier. This type of table inspired Molitor, and his models are among the most confident in his *œuvre*. Few, however, are stamped, but several series can be reconstructed through an analysis of style.

Circular in shape, tables 166 and (*99*) are his earliest models. Each table leg is composed of a console and a cabriole stanchion. A large rail supports the marble top which is encircled by an ormolu gallery. The use of mahogany and ormolu ornamentation on table (*100*) suggests a date between 1785 and 1790. The same design principles are expressed even more clearly in (*99*). Through its smooth, polished surfaces and the absence of ormolu decoration, the linear development of the leg is particularly important.

168
Sketch of a *guéridon* from a
source book by an unknown
*ébéniste*. The influence of
Molitor's design, 167, is clear.
Musée des Art Decoratifs,
Cabinet des Dessins

Although it is related to the preceding model, it announces a new conception. The two variants of 131 and 167 reveal the rigour of the aforementioned forms. The works differ in the junction of the legs and the lower
circular shelf: this is either connected directly to the legs or is carried by small
consoles. The model rests simply on three legs; the bipartite construction of
the legs with console and stanchion is replaced by an elegant, sinuous outline. Many variants exist of this model, which was widely distributed. It is
also possible that it was manufactured by other *ébénistes*. The discrepancies in
quality can often be considerable.

The form of model 172 is an interesting variant. Four carved monopodia, representing female busts *à l'égyptienne* rest on tapering legs which
support the top. The monopodia are linked by the intricate, curved lines of
the stretcher. Superbly carved and chiselled ormolu mounts ornament the
piece. From the table centre a carved mahogany vase emerges, surmounted
by a smaller circular tier. The lambrequin frieze encircling the top is reminiscent of one ornamenting candelabra executed by the *bronzier* Rémond
between 1781 and 1783, destined for the *cabinet turc* of the comte d'Artois.
Caryatids or female figures supporting *guéridons* and consoles are part of the
Antique and Oriental vocabulary; they appear in Dugourc's pre-Revolutionary sketches. A *guéridon* now at Pavlovsk, is adorned with similar caryatids in
porcelain executed by the St Petersburg porcelain factory in 1789. The
design of *guéridon* 23 corresponds, in terms of its tapering legs, stretcher and
its narrow rail to that of *guéridon* 44 and 172. The monopodia have been
replaced by terms, identical examples of which flank the fall front on *secrétaire* 17. *Guéridons* 62 and 118 are the most interesting examples of the evolution towards new forms. In order to lighten the appearance of the
structure, Molitor dispensed with the top rail; the table legs were joined by
metal braces directly to a thin frame on which the top rested. A delicately

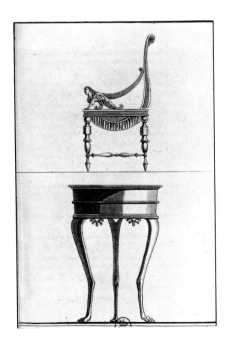

169
Table on legs carved in the
form of animal hocks,
reproduced in *Le Tableau
général du goût*, 1797.
Bibliothèque Nationale

wrought stretcher links the carved paw feet and, with the mid-height bronze ring, constitutes the only reinforcement on 62. On 118 the centrally placed ring, (this time in wood) is wider and acts as the only support since the stretcher has been eliminated. The curve of the legs is masterfully carved, terminating in griffin or ram's heads, inspired by models of Antique bronze furniture. They are carved in solid mahogany and are reminiscent of the use made of bentwood which was adapted and popularized by Michel Thonet from 1836 onwards. The top of 118 rests on ram's heads; Molitor drew his inspiration here from Etruscan *rhytons* illustrated in various contemporary engravings 116. On the piece attributed to Molitor – (*121*) – legs take on the form of monopodia which support a traditional rail structure. This marriage of the two concepts, despite its exceptional quality of execution, does not have the same adept, innovative quality as 44 and 171.

Tables supported by monopodia were widely depicted in paintings of Antique and mythological scenes. In 1797 the *Tableau général du goût* announced 'two table designs, the feet are formed by carved hocks ...'. Assisted by documents, we can date the outstanding design for a *table à manger* 171 to *c.* 1797. It is a remarkable replica of a marble, Antique table, with oversized hocks carved *en rond de bosse* which rest directly under a narrow rail. The solid mahogany oval top overhangs the rest of the piece. These characteristics and the total abandonment of bronze ornament make the table a prototype for new forms. The table (*113*) has faceted brass inlays on all surfaces, which also appear on the top of the legs of the chair (*168*). Each element of the legs is covered; the wood becomes the foil for the numerous

170
Detail of *guéridon* 62, the scrolls terminate in griffin heads (cat. 105).

171
Unusual *table à manger* with a slightly ovoid top. It is supported on monumentally carved animal hocks (cat. 116).
Formerly Collection Galerie Gismondi

172
(opposite) *Table à thé* with a double top, resting on carved, mahogany caryatids. The design corresponds to one delivered to the Château de Saint-Cloud in 1803 (cat. 96).
Private collection

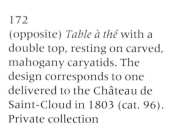

173
Fashion plate from the year X
(1801), featuring a *guéridon*,
(on which the subject's hand
is placed) which is
comparable to Molitor's
*guéridon* 175.
Bibliothèque Nationale

inlays. A comparison of *guéridons* by Molitor and other *ébénistes*, highlights the former's perfect mastery of outline and originality. Tables (*117*) to (*120*) display simpler endeavours by the *ébéniste*, closer to the later Louis XVI style. They were executed in the typical forms of the period – a top resting on a rail and tapered legs – in this sense they correspond to the design which predominated until the turn of the century. *Guéridon* 175 is supported on a central leg, carved in bas-relief and painted *à l'antique* in colours resembling those adorning the *lit de repos* 68. There are no stamped *guéridons* from the Empire period, but the Kassel models can help us form an idea of Molitor's production during this period inasmuch as they were conceived and delivered in a series, and that the suite still exists today. The forms are heavier and are constructed in the same way. They are composed of applied architectural elements, identical to those used in the *ébéniste's* other works of the same period. The massive legs of tables 176 and (*111*) and of commode (*33*) are the same; the table rail is adorned with the same ormolu mounts as the rail on console 47, also at Kassel. The ebony *guéridon* 174 belonged to the Choiseul-Praslin family; it was probably commissioned around 1815 by Lucie de Choiseul-Praslin, when she married the prince Charles Juste de Beauvau, to complement the lacquer furniture inherited from her mother in 1808. This table and its identical pair were included in the inventory drawn up after the daughter's death in 1834. The ormolu ornaments with swan motifs applied to the rounded corners of the triangular base match those on the escutcheons of 146 and 147.

During the thirty years of Molitor's professional activity, his small tables underwent as complete an evolution as his larger pieces. In addition to Molitor's most important models, we have encountered a significant number of variants and original forms, the fruits of the *ébéniste's* singularly creative imagination. In general, the table models adhere to the design concepts of the Louis XVI period; they rest on tapering legs, be they of rectangular or round section, plain or fluted. The occasionally surprising modifications of style and construction realized on certain forms are, however, particularly innovative 127, 177 and (*139*).

The idea behind the *table à écrire* and the *table de toilette* 21 and (*124B*), among the pieces made for the Choiseul-Praslin family, is very similar to that of a small table which the *marchands-merciers* sold in their shops. The marquetry top was certainly inspired by English designs; the placing of the two overlapping ovals, by Japanese lacquer work. The small *tables à café* (*136*) and (*137*) possess all the attributes of standard models of the Louis XVI period. The employment of mahogany, chiselled mounts and fine *baguettes* in bronze leads us to place these works during the years 1788 and 1795. Conceived under the influence of English designs, the small *guéridon* (*138*) corresponds to a model common in the 1780s: the use of plain veneer, the marble top, the absence of ornament, a polygonal stem and three legs originating from a wide base.

174
Ebony *guéridon* probably purchased by Lucie de Choiseul-Praslin, to complement the lacquer furniture she inherited from her mother (cat. 115). Private collection

Due to their original shape, two models merit a special place in Molitor's *œuvre*. The small *table à écrire* (*125*) is made in the traditional manner, but the *ébéniste* has altered the way in which the table is divided into three. The central section, instead of projecting, is slightly recessed. This work exemplifies the ingenuity of its creator who, playing on the public's expectation of conventionality, surprises by reversing traditional forms. The *serviteur* (*139*) is one of the most delightful of his small pieces of furniture, its three tiers seem suspended between the finely shaped, fluted stanchions which compose the light, fluent framework.

When compared to (*99*), the particularities of *guéridon* 177 assist us in grasping the evolution of forms: the later piece presents a simplified,

175
(above) *Guéridon* featuring decoration on the central support reminiscent of sculpted reliefs adorning the uprights of Molitor's *lits de repos* (cat. 114).
Formerly Blairman and Sons, London

176
*Guéridon* which belonged to Jérôme, King of Westphalia (cat. 110).
Schloss Wilhelmshöhe, Kassel

reduced version of the earlier one. The stress placed upon the outline becomes more marked and is reminiscent of the Oriental tendencies of the *goût turc* as Dugourc depicts them in his drawings. Moreover, these shapes were previously unknown in *ébénisterie*; somehow they seem to anticipate the design which was to predominate during the 1920s. Tables 127 and (*141*) present a novel shape: the tripod feet and wide base recall English models. Encased by fine, curved columns, a small, triangular structure fitted with a drawer serves as an additional point of support. Molitor's creative, innovative spirit is expressed fully in this unconventional treatment of a standard table model.

The *pupitres à musique* 129 and (*143*) rest on a triangular plinth. The shaft, with fluting along its whole length and the total absence of ornament, lead us to date this model to between 1790 and 1800.

Some of Molitor's pieces are characterized by delicate frameworks, with particularly graceful supporting elements, conferring an impression of lightness. This approach is opposed to traditional construction where a solid appearance is desired, as expressed in the preponderance of legs and rails.

177
Kingwood *guéridon* with brass inlays. The fluid lines of the legs are typical of the interest in outline after 1790. In this case inspiration is drawn from Oriental motifs (cat. 109). Private collection

178
(opposite) *Jardinière* belonging to Jérôme, King of Westphalia. The carved caryatids and the choice of ormolu mounts support an attribution to Molitor (cat. 153B).
Schloss Wilhelmshöhe, Kassel

179
*Tables vide-poches* were listed in Molitor's 1796 inventory. This model can be dated to the pre-Revolutionary period due to its diamond-shaped marquetry (cat. 146B). Private collection

The employment of stanchions considerably streamlines the strict tectonic elements based on circular or sinuous lines, the key to the elegant design of *table de travail* 132 lies in the realization of the stanchions. The circle *leitmotiv* is expressed in three interlaced marquetry circles on the middle of the uprights. The light construction, providing easy mobility, and its artistic realisation metamorphose this small work into a refined *cabinet de dame*.

Highly favoured before the Revolution, the *tables vide-poche*, for example 179 covered with citronwood marquetry correspond to tables which were in vogue from 1785. The sides which carry the top tray *en caisson* are only joined by a lower oval shelf. Obviously this type of construction would be unpracticable without the use of hidden, metal pieces which support the structure. The *tables de lecture* 123 and (*149*) have a distinctive narrow, elongated profile. The fragile-looking components are all rounded; the uprights and the middle stretcher provide the necessary stability. The concept of table 25 seems to be influenced by English sources. The use of ebony veneer and a drawer the full length of the rail are identical to those employed on cabinet 53 and (*66*). We can suppose that the table dates from the *Directoire* period by virtue of the large palm fronds adorning the uprights and the bell feet.

Tables 55 and (*135A and B*) are classified among the later works, after 1810. By the copying of individual elements, particular decorative motifs and the probable re-employment of ormolu mounts recovered from dismantled works, these tables seem to date from the pre-Revolutionary period; due to the evolution of forms and proportions, and their novel combinations of certain isolated components, they do not attain the perfection of their pre-Revolutionary models, however. The openwork stretcher, the baluster legs and the ormolu mounts applied on the drawer front of 55 are reminiscent of Molitor's own early works as well as those of Weisweiler. The stretchers are heavy, pronounced and lack traditionally-applied ormolu mounts on their upper edges (see 23 and 44). The Egyptian granite top is set back from the edge; the ormolu capitals and the palmette friezes feature Empire motifs. (*135A and B*) are classified among the late works. With the use of ebony, tapering legs and various ormolu mounts, the *ébéniste* attempts to achieve the luxurious appearance of his pre-Revolutionary works. However, the discrepancies in detail and the use of conflicting stylistic elements are unsatisfactory. *Guéridon* (*144*) is a strikingly original example of his late works. Positioned on each extremity of the triangular base is a bronze recumbent lion, originally designed to adorn *chenets* or fire dogs. A round top rests on a central cut crystal balustre.

180
Mahogany table *vide-poche*, unstamped but its unusual shape is reminiscent of other works by Molitor.
Private collection

Miscellaneous furniture and small objects

*Jardinières*, 37 and 178, screens and small boxes, 125, complete the wide range of products issuing from Molitor's workshop. The following few articles are all of excellent craftsmanship, and observe the same stylistic evolution as the larger pieces. *Jardinière* 37 is most probably contemporary with cabinets 34, 53, 152. Its exterior is decorated with ormolu mounts that we can identify as pre-Revolutionary. It was actually destined to be a musical clock case but was later transformed into a *jardinière* – a fact which can be deduced from the subject matter of the ormolu ornamentation: Apollo is represented on the central plaque and lyres adorn the sides. The stand consists of pillars and a base, both decorated in ormolu. Dating from the Empire period, the *jardinière* is a splendid example of the re-use of older elements. The ormolu motifs are comparable to the pre-Revolutionary production of

181
*Guéridon* featuring ormolu mounts similar to those employed by Molitor. The caryatids are in patinated bronze (cat. 134).
Private collection

182
(opposite) Detail of *fauteuil*. The griffin motif is finely carved *en rond de bosse* (cat. 164).
Musée Marmotan, Paris

183
(opposite, below left and right) *Fauteuil* featuring distinctive tapering legs terminating in carved paw feet, with straight set-back armrests and magnificently shaped backrest (cat. 165).
Private collection

184
(opposite, below centre) Chair *ensuite* with *fauteuil* 183 (cat. 166).
Private collection

Thomire and Rémond adorning a medal cabinet executed by Beneman for
Louis XVI *c.* 1791.

The only fire screen, (*154*) is ornamented with a Sèvres bisqué medallion. A side flap transforms it into a small writing table. The tea caddy, 125
is the only one of its type catalogued. The various mahogany boxes listed in
the 1796 inventory and the *chaufferettes* in the form of books mentioned in
Molitor's early advertisements also come to mind.

Molitor also made storage cases for furs, in citronwood lined with sandalwood, for the comtesse de Lamarck (*doc* 3). From contemporary documents it seems that the *ébéniste* produced a large array of pieces,
unfortunately we can only present the reduced number of extant known
works. Under heading 93 in the inventory drawn up after his death, mention is made of '*une couchette en bois d'acajou à bateau et à têtes bronzées*' and
elsewhere, '*deux couchettes en bois de rapport*'. *Table de chevet* 115 is part of a
bedroom suite, which would lead us to the assumption that the *ébéniste* produced bedsteads, although none have been found to this day. Despite the absence of *tables tronchin* in Molitor's *œuvre*, we know of a large architect's table
fitted with several mechanisms, now in a private collection (*123*).

Seat Furniture

One of the changes ushered in by the Revolution for *ébénistes* was the newly-
acquired right to make seat furniture, an activity which had been previously
prohibited by their Guild's by-laws and strict trade demarcations. Conversely, joiners had not been allowed to produce large veneered pieces
before 1791. Profiting from their new found liberty after the abolition of the
Guild, certain workshops launched themselves in the production of formerly prohibited items, and Molitor was among the first to make seat furniture; five different models are catalogued, as well as four different *lits de
repos*. In contrast to the fluid structures of the Louis XV period, the form of

186
Mahogany *lit de repos* with
chimera reliefs on the
uprights (cat. 162).
Private collection

the neo-classical seats was characterized by an individual treatment of each element. The basic design of the chair is enlarged in width and depth, and fitted with armrests. Influenced by the Antique Greek design – the *klismos* – the chair elaborated by Molitor was faithful to the engravings of antiques unearthed by archaeological diggings, fitted with sabre legs and a concave back, which then becomes a field for ornaments or painting. Molitor's seat-backs were inlaid with geometrically patterned brass string inlay motifs derived from English sources. The edges of various components were framed by brass *ovoli baguettes*. At the end of the eighteenth century, numerous contemporary illustrations of the *klismos* chair attest to its enormous success. The twelve chairs supplied to the *Garde-Meuble* in 1810 are a derivative of the *klismos* model with concave backs. This commission exemplifies the long period of production of this type of chair which was later manufactured less expensively – in walnut to be used as an office chair (*doc* 7).

*Lits de Repos*

Two models of *lits de repos* are catalogued, derived from the Ancient design.

186
Mahogany *lit de repos* with
chimera reliefs on the
uprights (cat. 162).
Private collection

187
Uprights of a *lit de repos*
showing griffins carved in
relief (cat. 157).
Private collection

Here again the exact source comes from painted vases. The sculpted natu-ralistic hock legs support the rail which terminates on both ends with el-egant, scrolled backs. The models are differentiated by the use of a double or single back; in the latter case, an oblique board prevents the mattress from sliding. Differences arise concerning carved bas-reliefs on one or both sides, and in the nature of the sculpted elements: griffins, chimera or aquatic mon-sters. The backs *en planche* are also sometimes adorned by carved elements. Molitor employed a gorgon's head, on rectangular or diamond-shaped fields. The bottom edge of the back of 187 is adorned with carved *laminae* re-sembling those found on antique breastplates. His most prestigious models are 186, 187 and (*156A*) with bas-reliefs carved in solid mahogany. Other models have applied carved motifs, in walnut or lime; these reliefs are pat-inated in verdigris and are highlighted once applied to the darker mahogany 68. The craftsmanship of the carving is extraordinary, akin to the orna-mental elements on a seat signed by Demay, (in the Musée Carnavalet in Paris). Indeed, Demay is listed as a supplier to the workshop in the 1796 inventory. 27 and (*159*) are the only examples which have decorated semi-circular supports under the centre of the rail.

*Armchairs and Chairs*

Three models of chairs and armchairs inspired by the *klismos* are catalogued. Now in the Musée Marmottan in Paris, the armchairs 72 have tapering, baluster legs, with the armrests reposing on the tips of the uplifted wings of griffins carved *en rond de bosse* 182. All that remains of the original brass ornamentation are *baguettes* and shoes for the feet of the legs. An engraving from year VI depicting a similar piece allows us to date the chair to *c.* 1797–98. Another model has also been listed: a matching chair and armchair, with tapering baluster front legs resting on carved paws. The wide and high back with its slender curve is the embodiment of elegance. The straight armrest reposes on the vigorous curve of the upright 183 and 184. The examples which most faithfully imitate the Antique chair are 45, 73, 112 and 185. The concept of the *klismos* chair is dominated by the rational relationship between the individual shapes and the decoration, applied or inlaid. Whatever the treatment of the model – ornate or restrained – the tectonic components are exploited to the limits of severity. Molitor's mastery is here revealed at its best in the use of mahogany. The basic model can receive inlays or ornaments on the seat rail, leg fronts, or back. Five different versions exist, with various shapes and decoration. The seat is supported by a frame and can be upholstered in silk, leather or horsehair. Models 128 and (*173*) are probably influenced by English sources. The shield back is reminiscent of chairs designed by Robert Adam for the vestibule of Byram House, Yorkshire, in 1780. Other engravings of work by English designers could have inspired Molitor, such as those by Hepplewhite which reached the four corners of the continent soon after their publication in 1787.

Probable attributions and workshop pieces

Since a considerable number of unstamped pieces do show similar characteristics to those of known pieces by Molitor, it is possible to argue that in some cases these pieces might have been produced in his workshop 180. One such piece is a console table which is very close in appearance to the stamped consoles, 95 and (*90*). In this case, however, the table is signed by Demay who, while during the Consular period was known as a chairmaker, also collaborated with Molitor's workshop.

On stylistic grounds again, a *secrétaire* and a commode *en suite* from the Directoire period, also lead use to think that they were made in Molitor's workshop 189.

Another sideboard, now in a private collection, is especially notable since it bears Molitor's stamp in no less than three separate places. Since it is clearly of English origin, it can be assumed that it was shipped to France where Molitor removed the original ornaments and replaced them with ormolu lions' head mounts of Parisian origin. The stamps would have been applied at this time.

Several pieces by Molitor have inspired later cabinet-makers. We know of pieces made by the late-nineteenth-century *ébénistes* Henri Dasson and Grohé Frères that clearly reflect the impact of Molitor's stylistic approach. Several copies of *guéridon* 44 are also known from the end of the nineteenth century and more recently, in 1988, a Parisian gallery has made copies of the *Klismos* chair 45, 73 and (*167*), in painted beech.

188
An example of the many known copies made of *guéridon* 172.
Private collection

189
*Secrétaire* and *en suite*
commode from post-
Revolutionary period. Due to
stylistic similarities it is
possible that they were made
by Molitor.
Collection Galerie Fabre

# Catalogue

All measurements are given in centimetres, in order height, width and depth, when known. Round/oval tables have two measurements, height and diameter, when known. Cross references in the catalogue are to other catalogue numbers. The numbers in brackets alongside the catalogue numbers refer to illustrations in the main text.

2

3

**Three-door commodes**

1 *(137)*
**Commode, stamped** *B. Molitor: c. 1788–92*
Cuban mahogany, oak, ormolu mounts and *griotte* marble;
92×137×62
   *Provenance:* Formerly Villefranche Collection; sold at Crédit Municipal, Paris, 26 Nov 1970, no. 17 repr.; private collection.
   *Literature: Les chefs-d'œuvre des grands ébénistes 1790–1850,* Musée des Arts Décoratifs, exhibition catalogue, 1951; P. Guth, 'La carrière brisée d'un ébéniste d'avant-garde B. Molitor, '*Connaissance des Arts,* vi, p. 70 1957; *Les ébénistes du XVIII siècle,* Paris, 1965, p. 318; D. Ledoux Lebard, *Les ébénistes parisiens, leurs œuvres et leurs marques 1795–1870,* Paris; 1984, p. 488; A. Pradère, *Les ébénistes français,* Paris 1989, p. 427.
   *Exhibited* Musée des Arts Décoratifs, Paris, 1951: *Les chefs-d'œuvre des grands ébénistes 1790–1850.*

2
**Commode, stamped** *B. Molitor* **and** *E. Levasseur; c. 1785–88*
Lacquer panels, ebony, oak, ormolu mounts, pewter and marble;
86×120
   *Provenance:* Sale, Château d'Ermenonville, 8 March 1933, no. 108 repr.

3A and B
**Pair of commodes, stamped** *B. Molitor; 1789–93*
Mahogany, ormolu mounts and marble;
90×138
   *Provenance:* Sold at Demonts, Paris, 23 May 1921, no. 237.

4A and B *(15)*
**Two commodes stamped** *B. Molitor; 1788–93*
Mahogany, oak, ormolu mounts and grey marble;
4A: 90×152×53, (4B measurements unknown).
   *Provenance:* Private collection.

5 *(63 and 66)*
**Commode, stamped** *B. Molitor; 1797–1803*
Japanese lacquer panels, ebony, oak, matt ormolu mounts and yellow Sienna marble;
95×140×55
   *Provenance:* Made for Antoine-César de Choiseul III, duc de Praslin; in 1808, placed in the bedroom of the duchesse de Praslin, née Charlotte O'Brian de Thomond, then removed to the residence of Lucie-Virginie de Choiseul-Praslin, wife of Charles-Juste, prince de Beauvau. Private collection.
   *Documents:* A.N. Min. Cent. LVIII-638, -639, LVIII-739, LIV-1369
   *Literature:* D. Cooper, *Trésors d'art français dans des collections privées,* Zurich, 1965, p. 302, repr.; U. Leben 'Choiseul-Praslin furniture by Molitor' In *f.H.S.,* xxvii, 1991.

6 *(151)*
**Commode, attributed;** *c. 1800–03*
Ebony, lacquer panels, ormolu mounts, marble and a signed lock by Fichet;
84×134×47
   *Provenance:* Sold at Christie's New York, 7 Feb. 1988, no. 288 transformed

and enriched with bronzes; sold at Franco Semenzato, Rome 23–25 May 1990, no. 144.

**Commodes with drawers**

7 (75)

**Commode, attributed;** *c. 1787–92*
Ebony, lacquer panels, ormolu mounts, pewter, mother of pearl and marble; 96.5×136×60.5

*Provenance:* Acquired for the future George IV through the intermediary Monsieur Wattier and delivered in December 1816 with 68A and B to Carlton House. Windsor Castle, Collection of H.M. the Queen.

*Literature:* G.F. Laking, *The Furniture of Windsor Castle*, London, 1905, *fig* 42; U. Leben 'Die Werkstatt B. Molitor,' *Kunst und Antiquitäten*, iv, 1987, repr. p.52.

8

8

**Commode, stamped** *B. Molitor; c. 1787–90*
Mahogany, ormolu mounts and marble; 92×127×60

*Provenance:* Formerly Grognart and Joinel Collection, Paris.
*Literature:* Guth, 'La carrière brisée . . .,' 1957, repr.

9

**Commode, stamped** *B. Molitor; c. 1787–90*
Mahogany, ormolu mounts and marble.
*Provenance:* Private collection.
*Literature:* M. Burckhard, *Le Mobilier Louis XVI*, Paris, p. 39. repr.

10

**Commode, stamped** *B. Molitor; c. 1787–95*
Mahogany, ebony, ormolu mounts and grey marble; 89×132×62

*Provenance:* Sold at Galerie Charpentier, Paris, 2 Dec. 1955, no. 86. A commode with three rows of drawers in mahogany and ebony veneers. The middle section is slightly extended; the fluted legs are decorated with ormolu decorations; grey marble top; period Louis XVI.

11

**Commode, stamped** *B. Molitor; c. 1788–93*
Mahogany, ormolu mounts and marble.
*Provenance:* Private collection. With various old inventory references. A commode with three rows of drawers, flanked by fluted vertical uprights on the front and fluted pilasters behind. The edges of the drawers are decorated with fine ormolu mounts.

12

**Commode, stamped** *B. Molitor; c. 1788–92*
Mahogany, ormolu mounts and marble; 84×132×63

*Provenance:* Sold at Béthune, 28 Sept. 1980, no. 86, repr.

13

**Commode, stamped** *B. Molitor; c. 1788–95*
Mahogany, citronwood, amaranth, ormolu mounts and marble; 82×83×40

*Provenance:* Sold at Versailles, 11 June 1969, no. 228. The commode is fitted with three front drawers and rests on four tapering legs. Mahogany uprights fluted *à chandelles,* ormolu mounts, grey Saint Anne marble.

### 14
**Commode, attributed to Molitor;** *c. 1785–89*
Mahogany, ormolu mounts and marble;
86.5×130×59.5
> *Provenance:* Sold at Sotheby Parke-Bernet New York, 17 May 1980, no. 320, repr.; The Garbish Collection.

### 15 (*143*)
**Commode, stamped** B. Molitor **and** *J.M.E., (Guild monogram); c. 1788–91*
Mahogany, oak, ormolu mounts, brass and Saint Anne marble;
86×120×61
> *Provenance:* Sold at Christie's, Monaco, 7 Dec. 1985, no. 61, repr.

### 16
**Commode, stamped** B. Molitor; *c. 1789–96*
Mahogany, ormolu mounts and white marble;
86.5×102×56
> *Provenance:* Sold by Daussy Ricqlès, Paris, 24 Dec. 1990, lot 239, repr.

### 17
**Commode, stamped** B. Molitor; *c. 1788–92*
Speckled mahogany, ormolu mounts and marble;
84×125×61
> *Provenance:* Sold at Château de X, Deauville, 20 April 1987, repr.
> *Literature:* 'Le guide du marché de l'art,' *Gazette de Drouot*, Paris, 1988.

### 18 (77)
**Commode, stamped** B. Molitor; *c. 1798–1803*
Citronwood, oak, ormolu mounts and marble;
84×133×65 (*en suite* with 57)
> *Provenance:* Sold at Franco Semenzato, Rome, 22 March 1990, lot 225, repr. Private collection.

### 19
**Commode, stamped** B. Molitor; *c. 1803–05*
Mahogany, ormolu mounts and white marble.
> *Provenance:* Private collection.

### 20A
**Commode, stamped** *twice* B. Molitor; *1802*
Mahogany, oak, ormolu mounts, brass, anthracite and marble;
93×96×40.5
> *Provenance:* Private collection.

### 20B
**Commode, attributed to Molitor;** *1805–10*
Mahogany, oak, beech, ormolu mounts and grey marble;
91×95×42
> *Provenance:* Private collection.

### 21
**Commode, attributed to Molitor;** *1802*
Mahogany, oak, beech and pine, ormolu mounts, and marble;
93×112×51

16

19

20B

21

*Provenance:* Musée des Arts Décoratifs, Paris, inv. no. 28436, bequeathed by Mme David Nillet, 1933

*Literature:* C. Bizot, *Mobilier Directoire et Empire,* Paris, p. 73, repr.; N. Apra, *Il mobile Impero,* Novara, 1970, *fig* 39; A. Stone. *Antique Furniture,* London, 1982, p. 211, repr.

22

**Commode, attributed to Molitor;** *1803–05*
Mahogany, ormolu mounts and grey marble;
89×132×61

*Provenance:* Sold at Sotheby Parke-Bernet, New York, 7 May 1983, no. 126, repr.

23

**Commode, stamped** *B. Molitor; c. 1803–08*
Mahogany, ormolu mounts and white marble;
89×132×61

*Provenance:* Private collection. The massive body rests on a high base. Two rail-less drawers are flanked by ormolu Egyptian terms which support the entablature drawer. The quality of the veneer is exceptional.

24 (*50*)

**Commode, stamped** *B. Molitor; 1811*
Burr elm, oak, ormolu mounts and dark grey marble;
98×130×64

*Provenance:* Formerly Roger Imbert Collection.

*Literature: Les chefs-d'œuvres . . .,* Musée des Arts Décoratifs, exhibition catalogue, Paris, 1951, no. 163, not repr.; Ledoux-Lebard, *Les ébénistes parisiens . . .,* Paris, 1984, p. 488; U. Leben, B. Molitor: Leben und Werk eines Pariser Ebenisten, '*Hémecht*, iv, Luxemburg, 1986; U. Leben, 'Une commande Impériale à Bernard Molitor,' *L'Estampille,* xii, 1986, p. 43, repr.

25

**Commode, stamped** *B. Molitor; 1811*
Burr elm, oak, ormolu mounts and marble;
100×130×65

*Provenance:* On 31 May 1811, Molitor received a commission for two commodes and two *secrétaires* (*63A* and *B*) for the price of 450 *francs* each. They were delivered to the *Garde-Meuble* on 27 August 1811. The inventory records confirm their presence in there a year later. In June 1814, a commode 'no. 17157' and a *secrétaire en suite* were removed to Saint-Cloud. They appear in the Château inventories of 1824 and 1828, in the suite of the duchesse de Reggio's lady-in-waiting. After the destruction of the Château in 1879, the furniture was transferred to the *Mobilier National,* in whose inventory the commode is mentioned. Since 1951, there is no information concerning its exact location; Château de Saint-Cloud, Mobilier National, inv. 1894, no. GME 7142.

*Documents: A.N.:* 02 522, 02 513, 02 586, 02 616, 02 627, 02 601, 03 2082, AJ19 306

*Exhibited:* Musée des Arts Décoratifs, *Les chefs-d'œuvre . . .* exhibition, Paris, 1951, no. 163.

*Literature:* See commode *24.* Although the commode is only known from descriptions, *24* (above) is similar enough to furnish a precise idea of its appearance.

26 (*32*)

**Commode, stamped** *B. Molitor; c. 1809–12*

Speckled mahogany, Cuban mahogany, ormolu mounts (probably by Thomire) and marble;
90×128.5×61.5
  *Provenance:* Sold at Versailles, 19 March 1989, no. 219. A similar commode in Cuban mahogany, with identical mounts on the drawers is part of the office furniture of Maréchall Berthier at Château Grosbois.
  *Literature:* U. Leben, 'La sobre élégance de B. Molitor,' *Connaissance des Arts*, CCCCLVI, Paris 1990.

**Two door commodes**

27 (*18*)
**Commode, stamped** *B. Molitor; c. 1788–92*
Speckled mahogany, oak, mahogany, ormolu mounts and *griotte* marble;
91 ×137 ×63
  *Provenance:* Commissioned by Antoine César de Choiseul III, duc de Praslin, see *sécrétaire à abattant 52*; private collection.
  *Documents:* A.N. Min. Cent. Et. LVIII-638, 768, XLVIII-989
  *Literature:* Guth, 'La carrière brisée ...', 1957, repr.; U. Leben, 'B. Molitor Leben und Werk ..', 1986, repr.; ibid, 'La sobre élégance ...', 1990.

28A (*10, 11* and *102*)
**Commode, stamped** *B. Molitor; 1789–90*
Ebony, Japanese lacquer panels, European lacquer, matt ormolu mounts, brass and turquin marble;
101×101×52.5
  *Provenance:* Private collection.
  *Marks:* Label: *The Rt Ho. The Lord Emly removed de Tervoe Limerick, Ireland.* Engraved metal plaque: *Lord Emly no. 7.*
  *Literature:* U. Leben, 'B. Molitor Leben und Werk ...', 1987, repr.

28B (*12*)
**Commode, attributed to Molitor;** *c.1789–90*
Ebony, Japanese lacquer panels, Chinese lacquer, ormolu mounts, brass and white marble; en suite with 28A
98×104×52
  *Provenance:* Sold at Palais Galliéra, Paris, 21 March 1969, no. 95, repr.; Museum of Art, Carnegie Institute, Pittsburgh, Pennsylvania, no. 70.7.20, gift of Alisa Mellon Bruce, 1970.
  *Literature:* D.T. Owsley, 'French Furniture from Régence to Louis XVI,' *Apollo*, London, Aug., 1973, p. 84.

28B

29A (*144*)
**Commode, stamped** *B. Molitor* **and** *J.M.E.,* **(Guild monogram);** *1788–91*
Mahogany, ormolu mounts and Saint Anne marble;
107×132×53
  *Provenance:* Collection Galerie J. Perrin.

29B
**Commode, attributed to Molitor;** *c. 1790*
Mahogany, ormolu mounts and white marble;
98×130×62
  *Provenance:* Sold at Galliéra, Paris, 11 Dec. 1961, no. 175, repr.

30 (*145*)
**Commode, stamped** *B. Molitor; c. 1800–03*

29

Cuban mahogany, gilded wood, ormolu mounts and marble;
95×128×61

*Provenance:* Sold at Sotheby Parke-Bernet, Monaco, 23 June 1987, no. 2125, repr.; Christie's, Monaco, 7 Dec. 1987, no. 189, repr.; Sotheby Parke-Bernet, New York, 21 May 1988, no. 158, repr.

31 (*28* and *29*)

**Commode, stamped *B. Molitor*, c. 1800–02**
Cuban mahogany, ormolu mounts and *griotte* marble;
92×134×62

*Provenance:* Private collection; traditionally considered as coming from the Parisian residence of Napoleon's general, baron Paul Grenier.

32

**Commode, attributed to Molitor;** *c. 1800–03*
Mahogany, ormolu mounts and marble;
92×132

*Provenance:* Sold at Sotheby's, London, 11 March 1983, no. 103, repr.

33A

**Commode, attributed to Molitor;** *1809–12*
Mahogany, oak, ormolu mounts and marble slab (replaced after war damage);
97×129×64

*Provenance:* Acquired in Paris between 1809 and 1812 for King Jérôme. The inventory of the city residence in 1812 lists two pairs of commodes placed in the bedchamber of Katherina von Württemberg, Queen of Westphalia and in the *salon* of her ladies-in-waiting. Schloss Wilhelmshöhe, Kassel, inv. no. 20 411.

*Documents:* Archives of Land Hessen, Marburg, inventory of the Résidence Royale in Kassel, 1812, 7-i-106.

*Literature:* B. Foucart, 'Attirance et réaction dans les relations artistiques franco-allemandes entre 1800 et 1815,' *Francia: Schriften des deutschen Historischen Instituts*, Paris and Munich; 1972; G. Egger, *Beschläge und Schlösser an alten Möbeln*, Munich, 1977, *figs* 358–62; G. Kreisel and Himmelheber, 'Die Kunst des deutschen Möbels', vol iii, *Klassizsmus, Historismus, Jugendstil* Munich, 1973, p. 80.

*Exhibited:* Preussische Akademie der Künste zu Berlin, *Meisterwerke aus den preussischen Schlössern*, 1930, no. 315, two commodes.

33A

33B

**Commode, attributed to Molitor;** *1809–12*
Mahogany, oak, ormolu mounts and red marble;
95×130×63

*Provenance:* See commode *33A*; Schloss Wilhelmshöhe, Kassel, inv. no. 20 412, room 12.

33C and D

**Pair of commodes, attributed to Molitor;** *1809–12*
Mahogany, ormolu mounts and white marble;
96×144×65

*Provenance:* See commode *33A*; Schloss Fasanerie-Fulda, Kurhessische Hausstiftung no. 3110 A and B.

33E

**Commode, attributed to Molitor;** *c. 1809–12*
Mahogany, ormolu mounts and marble;
92×145×64

*Provenance:* Private collection.

*Literature:* F. Brunhammer and Fayet, *Meubles et Ensembles Directoires et Empire*, Paris, 1965, p. 58. repr.

### 33F
### Commode, attributed to Molitor
Mahogany, ormolu mounts and marble.
> *Provenance:* Château de Daubeuf, Normandy.
> *Literature: Merveilles des Châteaux de Normandie*, Collection Hachette, Paris, 1966, p. 19, repr.

### 34
### Commode, attributed to Molitor; *c. 1808–14*
Mahogany, ormolu mounts and marble;
96×144×65
> *Provenance:* Sold at Drouot, Paris, 7 May 1963, no. 108, repr.
> *Marks:* Stamped *Mme J.*

34

## Dessertes

### 35
*Desserte,* stamped *B. Molitor; 1790*
Speckled mahogany, mahogany, brass, ormolu mounts and Saint Anne marble;
102×188.5×62
> *Provenance:* Sold at Versailles, 13–14 May 1970, no. 209, repr.

35

### 36
*Desserte,* attributed to Molitor; *c. 1805–10*
Mahogany, oak, ormolu mounts and marble;
96×191×59
> *Provenance:* Sold at Drouot, Paris, 23 June 1965, no. 170, repr.

### 37
*Desserte,* attributed to Molitor; *c. 1808–10*
Mahogany, ormolu mounts and yellow marble;
102×200×61
> *Provenance:* Sold at Sotheby Parke-Bernet, Monaco, 12 Dec. 1983, no. 1825, repr.

36

### 38 (69)
*Desserte,* stamped *B. Molitor; 1790*
Cuban mahogany, ormolu mounts and marble;
94×176×62
> *Provenance:* Sold at Christie's, Monaco, 18 June 1989, lot 199 repr. Private collection.
> *Marks:* Stamped: *A.B.*

37

### 39
*Desserte,* stamped *B. Molitor; 1790*
Cuban mahogany, ormolu mounts, marble and Sèvres bisque medallions.
> *Provenance:* Private collection.
> *Literature:* 6 Janneau, *Le style Directoire . . .*, Mobilier et Decoration, Paris, 1938; *Connaissance des Arts,* no. 27, May 1954, p. 49 repr.

## One-door commodes

### 40
### Commode, stamped *B. Molitor; c. 1788–92*

40

Palissander wood, mahogany, ormolu mounts, white marble;
93×73.5×48

*Provenance:* Musée de l'Armée, Paris, inv. no. Cc 286 26, gift of M et Mme Rosenthal and M Marchand. The commode was placed in the museum as part of the reconstitution of Général de Lafayette's office. It is probable that it was part of the furnishings of de Lafayette's mansion on the rue de Lille which he had richly furnished between 1782 and 1792. It reflects La Fayette's taste for the sober, refined Republican style, a taste which he developed following his return from America in 1782.

### 41A and B (65)
**Pair of commodes, stamped** *B. Molitor; c. 1976–1802*
Japanese lacquer panels, ebony, pine, oak, sandalwood, ormolu mounts and Sienna marble;
*41A:* 95×78×55; *41B:* 93×82×50

*Provenance:* Originally commissioned by Antoine-César de Choiseul III, duc de Praslin. See commode 5; private collection.

*Literature:* D. Cooper, *Trésors d'art français . . .* 1965, p. 302, repr.

### 42 (146)
**Commode, attributed to Molitor;** *1802*
Cuban mahogany, ormolu mounts and marble;
94×71.5×52

*Provenance:* Sold at Finarte, Milan, 22 Feb. 1989, no. 7, repr.

### Other commodes

### 43
*Semainier,* **stamped** *B. Molitor; c. 1788–95*
Mahogany, marble.

*Provenance:* Private collection.

*Literature:* D. Ledoux-Lebard, *Les ébénistes . . .* 1984. A mahogany *semainier* fitted with six drawers, fluted canted corners, turned feet, and marble top.

44

### 44A
*Chiffonnière,* **attributed to Molitor;** *1803–09*
Mahogany, ormolu mounts and white marble;
167×97×48

*Provenance:* Sold at Sotheby Parke-Bernet, New York, 24 May 1985, no. 187, repr.

### 44B (148)
*Chiffonnière,* **attributed to Molitor;** *1803–09*
Mahogany, ormolu mounts and white marble;
160×95×46

*Provenance:* Sold at Christie's, New York, 1 Nov. 1990, no. 171

### 45A
*Chiffonnière,* **stamped** *B. Molitor; c. 1787*
Tulipwood, rosewood, satinwood and mahogany;
74×41

*Provenance:* Mentmore Sale, Sotheby's, London, 18–20 May 1977, no. 519, repr.

45B

### 45B
*Chiffonnière,* **stamped** *B. Molitor; 1787–89*
Tulipwood, rosewood, satinwood, harewood, mahogany, oak, beech, pine,

ormolu mounts and marble;
73×41×31
> *Provenance:* Private collection; *en suite* with *chiffonnière 45A.*

## 46 (*115*)
***Table de chevet*, attributed to Molitor; *1803–05***
Mahogany, ormolu mounts (in part by Claude Galle) and marble;
82×242×42
> *Provenance:* Sold at Sotheby Parke-Bernet, Monaco, 13 Dec. 1983, no.
> 486, repr. It is part of a suite of bedroom furniture, some of the pieces of which
> are stamped *B. Molitor.* Private collection.

### Secrétaires à abattants

## 47 (*14*)
*Secrétaire à abattant*, **stamped** *B. Molitor; c. 1787–89*
Speckled mahogany, mahogany, ormolu mounts and white marble;
127×74
> *Provenance:* Private collection; sold at Sotheby Parke-Bernet, Monaco,
> 21–22 June 1978, no. 30, repr.; formerly Alphonse de Rothschild Collection.
> Probably part of the commission by Antoine-César de Choiseul Praslin (see
> commode 5).
> *Documents:* A.N. Min. Cent. Et. LVIII-847.

## 48 (*5*)
*Secrétaire à abattant*, **stamped** *B. Molitor; 1787–90*
Mahogany, ormolu mounts and marble.
> *Provenance:* Bibliothèque Musée des Arts Décoratifs, Collection Maciet,
> Paris, 339/v, repr.

## 49 (*13*)
*Secrétaire à abattant*, **stamped** *B. Molitor; 1789–91*
Mahogany, ormolu mounts, white marble and Sèvres bisque plaques;
119×103×34
> *Provenance:* Private collection.
> *Literature:* Y. Brunhammer, *Le Mobilier Louis XVI*, Paris 1965, p. 58;
> U. Leben, 'La sobre élégance . . .', 1990.

## 50
*Secrétaire à abattant*, **attributed to Molitor; 1788–90**
Mahogany, ormolu mounts, white marble and Sèvres bisque medallions;
108×97×40
> *Provenance:* Sold at Versailles, 11 May 1975, no. 158, repr.

## 51 (*138*)
*Secrétaire à abattant*, **stamped (twice)** *B. Molitor; 1788–92*
Cuban mahogany, speckled mahogany, matt ormolu mounts, and marble;
143×96×42 (*en suite* with 1)
> *Provenance:* Formerly Villefranche Collection; sold at Crédit Municipal,
> Paris, 26 Nov. 1970, no. 7; private collection.
> *Literature:* Guth, 'La carrière brisée . . .', 1957; ibid 'Le Château de
> Villarsceaux,' *Connaissance des Arts*, civ, Paris 1960, repr.; *Les ébénistes du XVIII
> siècle*, Collection Connaissance des Arts, Paris 1963; C. Fregnac, *Les styles
> français*; Collection Connaissance des Arts, Paris 1975, repr.; Ledoux-Lebard,
> *Les ébénistes parisiens . . .*, 1984; A. Pradère, *Les ébénistes français*, 1989.
> *Exhibited:* Musée des Arts Décoratifs: *Chefs-d'œuvre . . .*, 1951, no. 159.

53

53B

52 (*17*)
*Secrétaire à abattant*, **attributed to Molitor;** *c. 1790–98*
Mahogany, speckled mahogany, matt and burnished ormolu mounts and Spanish Brocatelle marble;
146×102×46
    *Provenance:* Originally commissioned by Antoine-César de Choiseul III, duc de Praslin, (see *doc 5*); Vaux-Praslin Sale, 10 April 1876, no. 202; Ojeh-Wildenstein sale, Sotheby Parke-Bernet, Monte Carlo, 25–26 June 1979, no. 79, repr.; The Cleveland Museum of Art, The Thomas L. Fawick Memorial Collection.
    *Literature:* Ledoux-Lebard, *Les ébénistes parisiens. . .* 1984; U. Leben, 'L'atelier de Bernard Molitor sous la Révolution,' *L'Estampille*, CLXXVII, 1985; ibid. 'Die Werkstatt . . .', 1987.

53
*Secrétaire à abattant*, **stamped B. Molitor;** *c. 1789–95*
Mahogany, ormolu mounts and marble;
149×95×40.5
    *Provenance:* Sold at Sotheby Parke-Bernet, Florence, 24 May 1979, no. 1416, repr. Another example of the same model with slight variations exists in a private collection.

53B
*Secretaire à abattant*, **stamped twice B. Molitor,** *1790–1800*
Speckled mahogany and marble;
142×95.5×38.5
    *Provenance:* Private collection.

54 (*133*)
*Secrétaire à abattant*, **stamped (four times) B. Molitor;** *c. 1789–98*
Mahogany and marble;
137×94×38
    *Provenance:* Collection Gallery Daxer and Marshall.
    *Literature:* J. Nicolay, *L'art et la manière des maîtres ébénistes français du XVIIIème siècle*, Paris, 1956, repr.

55
*Secrétaire à abattant*, **stamped B. Molitor;** *c. 1800*
Ebony, mahogany, Japanese lacquer panels, matt ormolu mounts and *pietra dura* inlay.
    *Provenance:* Choiseul-Praslin sale, Paris, 9 May 1808, no. 58.
    *Documents:* A.N. Min. Cent. LVIII-638.
Described in the sale catalogue as being 'a large *secrétaire à abattant*, designed and executed by Molitor in Paris. Simple in style and meticulous in detail, this piece of furniture is formed of old lacquer panels framed in pietra dura work, applied to the ebony body. The upper and lower portions have drawers veneered with lacquer of the same quality. A handsome mahogany entablature forms a large well-hidden, drawer, closing with the same lock as the *secrétaire*, which is only decorated with a few mouldings and capitals in matt ormolu. This piece alone would give an idea of the great talent of this artist who has executed the most beautiful works, which are valued as much for their appearance as for the usefulness of their imaginative interior details.' *Doc B.N.*

56 (*140*)
*Secrétaire à abattant*, **stamped B. Molitor;** *c. 1799–1801*
Speckled mahogany, mahogany, sandalwood, ormolu mounts and marble;
164×100×41
    *Provenance:* Private collection.

*Literature:* D. Ledoux-Lebard, *Les ébénistes parisiens . . .*, 1984, p. 490, repr.

**57** (*76* and *103*)
*Secrétaire à abattant,* stamped *B. Molitor; c. 1799–1803*
Satinwood, mahogany, ormolu mounts and marble;
147×100×47, (*en suite* with 18)
   *Provenance:* Sold at Franco Semenzato, Rome, 22 March 1990, lot 224.
Private collection.

**58** (*70*)
*Secrétaire à abattant,* stamped *B. Molitor; 1803*
Mahogany, ormolu mounts, brass and marble;
132×60.5×29.5
   *Provenance:* Private collection.
   *Literature:* U. Leben, 'La sobre élégance . . .', 1990.

**59**
*Secrétaire à abattant,* attributed to Molitor; *1802–04*
Mahogany and ormolu mounts;
131×70×41
   *Provenance:* Sold at Sotheby Parke-Bernet, Geneva, 4 Dec. 1983, no. 379, repr.

**60** (*149*)
*Secrétaire à abattant,* attributed to Molitor; *1806–10*
Mahogany, ormolu mounts and marble;
145×96×44
   *Provenance:* Sold at Sotheby Parke-Bernet, New York, 16 June 1978, no. 154, repr.

**61A**
*Secrétaire à abattant,* stamped *B. Molitor; 1790–98*
Mahogany, ormolu and marble;
124×63×32
   *Provenance:* Sold at Versailles, 30 March 1980, no. 144.

**61B**
*Secrétaire à abattant,* attributed to Molitor, *c. 1790–98*
Mahogany, bronze, brass and marble;
123×64×32
   *Provenance:* Château de la X sale, Deauville, 20 April 1987, repr.

**62** (*122*)
*Secrétaire à abattant,* stamped *B. Molitor; c. 1809–16*
Mahogany, Cuban mahogany, ormolu mounts, grey marble;
122.5×109×38
   *Provenance:* Sold at Ile de'Adam, 6 Dec. 1987, no. 22; Versailles, 12 March 1989, no. 138, repr. Private collection.

**63A** (*46*)
*Secrétaire à abattant,* stamped *B. Molitor; 1811*
Burr elm, ormolu mounts and black marble (added later);
137×92.5×38
   *Provenance:* Ministère de la Marine, Paris, *Mobilier National,* 1894 inventory, no. M 531. The *secrétaire* was executed as part of the exceptional commission ordered by Napoleon from Parisian *ébénistes* in 1811 (see *25* and *63B*). It was 'temporarily' delivered to the Ministry on 28 July 1814, where it remains to this day.

63A

*Documents:* A.N. 02/513, 02/616, 02/601, 02/627.
  *Literature:* D. Ledoux-Lebard, *Les ébénistes parisiens* . . . 1984; Leben, 'B. Molitor Leben und Werk . . .', 1986; ibid 'Une commande Impériale à Bernard Molitor,' *L'Estampille*, xii, 1986.

**63B**
*Secrétaire à abattant*, **stamped B. Molitor; 1811**
Burr elm, ormolu mounts and white marble;
139.5 × 59 × 43.5
  *Provenance: Mobilier National*, GME 7143. The *secrétaire à abattant* was part of the exceptional order commissioned by Napoleon from Parisian *ébénistes* in 1811 (see 63A). It was delivered to the Château de Saint-Cloud in 1824 and stood in the apartment belonging to the Marèchalle Oudinole, duchesse of Reggio, who was lady-in-waiting to the duchesse de Berry, (daughter-in-law to Charles X). Later it was returned to the *Mobilier National*. Its present location is unknown.
  *Literature:* A.N. 02-513, 02-616, 03 2082, AJ 19 306.
  *Exhibited:* Musée des Arts Décoratifs, *Les chefs-d'œuvre* . . , no. 162.
  *Literature:* U. Leben, 'Bernard Molitor', *Hémecht*, no. 4, 1986, Luxemburg.

*Bonheurs-du-jour*

**64** (*105*)
*Bonheur-du-jour*, **stamped B. Molitor; c. 1795–1800**
Mahogany, ormolu mounts, brass, marble and mirror glass;
130 × 60 × 40
  *Provenance:* Private collection.

**65A** (*147*)
*Bonheur-du-jour*, **stamped B. Molitor; 1805–10**
Cuban mahogany and ormolu mounts;
132 × 81 × 40
  *Provenance:* Private collection.
  *Literature:* Y. Brunhammer, *Meubles et Ensembles* . . ., 1965, repr. p. 65.

**65B**
*Bonheur-du-jour*, **attributed to Molitor**
Cuban mahogany, ormolu mounts and marble;
133 × 82 × 40
  *Provenance:* Private collection.

**66A and B**
**Two** *bonheurs-du-jour*, **stamped B. Molitor; 1797–1802**
Ebony, Japanese lacquer panels, matt ormolu mounts (possibly by Thomire) and Sienna marble;
125 × 79 × 37
  *Provenance:* Originally commissioned by Antoine-César de Choiseul III, duc de Praslin. See commode 5; private collection.
  *Literature:* U. Leben, 'La sobre élégance . . .', 1990.

**67A and B** (*53* and *54*)
**Two** *bonheurs-du-jours*, **stamped B. Molitor; 1816–18**
Ebony, Japanese lacquer panels, European lacquer panels, mahogany, matt ormolu mounts (possibly by Thomire) and green Italian marble;
136 × 84 × 48
  *Provenance:* Musée du Louvre, Paris, inv. no. 5475 I and II, former inventory no. SC 1215, no. 10183; label: 80. After long negotiations, the pieces were acquired in 1820. They were delivered to the *Garde-Meuble* on 30 June

66

67

1820, and registered under no. 10 183 (A.N. AJ 19-612). On 27 July 1820 they were sent to Saint-Cloud and were placed in the *Galerie de Diane* in 1828 (A.N. AJ 19-612). The *galerie* was mainly furnished with pieces made by the *ébéniste* Boulle. At this point the *bonheurs-du-jour* were placed on a high plinth rather than on the original feet which are still in place on *68*. They were moved to the Louvre in 1870. Saint-Cloud inventory, 1828, A.N. AJ 19-306 nos. 1215-1216

> *Documents:* A.N. AJ 19-318, A.N. AJ 19-326, A.N. AJ 19-1155.
> *Exhibited:* Musée des Arts Décoratifs, *Les chefs-d'œuvre. . .*, 1951, no. 161.
> *Literature:* C. Dreyfuss, *Le mobilier français au Musée du Louvre*, catalogue,

Paris, 1921; ibid, *Le Mobilier du XVII et du XVIII siècles*, Paris 1922 nos. 152 and 153; Guth, 'La carrière brisée . . .', 1957; G. Van der Kemp, 'Contribution à l'étude de deux bonheurs-de-jour de B. Molitor,' *Archives de l'art français*, xxii, Paris, 1959, p. 349; Verlet, *Les ébénistes français . . .*, Paris, 1963, p. 316; Ledoux-Lebard, *Les ébénistes parisiens , . .*; A. Boutemy, 'Les secrétaires en cabinets,' *Bulletin de la société de l'histoire de l'art français 1970*, Paris, 1972; F.J.B. Watson, *Le mobilier Louis XVI*, Paris, 1983, repr.; U. Leben, 'L'atelier de Bernard Molitor . . .', 1985, repr.; U. Leben 'Die Werkstatt . .', 1987, repr.

### 68A and B (*34* and *35*)
*Bonheurs-du-jour* and *en suite* bookcase, stamped *B. Molitor; 1814–16*
Ebony, maple or stained pearwood, light mahogany, Japanese lacquer panels, European lacquer panels, matt ormolu mounts (possibly by Thomire) and red marble;
134×84×47

> *Provenance:* Collection of H.M. the Queen, Buckingham Palace, London. Acquired in Paris in 1816 through the intermediary of M Wattier for the future George IV. They were registered in the Carlton House inventory on 21 Dec. 1816.
> *Literature:* F.J.B. Watson, *Le mobilier Louis XVI*, 1963, *fig* 92, p. 118.

### 69 (*152*)
*Bonheur-du-jour*, stamped *B. Molitor; 1814–18*
Kingwood, maple, boxwood, tulip wood, citronwood, purpleheart, ormolu mounts (possibly by Thomire), three Sèvres porcelain plaques (painted by Dodin) and grey marble;
142.3×86.4×42
The front plaque ornamented the top of the Table Taschen which Alfred Charles de Rothschild bought in 1874; the porcelain plaques were removed from the damaged table for reuse elsewhere.

> *Provenance:* Alfred Charles de Rothschild Collection, London; 1874–84, purchased by Alfred Charles de Rothschild in Russia; 1927, The Henry E. Huntington Library & Art Gallery, San Marino, California, where it remains today.
> *Literature:* A.C. de Rothschild, *A Description of the Works of Art forming the Collection of Alfred de Rothschild II*, London, 1884, no. 98; R. Wark, *French Decorative Art in the Huntington Collection*, catalogue, San Marino, 1961, *fig* 67; A. Boutemy, 'Les secrétaires en cabinets,' *B.S.H.A.F.*, 1972, p. 96; Huntington Collection catalogue, p. 47, *fig* 68; G. Wilson, 'New Information on French Furniture at the Henry E. Huntington Library and Art Gallery,' *J. Paul Getty Museum Journal*, iv, 1977, p. 29, repr.; D.H. Cohen, 'Four *tables guéridons* by Sèvres', *Antologia delle belli Arti*, xiii–xiv, Rome, 1980; D. Guillaume-Brulon, 'Les cabinets en porcelaine,' *L'Estampille*, Nov. 1983, repr. p. 44

## Secrétaires à cylindre

### 70 (*8, 9, 81, 82, 154*)
*Secrétaire à cylindre*, stamped *B. Molitor; 1788*

Cuban mahogany, black lacquer, matt ormolu mounts (possibly by F. Rémond), *griotte* marble;

136.2×177.4×87

> *Provenance:* Sold at Christie's, London, 16 May 1800, no. 101; Christie's, London, 12 Feb. 1801, no. 70; Cooper Family sale, Christie's, London, 22 June 1938, no. 38, repr.; Mortimer Schiff Collection; The J. Paul Getty Museum, Malibu, California, inv. no. 67DA 9;

> *Literature:* D. Cooper, *Trésors d'art français dans des collections privées*, Zurich, 1963, p. 189, repr.; A.M. Jones, *A Handbook of the Decorative Arts in the J. Paul Getty Museum*, Malibu, 1965, p. 21, pl 7; G. Wilson, *Decorative Arts in the J. Paul Getty Museum, Los Angeles*, catalogue, Malibu, 1977, repr.; A. Sasson and G. Wilson, *Decorative Arts – A Handbook of the Collections of the J. Paul Getty Museum*, Malibu, 1986.

### 71A

*Secrétaire à cylindre*, **stamped B. Molitor;** *c. 1788–92*
Cuban mahogany, ormolu mounts, brass and marble;
119×125×65

> *Provenance:* Baronne de Caix sale, Drouot, Paris, 11–12 June 1959, no. 210, repr.

> *Literature:* Comte de Salverte, *Les ébénistes du XVIII siècle*, 1934, repr. *Connaissances des Arts*, no. 194, 1968, p. 139.

### 71B (*134*)

*Secrétaire à cyclindre*, **attributed to Molitor;** *c. 1790–1800*
Cuban mahogany, ormolu mounts, brass and white marble;
140×159

> *Provenance:* Collection B.B. Steinitz.

### 72

*Secrétaire à cylindre*, **stamped B. Molitor;** *c. 1788–95*
Mahogany and marble;
width 115

> *Provenance:* Sold, Paris, 15 Dec. 1954, no. 75, not repr.

### 73

*Secrétaire à cylindre*, **stamped B. Molitor;** *c. 1788–95*
Mahogany.

> *Provenance:* Private collection.

### 74

*Secrétaire à cylindre*, **attributed to Molitor;** *1807–10*
Mahogany and ormolu mounts.

> *Provenance:* Bibliothèque du Musée des Arts Décoratifs Collection Maciet, 339, repr.

71A

*Bureaux plats*

### 75

*Bureau plat*, **stamped B. Molitor;** *1788–93*
Cuban mahogany, mahogany and ormolu mounts; probably a transformed *bureau à cylindre*;
74.5×157×70

> *Provenance:* Private collection.

### 75A

*Bureau plat*, **stamped B. Molitor;** *1788–93*

Spechelel and cuban mahogany and ormolu mounts.
*Provenance:* Birmingham Museum of Art, Alabama. Inv. 1991–104 from the Engenia Woodward-Hilt Collection.

**76** (*157*)
*Bureau plat,* stamped *B. Molitor; 1788–93*
Cuban mahogany and ormolu mounts;
160×74.5×79
*Provenance:* Pels-Leuden Gallery, Villa Grisebach, Berlin.

**77**
*Bureau plat,* stamped *B. Molitor; 1788–93*
Light speckled mahogany, mahogany and matt ormolu mounts; probably a transformed *bureau à cylindre;*
748×129×62.5
*Provenance:* Sold at Versailles, 1 Dec 1985, no. 127, repr.

*Pupitres* **and** *secrétaires de voyage*

**78** (*33*)
*Pupitre,* stamped *B. Molitor; 1814*
Mahogany and ormolu mounts;
138×89×59
*Provenance:* Sold at Drouot, Paris, 29 Nov. 1950, no. 146, repr.; Drouot, Paris, 23 June 1969, no. 75, repr. Private collection.
*Literature:* Ledoux-Lebard, *Les ébénistes parisiens . . .* 1960 repr.; G. Janneau, *Le meuble d'ébénisterie,* Paris, 1974, *fig* 217.

**79** (*156*)
*Pupitre de voyage,* attributed to Molitor; *c. 1808–12*
Mahogany and ormolu mounts;
100×49×26
*Provenance:* Sold in Sémur-en-Aixois, 18–19 May 1986, no. 251; Paris, Ader, 9 April 1990, lot 175.

**Armoires**

**80**
*Bibliothèque,* stamped *B. Molitor; c. 1787–92*
Mahogany, ormolu mounts and glass;
198×132×34
*Provenance:* Private collection.

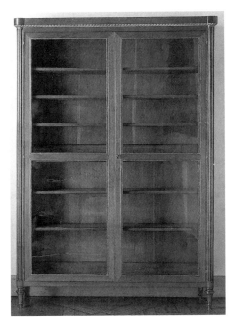
80

**81**
*Bibliotheque,* stamped *B. Molitor; c. 1788–95*
Mahogany, ormolu mounts and glass;
232×69.5×39
*Provenance:* Sold at Versailles, 28 Oct. 1979, no. 119, repr.

**82**
*Armoire,* stamped *B. Molitor; c. 1790–97*
Mahogany, ormolu mounts, steel and black marble;
160×93×38
*Provenance:* Private collection.

**83** (*130*)
*Armoire,* stamped *B. Molitor; c. 1799–1800*

81

83

85

85c

Cuban mahogany, oak, cherrywood, Saint Anne marble, brass;
143×86×42
> *Provenance:* Private collection.

**84**
***Armoire**, stamped B. Molitor; c. 1808–12*
134×82.5×38
> *Provenance:* Private collection.
> *Literature:* Fayet/Brunhammer, *Ensembles Directoire et Empire*, Paris, *c.*
1965, repr. plate 64

**Console tables**

**85A**
**Console table, stamped** B. Molitor; *c. 1788–95*
Mahogany, ormolu mounts, marble.
> *Provenance:* Formerly in the collection Bleustein-Blanchet. Possibly
destroyed by fire in 1971.
> *Literature: Connaissance des Art*, Nov. 1958, repr. p. 66

**85B**
**Console table, attributed to Molitor;** *c. 1788–95*
Mahogany, ormolu mounts and marble.
> *Provenance:* Private collection.
> *Literature:* C. Bizot, *Mobilier Directoire*, p. 77, repr.

**85C and D**
**Two console tables, attributed to Molitor;** *c. 1786–95*
Mahogany, ebony, brass, ormolu mounts, and marble;
91×128
> *Provenance:* Sold at Sotheby's, London, 20 June 1986, lot 97.

**86A (7)**
**Console table, attributed to Molitor,** *c. 1785–92*
Mahogany, ormolu mounts, marble and mirror glasses (added in the
nineteenth century);
85×155×56
> *Provenance:* The Toledo Museum of Art, Toledo, Ohio, Acc. 67,150, Gift of
Florence Scott Libbey. Acquired from Rosenberg and Stiebel, New York. Until
1938, the console table was part of the Baron Nathaniel de Rothschild
Collection in the Palais Rothschild, Vienna. After the war it passed to Baron
Alphonse de Rothschild, (nephew of Nathaniel) in New York until *c.* 1965.

**86B**
**Console table, attributed to Molitor;** *c. 1785–92*
Mahogany, ormolu mounts and marble;
85.5×134.6 (front), 165.7×58.5 (back)
> *Provenance:* Metropolitan Museum of Art, New York, no. 26.220.1.
Purchased in 1926 in Paris from the antiquarian Seligmann by Roger Fund.
> *Literature: Renaissance de l'Art Français des Industries de Luxe*, vi, 1923,
p. 340, repr.

**87 (*119*)**
**Console table, stamped (twice)** B. Molitor; *1803*
Mahogany, oak, pine, matt, ormolu mounts, white marble and mirror
(probably added at a later date);
94×123×48

*Provenance:* Musée National du Château de La Malmaison, M.M. 40-47-859, label no. 17. Removed in 1929 from the War Ministry located in the Hôtel de Brienne in Paris, to La Malmaison. The Hôtel de Brienne was the residence of Napoleon's mother, Madame Mère, during the Empire. This console table was possibly part of the furniture supplied to Saint-Cloud in 1803.

*Literature: La Malmaison, Le Passeport de l'art*, Paris, 1984, pp. 44–45, repr.; Guth, 'La carrière brisée . . .', 1957, p. 70 repr.

## 88A and B (95)
### Two console tables, stamped *B. Molitor; 1803*
Mahogany, oak, matt ormolu mounts, *griotte* marble and mirror;
90.5×92×91.5
*Provenance:* Private collection.

90

91

## 89
### Console, trace of Molitor's label, *1803–05*
Mahogany, oak, matt ormolu mounts, *griotte* marble;
90.5×80×43.5
*Provenance:* This was one of a pair said to have come from Château de Saint-Cloud, the pair having been destroyed during the war; Private collection.

## 90
### Console table, attributed to Molitor; *c. 1803–05*
Mahogany, matt ormolu mounts, black marble;
88.9×96.5
*Provenance:* Sold at Sotheby Parke-Bernet, New York, 17–18 Oct. 1963, no. 695, repr.; The René Fribourg Collection.

## 91
### Console table, stamped *B. Molitor; c. 1796–1803*
Ebony, lacquer panels, oak, matt ormolu mounts, Sienna marble and mirror glass;
103×115×41
*Provenance:* Originally commissioned by Antoine-César de Choiseul III, duc de Praslin; private collection.
*Documents:* A.N. LVIII-768, cf no. 5
*Literature:* D. Cooper, *Trésors d'art français . . .*, 1965, p. 302, Pillars resting on the high base support the entablature. The marble top is surrounded by a diamond-shaped decorated gallery; there is a mirror behind the two lacquer shelves. Two opposing griffins have between them a crown with a cypher A-C-P (Antoine-César de Choiseul Praslin) in the centre.

## 92A and B (51)
### Two console tables, both with labels *Molitor-Ebéniste*, c. 1809–11
Mahogany, ormolu mounts, white marble and mirror glass;
85×140.5×54 (92A); 85×140×58 (92B).* These two console tables, and the console tables 93 A and B and 93 C and D are the only known examples of pieces with their original labels in place.
*Provenance:* Schloss Wilhelmshöhe, Kassel, inv. vol. Ia, p. 188, no. 20 733 A and B. The consoles were acquired in Paris for Napoleon's youngest brother Jérôme, King of Westphalia. According to the 1812 inventory of the '*Palais de Napoleonshöhe*', they were placed in the '*salon de velours cramoisi*', on the ground floor of the north wing and were described as follows: 'A mahogany console decorated with ormolu with two winged lion heads, in carved and gilded wood, mirror glass in the back, white marble on top and the same underneath'. In 1933 the consoles were still in the garden-level reception room.
*Documents:* Inv. Napoleonshöhe, 1812, Landesarchiv Hessen, Marburg, 7-i-153.

*Literature: Guide du Schloss Wilhelmshöhe*, (edition 1933, Huth, 1962, E. Schulz 1968, Biehn); B. Foucart, 'Attirance et réaction . . .'; 'La Diffusion du Mobilier Empire,' *Forschungen sur westeuropäischen Geschichte*, Munich, 1973.

*Exhibited:* Preussische Akademie der Künste zu Berlin '*Meisterwerke aus den preussischen Schlössern*, no. 306, 1930.

### 93A and B (47)

**Two console tables, both with labels** *Molitor-Ebéniste*; (* see 92A and B)
*1809–11*
Mahogany, oak, matt ormolu mounts, white and grey veined marble and mirror glass;
83×135.5×51.5 (93A); 83×140.5×54 (93B).

*Provenance:* Schloss Wilhelmshöhe, Kassel, A inv. no. 10 755, B inv. no. 20 254; formerly listed under Z.32/60; Z.159/7; Z.36/11. The console tables arrived in Kassel between 1809 and 1812 for King Jérôme. In 1897 they were in the ground floor reception room.

*Literature:* F. Luthmer, *Sammlung von Innenraümen, Möbeln und Geräten im Louis XVI und Empire Stil*, Stuttgart, 1897, *fig* 12; Biehn, *Guide du Schloss Wilhemshöhe*, 1968.

### 93C and D (161)

**Two console tables, both with labels** *Molitor-Ebéniste* (*see 92A and B);
*c. 1809–11*
Mahogany, matt ormolu mounts, marble and mirror;
84×140×54.
*Provenance:* Schloss Bad Homburg von der Höhe, (C) inv. 22206, (D) inv. 22205; before the Second World War in Schloss Wilhemshöhe, Kassel Z-32/60. The consoles were part of the Parisian commission for King Jérôme.

*Literature:* L. De Groer, *Les arts décoratifs de 1790–1850*, Fribourg, 1985, p. 322, repr.

### 94

**Console table, attributed to Molitor;** *1803–07*
Mahogany, matt ormolu mounts and marble;
91×145

*Provenance:* Hôtel de Baye sale, Drouot, Paris, 19 May 1930, no. 94, repr.

### 95

**Console table, attributed to Molitor;** *1805–12*
Mahogany, ormolu mounts and marble;

*Provenance:* Sold at Versailles, 28 April 1968, no. 210, repr.

### Tables

### 96 (172)

*Table à thé*, **stamped** *B. Molitor; 1788–92*
Mahogany and matt ormolu mounts;
94×101

*Provenance:* Madame de la Madriére Collection; sold at Versailles, 8 Dec. 1974, no. 252, repr.; sold at Ader Monte Carlo, 11 Nov. 1984, no. 92, repr.; private collection.

*Literature: Connaissance des Arts*, Sept. 1957, repr.; Les ébénistes parsiens . . . , 1984, p. 491.

### 97 (44)

*Guéridon*, **attributed to Molitor;** *1788–1803*
Mahogany, matt ormolu mounts and white marble;
73×94

*Provenance:* Musée du Château de Versailles, Petit Trianon, inv. 1894 no. T 512 C, PT-TR 7748; Mark of 'Palais de Saint-Cloud', Empire period; former inv. nos. of Fontainebleau, 19th century: F-1041, F-1924, F-19537, F-20876.

*Documents:* In the 1807 inventory of the then 'Palais de Saint Cloud,' a table is described which corresponds exactly to this *guéridon:* a *table à thé*, with two tiers [later crossed out], in figured mahogany, feet with paws, four cross rails, ornamented with ormolu gallery, mouldings and capitals, and castors, 600, -F H: 72 cm D: 93 cm (A.N. AJ 19 292).

The fact that the mention of the tier was crossed out suggests that the wooden, double table top was modified and later replaced by the present marble top. The *guéridon* remained at Fontainebleau during the nineteenth century where its inventory number changed several times. It was only in 1874 that it was removed to the Petit Trianon at Versailles.

*Literature:* S. de Ricci, *Der Stil Louis XVI,* Stuttgart, 1913, repr.; E. and W. Hessling, *Le Style Directoire*, Paris, 1914, *fig* XVI; E. Dumonthier, *Documents d'Art – Mobilier National Français: Les tables, styles Louis XVI et Empire*, Morance, 1924, *fig* 13; P. Avril, *L'ameublement parisien pendant la Révolution*, Paris, 1924, *fig* 38; F. Kimball, *Le Style Louis XV*, Paris, 1949, *fig* 274.

### 98 (23)
**Guéridon, attributed to Molitor;** *1790–98*
Cuban mahogany and matt ormolu mounts;
73×90

*Provenance:* Musée Nationale du Château de Versailles, Cabinet Intérieur de la Reine, inv. 1885 no. VMB 884; Mark of Saint-Cloud, Empire period; former inv. nos. SC 7455, 1155, 1032, V-1530

In the Inventory of the then 'Palais de Saint-Cloud', taken on 14 Prairial year XIII (3 June 1805) a table in Empress Josephine's *grand salon* corresponds exactly to this piece: 'solid mahogany *guéridon* with openwork stretcher, matt gilt Egyptian heads and gallery. There is a description from 1809 of an identical *guéridon* in the *salon* of the Grand Maréchall de Saint-Cloud.

*Documents:* A.N. 02 730, AJ 19 292 B no. 1143.

*Literature:* E. Dumonthier, *Documents d'Art . . .* 1924, *fig* 12.

### 99
**Guéridon, stamped B. Molitor;** *c. 1789–95*
Mahogany, citronwood and brass;
74×82

*Provenance:* Sold at Drouot, Paris, 5–6 June, 1930, no. 230.

### 100
**Guéridon, attributed to Molitor;** *1785–88*
Mahogany, oak, ormolu mounts and white marble;
72×99

*Provenance:* Purchased by comte Nissim de Camondo in 1916; Musée des Arts Décoratifs, Paris; Musée Nissim de Camondo, Paris.

*Literature:* Y. Brunhammer, *Le Mobilier Louis XVI*, Paris, 1965; *Catalogue du Musée Nissim de Camondo, Paris*, 1985 no. 587; L. Chanson, *Traité d'ébénisterie*, Paris, 1988, pl 47.

### 101 (166)
**Guéridon, attributed to Molitor;** *c. 1785–88*
Mahogany, ormolu mounts and grey marble with blue vein;
72.5×100

*Provenance:* Sold at Sotheby Parke-Bernet, Monaco, 23–24 June 1985, no. 877.

99

100

102
*Guéridon*, stamped *B. Molitor; c. 1790–1800*
Mahogany, ormolu mounts, brass and marble;
73×93
> *Provenance:* Sold at Versailles, 7 June 1973, no. 144, repr.
> *Literature:* Ledoux-Lebard, *Les ébénistes parisiens . . .*, 1984.

103A (*131*)
*Guéridon*, stamped *B. Molitor; c. 1790–1800*
Mahogany, ormolu mounts, brass and white marble;
71×91
> *Provenance:* Private collection.

103B (*167*)
*Guéridon*, stamped *B. Molitor; c. 1790–1800*
Mahogany, ormolu mounts, brass and marble.
> *Provenance:* Former Collection Levy.

104
*Guéridon*, attributed to Molitor; *1790–1800*
Mahogany, ormolu mounts, brass and grey marble with blue vein;
70×81
> *Provenance:* Private collection.

105 (*62* and *170*)
*Guéridon*, stamped *B. Molitor; 1795–1800*
Mahogany, oak and ormolu mounts;
75×95
> *Provenance:* Acquired around 1795–97 by Thomas Merlin, businessman and founder of the newspaper *Le Débat*, to furnish his *hôtel* at 11 rue Louis le Grand. Private collection.
> *Literature:* M. Burckhard, *Le Mobilier Louis XVI*, Paris; U. Leben, 'B. Molitor, Leben und Werk . . .', 1986, p 573, repr.

106 (*118*)
*Guéridon*, stamped *B. Molitor; c. 1795–1800*
Mahogany, ormolu mounts, and white marble.
> *Provenance:* Formerly Collection Roger Imbert.
> *Literature: Art Treasures*, Parke-Bernet Galleries, exhibition catalogue, New York, 1967, no. 275; Ledoux-Lebard, *Les ébénistes parisiens . . .* 1984.

107
*Guéridon*, attributed to Molitor; *c. 1795–1803*
Mahogany, brass, ormolu mounts, and white marble;
95×82.5
> *Provenance:* Sold at Paris, 25 March 1974, no. 103, repr.

108
*Guéridon*, attributed to Molitor; *c. 1795–1803*
Mahogany, ormolu mounts and grey marble;
74×81
> *Provenance:* Sold at Paris, Drouot, 9 March 1987, no. 282.

109 (*177*)
*Guéridon*, stamped *B. Molitor, c. 1790–1803*
Kingwood and brass;
70.5×80
> *Provenance:* Sold at Christie's, London, 23 June 1988, no. 67.

107

112

110 (176)
*Guéridon*, attributed to Molitor; *c. 1809–12*
Mahogany, ormolu mounts and white marble;
72×80
  *Provenance:* Schloss Wilhelmshöhe, Kassel, inv. no. 20 367; formerly 32/47; 216/8. Part of the Parisian-manufactured furniture supplied for King Jérôme between 1809 and 1812.

111
*Guéridon*, attributed to Molitor; *c. 1809–12*
Mahogany and ormolu mounts;
77.5×101.5
  *Provenance:* Schloss Bad Homburg von der Höhe, Hauptverwaltung, inv. no. 22317; formerly Wilhelmshöhe 148/44. Part of the furniture made in Paris for Jérôme, King of Westphalia between 1809 and 1812.
  *Literature:* F. Luthmer, *Sammlung von Innenraümen ...*, 1897, *fig* 11.

112
*Guéridon*, attributed to Molitor; *c. 1809–12*
Mahogany, matt ormolu mounts and dark coral marble
  *Provenance:* Schloss Wilhelmshöhe, Kassel, inv. no. 20 750; before Second World War: Residenz Palast, Kassel, inv. Res. Pal. Z. 102/3x. See 33, 52, 93, 111.

113
*Guéridon*, attributed to Molitor; *c. 1790–1800*
Mahogany, ormolu mounts, polished brass and white marble.
  *Provenance:* Private collection, (courtesy of Partridge Archives, London).

114 (175)
*Guéridon*, attributed to Molitor
Mahogany and ormolu mounts;
74.5×95.7.
  *Provenance:* Private collection (courtesy of Blairman and Sons Archives, London).

115 (174)
*Guéridon*, attributed to Molitor; *c. 1815–19*
Ebony, ormolu mounts and green porphyry marble.
  *Provenance:* Château d'Haroué, Lorraine.
This *guéridon* and another *en suite* were purchased by Lucie-Virginie de Choiseul-Praslin to complement the lacquer furniture, inherited from her mother (see 5).
  *Documents:* A.N. Min. Cent. Et. LIV-1369.
The *guéridon* has a triangular plinth resting on ball-and-claw feet. A central baluster supports the round top decorated with a palmette frieze similar to the one on 67A and 67B.

116 (171)
*Table à manger*, stamped *B. Molitor; c. 1797–1800*
Cuban mahogany;
depth 130
  *Provenance:* Formerly collection Gismondi.
  *Literature:* 'Les Tables à manger,' *Trouvailles*, XXXXIII, 1983, p. 24, repr.

117
*Table à manger*, stamped *B. Molitor; c. 1788–1800*

118A

118B

118C

121

Mahogany and ormolu mounts.
    *Provenance:* Private collection.

## 118
*Table à jeux circulaire,* **stamped B. Molitor; 1788–1800**
Speckled mahogany and ormolu mounts.
    *Provenance:* Private collection. Since its original acquisition the table has remained in the Foucault family.

## 119 (*126*)
*Table à dejeuner* or *à en cas,* **stamped B. Molitor; c. 1790–1800**
Mahogany;
68.5×96.5
    *Provenance:* Private collection.

## 120
*Table de bouillote,* **stamped B. Molitor; c. 1790–1800**
Mahogany;
75×120
    *Provenance:* Sold at Paris, 28 May 1948, no. 103. Sale catalogue description, *'Table de bouillote en bois de placage d'acajou, reposant sur trois pieds gainés et se développant sur un quatrième.'*

## 121A
*Table à jeux,* **attributed to Molitor; c. 1795–1803**
Mahogany, ormolu mounts and brass;
75×109.5×53
    *Provenance:* Sold at Drouot, Paris, 26 June 1981, no. 56, repr.

## 121B
*Table à jeux,* **attributed to Molitor; c. 1795–1803**
Mahogany and brass;
72×111
    *Provenance:* Sold at Chartres, 24 May 1987, no. 137, repr.

## 121C
*Table à jeaux,* **attributed to Molitor, c. 1795–1803**
73×112
Mahogany, ormolu mounts
    *Provenance:* Collection Gallery Didier Aaron

## 122
*Table à jeux,* **stamped B. Molitor; c. 1788–1800**
Mahogany;
75×87×42
    *Provenance:* Sold at Versailles, 23 June 1986, no. 94. *'Table à jeux en bois de placage d'acajou, piedes fuselés et cannelés.'*

## 123
*Table d'architecte,* **stamped B. Molitor**
Mahogany.
    *Provenance:* Private collection.

## 124A
*Bureau de dame,* **stamped B. Molitor; c. 1788–96**
Citronwood, ebony, purpleheart, mahogany, sycamore and amaranth;
71.1×81.3×43.2

124A

125

126

*Provenance:* Originally commissioned by Antoine-César de Choiseul III, duc de Praslin; sale, Paris, 23 April 1877, no. 485; Oppenheim Collection sale, Christie's, London, 10 June 1913, no. 187; Huntington Collection, San Marino, acquired in 1916.

*Documents:* See 5.

*Literature:* P. Verlet, *Styles, meubles, décors ...*, 1972, repr.; R. Wark, *French Decorative Art ..., 1961, p 79, repr.;* F.J.B. Watson, *Wallace Collection – Catalogue of Furniture*, London, 1956, p. 175.

### 124B *(21, 22, 42)*
**Coiffeuse, attributed to Molitor;** *c. 1788–96*
Mahogany, citronwood, purpleheart, ebony, oak and ormolu mounts; 70.5×80.7×43.2 *(en suite* with 124A)

*Provenance:* Originally commissioned by Antoine-César de Choiseul III, duc de Praslin, (see 5); Béarn Collection sale, 13 Feb. 1873, no. 93; Wallace Collection, London, F321.

*Literature:* Watson, *Wallace Collection ...*, 1956, p. 174 *fig* 104; Verlet, *Les ébénistes français ...*, 1963, p. 316, repr; A. Gonzalez Palacios, *Gli ebanisti del Louis XVI*, Milan, 1966, *fig* 40; U. Leben, 'L'atelier de Bernard Molitor ...,' 1985, repr.

### 125
**Small bureau, stamped** *B. Molitor; c. 1788–95*
Mahogany, brass, ormolu mounts;
76×82×49

*Provenance:* Sold at Paris, Drouot, 20 Nov. 1985, repr.

*Literature:* U. Leben, 'B. Molitor Leben und Werk ...,' 1986, repr.

### 126
**Small bureau, stamped** *B. Molitor; c. 1788–95*
Mahogany, citronwood and ormolu mounts;
74×77×41.5

*Provenance:* Sold at Paris, 7 May 1936, repr.; Nicolay Collection.

*Literature:* Guth, 'La carrière brisée ...'; Nicolay, *L'art et la manière ...*, 1965, repr.

### 127
**Small bureau, attributed to Molitor;** *c. 1790–95*
Mahogany and ormolu mounts;
75.5×87.6×53.3

*Provenance:* Partridge Archives, London.

### 128
**Bureau, stamped** *B. Molitor; c. 1788–1800*
Ebony and ormolu mounts.

*Provenance:* Sold in Paris, 7 Dec. 1923, no. 116, not repr. Sale catalogue reads: '*Table bureau plaquée d'ébène, fermant à coulisse et garnie de bronzes, tel que rangs de piastres, galerie, encadrements, époque Louis XVI'*, from 1923 catalogue description.

### 129
**Small bureau, stamped** *B. Molitor; c. 1790–1800*
Mahogany and ormolu mounts.

*Provenance:* Sold at Versailles, 14 Nov. 1982, repr.

### 130
**Small bureau, stamped** *B. Molitor; c. 1785–90*
Rosewood, satinwood, amaranth, citronwood stained green, ebony and

ormolu mounts;
74.5×73.5×74.5

> *Marks:* Firebrand of Château de Maille.
> *Provenance:* Private collection.

### 131 (*132*)
**Table de travail**, stamped *B. Molitor; c. 1788–92*
Mahogany, citronwood, purpleheart and ormolu mounts;
74.5×82×38.5

> *Provenance:* Heim Collection; sold at the Hôtel George V, Paris, 22 Nov. 1987, no. 206, repr. Private collection.
> *Literature:* A. Theunissen, *Meubles et sièges du XVIIIᵉ siècle*, Paris, 1934, *fig* XLVI (Heim Collection); 'Le Guide du marché de l'art,' *La Gazette de Drouot*, 1988.

### 132 (*25*)
**Small *bureau plat*, stamped B. Molitor; c. 1797–1804**
Ebony, mahogany, satinwood and matt ormolu mounts;
72×97.5×52

> *Provenance:* Private collection.

### 133 (*55*)
**Salon table**, stamped *B. Molitor, 1814–18*
Mahogany, ormolu mounts and granite;
75×44×77

> *Provenance:* Formerly Hagenauer Collection.
> *Literature: Catalogue Biennale des Antiquaires*, Grand Palais, Paris, 1972, repr.; Ledoux-Lebard, *Les ébénistes parisiens, ...,* 1984.
> *Documents:* 'Une table en bois d'acajou, avec un tiroir pour écrire, le dessus en marbre granite gris, monté sur quatre balustres ou colonnes ornées de bronzes, ciselés et dorés au mat.' A.N. 03/1891, Dec 27, 1819 (cf. *Doc.* 13), 03/1885.

### 134 (*181*)
**Gueridon**, attributed to Molitor, *1805–10*
Mahogany and patinated bronze;
81×79

> *Provenance:* Sold at Sotheby's, New York, 30 March 1990, lot 159.

135

### 135A
**Writing table, stamped** *B. Molitor; c. 1812–18*
Ebony and ormolu mounts;
75×66×53.5, *en suite* with 135B

> *Provenance:* Sold at Versailles, 29 March 1981, no. 161, repr.

### 135b
*Table de toilette*, attributed to Molitor; *1812–18*
Ebony, ormolu mounts and marble;
76.5×66×66

> *Provenance:* Sold at Sotheby's London, 11 July 1980, no. 198, repr.

### 136
*Table à café*, stamped *B. Molitor; 1788–91*
Mahogany, oak, ormolu mounts and grey marble with blue veins;
74×57.5×32

> *Provenance:* Sold at Paris, 14 Dec. 1984, repr.; private collection.

### 137
*Table à café*, stamped *B. Molitor; 1788–93*

136

137

139

143

Mahogany, ormolu mounts and white marble.
    *Provenance:* Partridge Archives, London.

138
*Guéridon*, stamped *B. Molitor; c. 1788–1792*
Mahogany, ormolu mounts and marble;
74.5×33
    *Provenance:* Sold at Paris, 16 June 1981, no. 68, BIS repr.

139
*Table étagère*, stamped *B. Molitor; 1788–92*
Mahogany, ormolu mounts and brass;
110×58.5
    *Provenance:* Private collection.
    *Literature:* G. Janneau, *Le Meuble léger en France*, Paris, 1952, p. 226, repr.

140 (*127*)
*Guéridon*, stamped *B. Molitor; c. 1789–96*
Mahogany, ormolu mounts and *brèche d'Alep* marble;
82×44.5
    *Provenance:* Private collection.

141
*Guéridon*, stamped *B. Molitor; c. 1789–1800*
Mahogany, ormolu mounts and brass;
94×39
    *Provenance:* Surmount Collection sale, Drouot, Paris, 13 May 1912.
Identical to 140.

142
*Pupitre à musique*, stamped *B. Molitor; 1788–95*
Mahogany and brass;
height 78
    *Provenance:* Sold at Sotheby Parke-Bernet, Monaco, 23 Feb. 1986, no. 798.
Private collection.

142A and B (*129*)
*Pupitre à musique*, attributed to Molitor; *1788–95*
Mahogany and brass;
56×27
    *Provenance:* Private collection.

143
*Pupitre à musique*, stamped *B. Molitor; 1788–95*
Mahogany and brass.
    *Provenance:* Private collection.

144
*Guéridon*, stamped *B. Molitor; 1810–18*
Mahogany, patinated bronze mounts, cut glass and marble
    *Provenance:* Private collection.

144B (*162*)
Gate-leg table, stamped *B. Molitor and J.M.E., c. 1787–91*
Cuban mahogany and bronze;
72×91×73
    *Provenance:* Private collection.

**145A and B**

146C

147

145A and B
**Pair of *guéridons*, attributed to B. Molitor; *c. 1809–12***
Mahogany, ormolu mounts and marble;
90.7×39 (A); 93×36 (B)
    *Provenance:* Schloss Wilhelmshöhe, Kassel, inv. no. 20 392; formerly Residenz Palast, (A) Res. pal Z 130/20; (B) Res. Pal Z 130/12, 109/39. The *guéridons* were part of the furniture commissioned in Paris by King Jérôme of Westphalia.

146A
*Table vide-poche*, **stamped B. Molitor; *c. 1788–92***
Citronwood, purpleheart, mahogany and brass;
73.5×73.5×33
    *Provenance:* Private collection.

146B (*179*)
*Table vide-poche*, **attributed to Molitor; *c. 1788–92***
Citronwood, purpleheart and mahogany;
72×74×33.5
    *Provenance:* Sold at Sotheby Parke-Bernet, New York, 4 May 1984, no. 57, repr.

146C
*Table vide-poche*, **attributed to Molitor; *c. 1788–92***
Satinwood, purpleheart and mahogany;
72×74×34
    *Provenance:* Museum of Art, Carnegie Institute, Pittsburgh, Pennsylvania, Inc. no. 70.70.22. Identical unstamped models can be found in the *Museum für Kunsthandwerk*, Frankfurt and in the *Musée Jacquemart-André*, Paris (inv. no. D-367).

147
*Table vide-poche*, **attributed to Molitor; *c. 1791–93***
Mahogany, grey sycamore;
77×63×42
    *Provenance:* Alexander and Behrendt Archives, London

148 (*123*)
*Table à écrire*, **stamped B. Molitor; *c. 1788–95***
Mahogany;
71×168×35
    *Provenance:* Sold at Sotheby Parke-Bernet, New York, 6 Nov. 1982, no. 67, repr.

149
*Table de lecture*, **stamped B. Molitor; *c. 1788–1800***
Mahogany and bronze;
72.5×113×54
    *Provenance:* Private collection.

150
*Coiffeuse d'homme*, **stamped B. Molitor; *c. 1790–1800***
Mahogany, ormolu and marble;
81×100×58
    *Provenance:* Sold at Paris, 17 Dec. 1943, no. 36. '*Coiffeuse d'homme en acajou, d'epoque Louis XVI presente un plateau muni d'une glace et decouvre une tablette de marbre.*' (Description from 1943 Sales Catalogue.)

155

155 (open)

156A

**151**
*Table de malade (top only)*, stamped *B. Molitor* and *J.M.E.*, (Guild Monogram);
*c. 1788–91*
Mahogany and brass;
30.5×60×45
> *Provenance:* Private collection.

**152**
*Table de malade (top only)*, stamped *B. Molitor; c. 1788–92*
Mahogany, ormolu mounts and brass;
24×105×50
> *Provenance:* Private collection.

## Other furniture and small objects

**153 (37)**
*Jardinière*, stamped *B. Molitor; 1810–18*
Mahogany and matt ormolu mounts;
98×78×32
> *Provenance:* Sold at Sotheby Parke-Bernet, Monaco 3 May 1977, no. 43, repr.

**153B (*178*)**
**A pair of Jardinières, attributed to Molitor;** *1809–12*
Mahogany, carved and painted wood and bronze;
81×60
> *Provenance:* Part of the furniture acquired by Jérôme, king of Westphalia, Schloss Wilhelmshöhe, Kassel (Z–57/13).

**154**
**Screen, stamped** *B. Molitor; 1788–95*
Mahogany and Sèvres bisque plaque;
110×54
> *Provenance:* Chappey collection sale, Galerie Carpentier, Paris, 11 Dec 1958, no. 95, not repr.
> *Literature:* Ledoux-Lebard, *Les Ebénistes . . .*, 1984.

**155 (*125*)**
**Tea caddy, stamped** *B. Molitor; c. 1800–10*
Citronwood, mahogany, rosewood, sycamore, ebony and horn;
12×19×11.5
> *Provenance:* Private collection.
> *Literature: Connaissance des Arts*, 70, 1957, repr.

## Seat furniture

**156A**
*Lit de repos*, stamped *B. Molitor; c. 1799–1807*
Mahogany and beech;
84.5×163.5×64
> *Provenance:* J. Lefèvre Collection; private collection.
> *Literature:* Guth, 'La carrière brisée . . .,' 1957; Ledoux-Lebard, *Les Ebénistes . . .*, 1984.
> *Exhibited:* Musée des Arts Décoratifs: *Pierres précieuses de Paris*, Pavillon Marsan, Paris, 1946.

**156B (*27* and *68*)**
*Lit de repos*, attributed to Molitor; *c. 1799–1803*

Mahogany, walnut and metal mounts;
length 206

    *Provenance:* Collection B.B. Steinitz repr. Purchased by Général Nicolas-Antoine-Xavier Castella de Berlens during Napoleon's reign, for Schloss Wallenried.

    *Literature:* G. Diesbach, 'Le Château de Wallenried.' *Connaissance des Arts*, ii no. 192, Feb. 1968, p. 66.

**157** (*187*)
***Lit de repos*, stamped *B. Molitor; c. 1790–1807***
Mahogany, ebony and brass;
length 163 cm

    *Provenance:* Sold at Sotheby Parke-Bernet, Monaco, 17 June 1988, no. 667.

**158A** (*68*)
***Lit de repos*, attributed to Molitor; *c. 1799–1803***
Mahogany, walnut and cast metal mounts
length 206

    *Provenance:* See *156B*.

**158B**
***Lit de repos*, attributed to Molitor; *c. 1799–1807***
Mahogany;
length 206

    *Provenance:* Private collection.

162

**159**
***Lit de repos*, attributed to Molitor; *1800–07***
Mahogany;
160×60

    *Provenance:* Traditionally this piece belonged to Joseph Bonaparte, Napoleon's brother; private collection, damaged scrolled sides.

**160**
***Lit de repos*, attributed to Molitor; *c. 1799–1807***
Mahogany.

    *Provenance:* Private collection.
    *Literature:* G. Janneau, *Le siège*, Paris, 1974, *fig* 327.

**161**
***Lit de repos*, attributed to Molitor; *c. 1799–1807***
Mahogany;
87.5×207×64

    *Provenance:* Sold at Paris, 26 May 1967, no. 129
    *Literature:* 'Le Guide de l'acheteur,' *Connaissance des Arts*, III, 1968, repr.

**162** (*186*)
***Lit de repos*, stamped *B. Molitor; c. 1799–1807***
Mahogany and walnut;
89×205×63.5

    *Provenance:* Private collection.

**163A**
***Lit de repos*, attributed to Molitor; *c. 1799–1807***
Mahogany and walnut;
89×140×57

*Provenance:* Lefuel Collection.

*Literature:* Guth, 'La carrière brisée . . .,' 1957; 'Dictionnaire du siège,' *Connaissance des Arts*, XXXXVII 1960, p. 5; Janneau, *Le Siège*, Paris, 1974, p. 173; C. Bizot, *Mobilier Directoire . . .* Paris, repr.; P. Devinoy and M. Jarry *Le siège français*, Fribourg, 1973, *fig* 273; C. Fregnac *Les styles françaises*, Collection *Connaissance des Arts*, Paris, 1975.

### 163B
***Lit de repos*, attributed to Molitor; *1799–1807***
Mahogany;
> *Provenance:* In 1907, Gustave Duval Collection.
> *Literature: Décorations intérieures et meubles d'époques Louis XV, Louis XVI et Empire*, Paris, 1907–1909, vol 2, repr.

### *Fauteuils* and chairs

### 164A–F (*72* and *182*)
**Six *fauteuils*, stamped *B. Molitor; 1797–1803***
Mahogany and brass;
92×60×48
> *Provenance:* Musée Marmottan, Paris, inv. nos. 708–713.
> *Literature:* H. Lefuel, *Catalogue du Musée Marmottan*, 1934, inv. no 310 to 315, p. 87; Guth, 'La carrière brisée . . .,' 1957; *Dictionnaire du siège, Connaissance des Arts*, 97, 1960, p. 72, repr.; Verlet, *Les ébénistes français . . .*, 1963, p. 316; LXXXXVII, May 1960; Ledoux-Lebard, *Les ébénistes parisiens . . .*, 1984.
> *Exhibited:* Musée des Arts Décoratifs, Paris: *Les chefs-d'œuvre . . .'* 1951, no. 164; Institut Néerlandais, Paris: *La rue de Lille – l'Hôtel de Salm* exhibition, 1983, inv. no. 310, exhibited under no. 199, repr.

### 165A and B (*183*)
**Pair of *fauteuils*, stamped *B. Molitor; 1797–1803***
Mahogany.
> *Provenance:* Private collection.

### 166A–F (*184*)
**Six chairs, stamped *B. Molitor; c. 1797–1803***
Mahogany (*en suite* with 165).
> *Provenance:* Private collection.

### 166G–T
**Fourteen chairs, attributed to Molitor**
Mahogany (*en suite* with 166).
> *Provenance:* Sold at Palais des Beaux Arts, Brussels, 28–29 Sept. 1988.

### 167A–C
**Three chairs, stamped *B. Molitor; c. 1795–1800***
Mahogany and brass;
84×47×46
> *Provenance:* Private collection. They are part of a suite of at least six chairs and are numbered 1, 2 and 5.
> *Literature: Connaissance des Arts*, LXXII, 1958, repr.; Ledoux-Lebard, *Les ébénistes parisiens . . .*, 1984.

### 167D
**Chair, stamped *B. Molitor; c. 1795–1800***
Mahogany and brass.
> *Provenance:* Private collection.

168A–H

*Literature:* L. de Groer, *Les Arts Décoratifs 1790–1850*, Fribourg, 1986, p. 19.

167E–J
**Six chairs, attributed to Molitor;** *c. 1795–1800*
Mahogany and brass.
> *Provenance:* Private collection.
> *Literature:* C. Bizot, *Mobilier Directoire . . .* Paris, p. 17, repr.

168A–H (*185*)
**Eight chairs, stamped** *B. Molitor; c. 1795–1800*
Mahogany and brass;
85×48
> *Provenance:* Private collection.

169A–H
**Eight chairs, attributed to Molitor;** *c. 1795–1800*
Mahogany and brass.
> *Provenance:* Sold at Neuilly, 10 March, 1986, repr.; Nantes, 15 Dec. 1986
repr.

169I–J (*112*)
**Two chairs, attributed to Molitor;** *1795–1800*
Mahogany and brass.
> *Provenance:* Sold at Paris, 28 March 1990, no. 132.
The chairs are stamped *Henri Jacob.*

170A–F (*45*)
**Six chairs, attributed to Molitor;** *1800–05*
Mahogany.
> *Provenance:* Sold at Sotheby Parke-Berne, Monaco, 4 Dec. 1983, no. 52
repr. Private collection.

171A–D (*73*)
**Four chairs, attributed to Molitor;** *1795–1800*
Mahogany and brass;
85×47
> *Provenance:* Private collection. Acquired between 1795–1800 by the
businessman Thomas Merlin, for his Paris *hôtel* at 11 rue Louis le Grand.
> *Literature:* C. Bizot, *Mobilier Directoire . . .* (Paris, *c.* 1965), p. 10 repr.; P.M.
Favelac, *Aujourd'hui s'installer en Directoire – Empire*, Paris, (n.d.) U. Leben,
'B. Molitor Leben und Werk . . .,' 1986, repr.

172A–F (*128*)
**Six chairs, stamped** *B. Molitor; c. 1795–1800*
Mahogany.
> *Provenance:* Sold at Sotheby Parke-Berne, New York, 17 Nov. 1984, no.
295, repr.

173A–E
**Five chairs, stamped** *B. Molitor; c. 1795–1800*
Light mahogany.
> *Provenance:* Château Ingelmüster Belgium sale, 26–27 Sept. 1986, nos.
145–150, repr. in sale catalogue.

# Appendices

In the documentary material quoted below, italics indicate author's comments and document sources.

## Document 1

1.1    Le Sieur Molitor, Ebéniste, Cour de l'Orme à l' Arsenal, maison du sieur Lelièvre, sellier, possède pour la destruction des punaises, un secret qu'il à employé avec succès dans plusieurs maisons de cette ville. C'est une pommade qui n'a point d'odeur, qui n'incomode personne qui ne cause aucun dommage.
*Annonces, Affiches et Avis divers*, 21 Septembre 1778
B.N. V-28290

1.2    Le Sieur Molitor, Ebéniste, Cour de l'Orme à l'Arsenal à perfectionné ses chaufferettes dites "à la Comtesse", faites en forme de livre et dont on peut se servir partout, sans inconvénient et sans qu'elles puissent être aperçues.
La chaleur en est tempérée et dure longtemps. Prix 15 à 18 Livres celles en bois de noyer et 24 Livres celles en bois d'acajou.
*Annonces, Affiches et Avis divers*, 27.12.1781
B.N. V-28297

1.3    Le Sieur Molitor, Cour de l' Orme à l'Arsenal, continue de vendre avec succès, une pommade qui détruit les punaises sans causer aucune incommodité ni aucun dommage: il envoie en ville et en province avec un imprimé qui indique la manière de s'en servir.
*Petites Annonces, Affiches et Avis divers*, 9 Septembre 1786.
B.N. V-28314

## Document 2

Déclaration de Vol de divers effets appartenant aux Messieurs Molitor, le 2 janvier 1788

L'an 1788, le mercredi 2 janvier, quatre heures de la relevée, en notre Hôtel et pardevant nous Claude Leroy, Conseilleur du Roy au Chatelet de Paris sont comparant Sieurs Bernard Molitor, ébéniste et Michel Molitor, aussi ébéniste, demeurant à Paris, Cour de l' Orme à l'Arsenal, maison de la veuve Lelièvre assisté du Sieur Jean Baptiste Vogt, secrétaire interprète du Roy pour les langues étrangères, demeurant à Paris rue St. Denis N°381, attendu qu'ils sont allemands et qu'ils ne prononcent pas la langue française.
Les quels ont déclaré par l'organ dudit Sieur Interprète que le trente et un décembre dernier à six heures du soir, ils s' étaient apperçu qu'ils leur avaient été volés dans leur atelier sans effraction, mais avec une fausse clef, les effets qui suivent. Savoir, audit Bernard Molitor une redingotte neuve de drap gris foncé, avec boutons de poil de chèvre jaune et queues bordée de cordonnes de soie jaune, une chemise garnie de mousseline très fine à manche en amadisle, deux mouchoirs, dont un rayé bleu et blanc et l'autre blanc marqué B.M., une chaîne d' acier anglais à deux branches avec un mousqueton de cuivre jaune et clef de cuivre.

Et audit Michel Molitor une montre de Paris, à boite d'argent avec cordon de soie verte du nom de Foulay gravée sur le cercle de verre, une culotte de velours noire, presque neuve doublée de toile de coton, avec boucles de jarretières d'acier à la culotte, et un parapluie de soie verte à dix branches.

Qu'ils ignorent qui est l'auteur du vol, faisant la prompte déclaration pour rendre hommage à la vérité nous ont requis acte......................et ont signé avec ledit interprète M. Molitor, B. Molitor, Vogt Molitor.
A.N. Y 14436

## Document 3

Reçu fait à la comtesse de Lamarck
Mémoire d' ébénisterie fait et fournis pour Madame de Lamarck à St. Germain par Molitor
Ebéniste demeurant à Paris rue de Lille ci-devant rue Bourbon Faubourg St. Germain.
Savoir,
-       Fait et fournis deux coffres en bois de santal plaqué et bois jaune, orné de filéts blancs et noirs avec les serrures à 36 Livres chaque... 72 Livres
-       Plus le 28 avril 1792 rétablie et repoly à neuf un nécessaire et une table à patin, en bois d'acajou le tout pour la somme de... 12 Livres
-       Plus le 13 février 1793 fait et fournis une table à consolle de 5 pieds 4 pouces de long, garnie de bronze avec un dessus de marbre blanc, prix convenu avec Madame... 450 Livres
-       Plus le 10 juin 1793 envoyé un ouvrier à St. Germain pour rétablir les meubles de Madame avoir employé 21 jours à 4 Livres par jour fait la somme de... 105 Livres
-       Plus avoir fait redoré les bronzes de plusieurs meubles deboursé pour ceci... 80 Livres
-       Plus paié à mon ouvrier trois voyages de Paris à St.Germain à cinq Livres par voyage...15 Livres
-       Plus un voyage que j'ai fait de l'ordre de Madame pour ceci 12 Livres
Total : 746 Livres
Vérifié les articles contenus audit mémoire, lesquels j'ai reconnuy véritable et modéré ledit à la somme de sept cent Livres à St. Germain en Laye ce trente juin mil sept cent quatre vingt treize (30.6.1793) Laborde
Reçu le montant du mémoire arrêté de l'autre part des mains et des deniers du citoyen Says.
A Paris ce decadé Frimaire l'an second de la République française une et indivisible. Molitor
9 Décembre 1793
A.N. T 769

## Document 4

*Inventaire après décès (extraits)*
Julie Elisabeth Fessard, première femme de Bernard Molitor
Troisième jour complémentaire de l'an IV (19.9.1796)

L'An quatre de la République française, le troisième des jours complémentaires, trois heures de relever, à la requête de Bernard Molitor, ébéniste à Paris, y demeurant rue de Lille N°576, section de la fontaine de Grenelle, en son nom à cause de la communauté de biens, qui a existé entre lui et Julie Elisabeth Fessard, son épouse veuve en première noces de Jacques Bonnaventure Verdier, notaire à Milly, en Gatinois et sans enfants de son premier mariage, aux-termes de contract de marriage passé devant Lecointre, qui en a la minute, et son confrère, notaires à Paris le sept juin 1788. Led. Molitor, encore au nom et comme tuteur d'Anne Julie Molitor, sa fille mineure et de lad. défunte son épouse, enfant unique de leur mariage à l'effet de régir et administrer ses personnes et biens. En présence de Claude Fessard demeurant à Paris rue Perdue N°2 division du Pantheon, oncle maternel de lad. mineure Molitor, à l' effet de stipuler et deffendre ses droits et interêts dans tous les cas ou ils se trouvent contraires à ceux dud. Molitor. Led. Molitor père, nommé à lad. qualité de tuteur, et led. Fessard oncle maternel, nommé à lad. qualité de subrogé tuteur delad. Molitor le tous de l'avis des parens et amis de lad. mineure, reçu par procès verbal du juge de paix de la division de la fontaine de Grenelle, en date du 22 Fructidor de l'an IV de la République française, enregistré à Paris par Carrou le même jour dont expédition en bonne forme de livrée par notte greffier de lad. justice de paix représenté par led. Molitor père, est demeurée y annexée après avoir été de lui signé et paraphé, en présence des notaires soussignés. Lad. mineure Molitor habile à se dire et porter, seule réprésentante et unique héritière de lad. Julie E. Fessard sa mère. A la conservation des droits et actions des parties en noms et qualités et de qui il appartiendra, il va être par les notaires à Paris sousignées, procédé ensuite du présent intitulé à l'inventaire, fidèle et exacte description de tous les meubles meublants, ustensiles de ménage, habit, linge, effets, argenterie, bijoux, deniers comptant titre papiers renseignements et tous objets generallement quelconques appartenant à la communauté entre led. Molitor et sa femme à la succession de la dernière le tout trouvé et étant dans les lieux cy après designés dépandant de la maison rue de Lille N°576 où demeure led. Molitor, appartenante au citoyen Trompette dans lesquelles lieux lad. femme Molitor est decedée le 15 Fructidor de l'an IV de la République française.

Sur la représentation et mise en évidence, qui se faite du tout aux notaires, sousignées par led. Molitor père, de tout dire représenter et déclarer, sans en rien exempter ni réserver et de n'avoir ni détourné par quique c'était sous les peines aud. cas introduites qui lui ont été expliqué et qu'il a dit connaître led. serment preté entre les mains de Rouen, l'un des notaires soussignés en présence de son confrère.

La prise des choses y sujeter sera faite par Pierre André Auger expert priseur, demeurant à Paris rue Sauveur N°1 division de bon conseil qui fera lad. prise en égard des marchandises et objets de l'état dud. Molitor en sad. qualité d'ébéniste ils seront prises par led. Auger en présence et de l'avis du citoyen Etienne Trompette dem. à Paris sad. maison rue de Lille 576, où est procédé au présent inventaire, et de Joseph Sintz ébéniste demeurant rue neuve des petits champs N°74, division de la butte des moulins, pour deux experts jointoiement choisis par led. tuteur et subrogé tuteur et qui donnerons leurs avis sur leur âme et conscience et ont signé sous toutes réserves protestations et deffenses respectives et de droit en ces présentes, mots sont rayés.

Comme aussi après serment pareillement fait en présence des notaires sousignés entre les mains dud. Rouen l'un d'eux par Michel Molitor, cousin germain dud. Molitor père demeurant avec lui et son épouse antérieurement au décès de celle-ci et qui a continué de rester avec led. Molitor père jusqu'à ce moment de n'avoir rien pris ni détourné et de n'avoir point connaissance qu'il ait été rien détourné, parceque ce soit sous les peines audit car introduites qui lui ont été expliqué et pareillement connaître et soussigné les présentes: B. Molitor, Trompette, Anger, Fessard, Sintz, M. Molitor Rouen...

(*suit la prisée*)

Dans un petit caveau, .....

Dans une chambre, au rez-de-chaussée, éclairée de deux fenêtres sur la rue servant en même temps d'atelier ...

(*suivent les ustensils de cuisine*)

Dans un salon à l'entresol éclairé de deux croisées donnant sur la rue

Item, deux chenets à une branche, pelle et pincette de fer, une paire de mouchette d'acier, sur son porte mouchette de fer vernis, un petit bougeoir de cuivre argenté, deux flambeaux de cabinet à colonne avec bobèche, aussi de cuivre argenté, deux caraffes à eau de verre, une pendulle à cadran d'émaille, anonçant les phases de la lune, garnie de trois aiguilles marquant les quantièmes heures et minutes, sonnant les heures et demie, dans sa boîte de cuivre cy devant dorée et soutenus sur un pied de bois, p.l.t. 40 Livres.

Item, un petit coffret, à bonnet, en bois blanc fermant à clef, quatre chaises en bois de hêtre, à gerbe, paillée satinée, trois autres chaises de bois de hêtre, peint en vert aussi foncée, paille satinée p.l.t. 5 Livres.

Item un petit ballet de liseuse, un parassol à huit branches en taffetas rose, dans son étui de toile, quatre gravures, représentant divers paysages, dans leurs cadres de bois noirci, environ 18 pouces de large sur 15 de haut, deux autres de même grandeur sous verre blanc dont un représentant la paysanne bienfaisante, quatre dessins, dont deux en noir et deux en rouge aussi sous verre blanc, dans leurs cadres de bois noirci p.l.t. 12 Livres.

Item six fauteuilles un canapé garni de son matelat le tout foncé crin couvert en velours d'Utrecht à rayé, cramoise et jaune, deux oreillers en duvet couvert de même velours d'Utrecht le tout monté sur bois peint en gris, le velours d'Utrecht piqué de verre le t.p. 80 Livres.

A l'égard de deux tableaux peint sur toile, dont un représentant le portrait dud. citoyen Molitor et l'autre de la citoyenne sa fille, il n'en a été fait plus ample désignation, ni prisée et le présent article a été seulement tiré pour mémoire cy mémoire:

Dans une petite armoire, en boiserie à côté de la cheminée

Item, douze bouteilles, pleine de vinaigre blanc p.l.t. 31 Livres.

un plat, un saladier de fayence, une soupierre à anse, avec son couvercle un autre saladier;

deux assiettes et un plat le tout de fayence blanche, cinq tasses, une théière, le tout de terre anglaise p.l.t. 5 Livres.

Item une veilleuse à pompe, de fer blanc un bocal de gros verres noirs, deux petits couteaux dont un à manche d' écaille et l'autre d' ivoire blanc p.l.t. 1 Livre.

Item une table ronde ployante, en acajou, monté sur son pied en bois de noyer, un secrétaire en armoire, ouvrant à bascule, surmonté d'un tiroir fermé par bas par deux petites portaires, avec entrée de serrure de cuivre en couleur p.l.t. 60 Livres.

Dans un petit cabinet servant à coucher la citoyenne mineure

Item, un petit berceau, une paillasse de toile à carreaux bleu et blanc, un matelas de petite laine couvert de même toile, un oreiller de vieille plume couvert en vieux coutil, un draps de grosse toile de ménage un couvre pied piqué couvert en vieille toile blanche p.l.t. 8 livres.

Item, un miroir de toilette, une glace de dix pouces sur onze, dans son cadre de bois peint en blanc une chaise de commodité en canne, garnie de sa cuvette un petit oreiller rempli de plume couvert en coutil 41 Livres.

Dans une chambre à coucher, ayant son entrée par le sallon, eclairée d'une croisée sur la cour.

Item, une petite gravure sous verre blanc dans son cadre de bois noirci, un cruzifie en cuivre, encienement doré, sur sa croix, encore avec filles aussi de cuivre anciennement doré, une table de nuit, en bois de noyer, deux petites rideaux de croisée de toile vert d'environ un mettre et demie de large, sur un mettre et demie de haut avec treingle et anneaux 8 Livres.

Item, une couchette de quatre pieds à deux chevets et à colonnes de bois peints, en gris à fond sanglé, garni de roulettes à écaire, un sommier de crin couvert de toile à carreaux, deux matelas demie laine couvert aussi de toile à carreaux, un lit de bonne plume, couvert de coutil de florence un traversin de plume, couvert en même coutil, un petit oreiller du duvet, également couvert en coutil, deux draps dont un de grosse toile grise, et un autre de toile fine de ménage, une couverture en toile de coton à linteau bleu prise 130 Livres.

Item, un matelas de petite laine, couvert de vieille toille à carreaux de trois pieds de long p.l.t.10 Livres.

Dans une armoire en boiserie, pratique en lad. pièce

Item, de fers à repasser le linge, un porte manteau, un pot de nuit 1 Livre.

Dans une armoire en encoignure, pratique dans le sallon

Item, six bouteilles de différentes ratafias, deux autres bouteilles, vides, deux petites caraffes à liqeur, en cristal avec leurs bouchon, contenant aussi différentes ratafiats, deux bocaux de grosse verre, vides dans lequelles il y a peu de liqeurs 15 Livres.

Item, quatre petit rideaux de croisées de mousseline rayé, d'un sur environ un mètre de haut avec treingle et anneaux 2 Livres

Dans la chambre de la mineure cy devant nomme

Item, deux petits rideaux de croisée de toile verte, d'environ un mètre et demie de haut, avec treingle anneaux 2 Livres.

Dans une antichambre

Item, un vieux lit de sangle, un miroir de toilette, une glace de dix pouces sur douzes dans son cadre de bois brun, une autre miroire d'une glace, de dix huit pouces de large sur douze de haut, dans son cadre de bois sculpte doré 10 Livres.

Il a été vu que à tous ce dessus par double vacation de la réquisition, des parties pour accélérer jusqu' à neuf heures sonnées ce fait tous les objets cy dessus inventoriés et ceux restant à l'être du consentement dud. subogé tuteur en sa qualité ont continuité de rester en la garde et possession dud. Molitor père qui le reconnait et s'en charge pour en faire la représentation quand et à qui il appartiendra la vacation pour la continuation du présent inventaire a été remise et indique à demain quatrième jour complémentaire huit heures du matin

Et ont signés...Molitor, Fessard, Raguideau, Rouen, Anger

Et led jour quatrième de ceux complémentaires de l'an IV de la République française, huit heures du matin, en conséquence de l'indication portée en la clôture de la precédente vacation à ce jour et heure il va être par lesd. notaires à Paris sousignés, procédé en mêmes lieux requêtes présence et qualité que ci devant la continuation du présent inventaire de la manière ainsi qu'il suit.

Dans la chambre à coucher cydev. énoncée... suit la garderobe à l'usage dud. Molitor.... 20 Livres.

Sur des planches en tablettes, pratiques dans lad. pièce

Item, un petit coffres, en bois noir, fassot de lattes, deux volumes de livres allemand, secets des arts, une serpierre en toile verte avec agraphe en cuivre p.l.t. 2 Livres

Dans une armoire en boiserie, pratiqué dans le salon

Linge de maison ... (*description*) 6 Livres

Dans une autre armoire dépendant de lad. maison

Linge de maison ... (*description*) 88 Livres

Suivant les effets de garderobe a l'usage dela défunte Molitor

Description de la garderobe... 534 Livres

Dans un magazin, éclairé de deux croisée, donnant sur lad. rue

Item, une petite garniture de nécessaire, en maroquin vert un petit nécessaire, en acajou plaque garni de six rassoire, deux bras de cheminée, à deux branches de cuivre un petit roy à filer, avec son ratellier de cuivre enciennement argenté p.l.t. 50 Livres

Item une vielle housse de console en futaine de laine, trois vielles serviettes ouvrées, servant à couvrir différents meubles, une caisse en bois blanc, un poêle de fayence blanche avec portes d'entrée, four, et tuyaux de tôle p.l.t. 16 Livres

Item, un carreau en miroir d'une glace de dix pouces de large sur quatorze de haut encadré de baguette de bois, peint en gris un autre pareille p.l.t. 18 Livres

Item, un grand carreau d'un verre blanc, de deux pieds carré prises 4 Livres.

Item, un grand cadre de bois doré, un vieux tapis de liziere, un petit coffre d'environ quatre pouces de haut, sur six de large en acajou massif, avec serrure et charnière en cuivre sans clef 4 Livres.

Dans un secrétaire, cy devant inventorié, suivant les bijoux

Item, une paire de petits anneaux d'oreille, un anneau d'or, un œuf en casselette à éponge en or de couleur, un cœur en cristal avec cercle et charnière d'or, une paire de bouton de manche à petits points en argent, un bracelet de pierre, monté en argent sur sa gance de soye noir, un dez d'argent une tresse de soye et or, une paire de boucle à usage d'homme à conoure d'argent taille en pierre, avec rosettes à double chappe en acier 54 Livres.

Item une petite montre dans sa boîte d'or de Genève, unie à cadran d'émaille, garnie de ses deux eguilles marquant les heures et les minutes, un autre montre dans sa boîte d'or de Paris unie portant sur le mouvement le nom de Darliebe N°123 à cadran d'émaille garnie de ses deux eguilles marquant heures et minutes toutes deux avec chaînes de cuivre p.l.t. 120 Livres.

Item, une large montre dans sa boîte d'argent, unie portant sur la boîte len. 9754, à cadran d'émaille, garnie de ses deux eguilles marquant les heures et les minutes 36 Livres.

Suit l'argenterie

Item, une petite timballe et une grande, une cuillere à soupe, six cuilleres et six fourchettes à bouches, un petit couvert d'enfant, le tout d'argent poinçon de Paris, paisant ensemble six marcs six gros prises à juste valleur et sans crue, comme vaisselle plate poinçon de Paris à raison de 50 Livres 17 sous six denuser lemarc recuant lad. quantité aud. prisés la somme de 343,8 Livres.

( *Signatures de ...*) Molitor, Fessard, Anger, Raguideau, Rouen

Et le cinquième de ceux complémentaires........

Il va être procédé à l'inventaire prises et descriptions des marchandises, ustensiles de l'état dud. Molitor par led. Anger, en présence de l'avis desd. Trompette et Sintz experts choisis comme il est établie l'intitule du présent inventaire à l'effet de quoi les parties et qualités nous ont requis de procéder d'abord à l'inventaire des bois non ouvragés, existants dans un chantier appartenent à la succession de Salm, à côté des lieux qu'occupe led. Molitor, et ou est procédé au présent inventaire obtempèrant au quel réquisitoire nous sommes aussitôt transportés sur led. chantier ou étant a été fait cequi suis

Premièrement Mille huit toises courante de bois français et Fontainebleau, de moyenne qualité à quatre vingt dix Livres le cent fait neuf cent sept Livres quatre sous 907,4 Livres.

Item, vingt madrieres d'acajou, avec plusieurs feuillets feuilles de placage et bois jaune pesant ensemble quatre mille sept cent vingt Livres à vingt quatre Livres les cent fait mille cent trente deux Livres seize sous 1132,16 Livres.

Ne s'étant plus rien trouvé sur led. chantier nous sommes retournés chez led. Molitor pour continuer le présent inventaire étant nous avons fait ce qui suit

Dans l'atelier au rez-de-chaussée

Premièrement, huit établis avec six affutages, différents outils comme valets, scies, ciseaux, gouges et le tout en médiocre état estimé le tout ensemble 156 Livres.

Dans une chambre au premier étage, éclairée de deux croisées sur la rue de Lille

| | |
|---|---:|
| Item, trois tables à écrire non achevées | 108 L. |
| Item, deux à brelan en acajou | 120 L. |
| Item, deux petits bureaux de hazard, en acajou, dont un couvert d'un maroquin vert | 40 L. |
| Item, une table trictrac, à jeu triangulaire, de hazard aussi en acajou | 10 L. |
| Item, un bureau de quatre pieds, orné de bronze doré | 240 L. |
| Item, deux comodes, non garnies, dont une avec un dessus de marbre de languedoc, ensemble | 240 L. |
| Item, deux autres commodes, non garnies à dessus de marbre blanc veiné, ensemble | 260 L. |
| Item, deux idem. non finies, ornées de bronze, l'une doré et l'autre non doré, à dessus de marbre de couleur, | 700 L. |
| Item, deux secrétaires de trois pieds, ornés de bronze dont un doré, ensemble | 400 L. |
| Item, un idem. de trois pieds, en bois jaune, avec ornement feuille de chêne, à dessus de marbre chipolin, orné de bronze non doré prises ensembles | 250 L. |
| Item, un trictrac à mechanique, orné de bronze non doré | 150 L. |
| Item, deux armoires en bois jaune, à dessus de marbre de couleur, de trois pieds de large sur quatre pieds huit pouces de hauteur, dont l'une à tiroir, et l'autre à tablettes à coulisses prisés ensembles | 500 L. |
| Item, une bibliothèque de quatre pieds de longue, sur six pieds de hauteur, à crémaillère, prisés | 200 L. |
| Item, deux toilettes de femme, à dessus de marbre blanc, non finies et sans glaces ensembles | 200 L. |
| Item, deux guéridons, cerclés et dorés, prisés ensembles | 180 L. |
| Item, une petite table a pattin, orné de cuivre doré | 150 L. |
| Item, une idem, à pattin, non doré | 80 L. |
| Item, une table à manger, de quatre pieds huit pouces | 90 L. |
| Item, deux idem, creuses, l'une en acajou et l'autre en bois jaune, ensembles | 170 L. |
| Item, une idem, en bois gris | 50 L. |
| Item, trois id., non finies | 80 L. |
| Item, deux petites tables étagères, en bois gris, avec dessus de marbre, ensemble | 100 L. |
| Item, un guéridon, garnie en acier | 200 L. |
| Item, un id., à colonnes garnis en cuivre doré | 120 L. |
| Item, deux tables à écrire, à la Pompadour, en marqueterie, ornées de bronze, doré au mat, ensembles | 500 L. |
| Item, un secrétaire de femme, orné de bronze doré au mat | 1200 L. |
| Item, une table à déjeuner, à deux dessus, doré au mat | 400 L. |
| Item, un grand guéridon, octogone avec marbre griotte | 60 L. |
| Item, quatre chaises en acajou, garnies en crin noir | 86 L. |
| Item, une commode, en bois de rose | 70 L. |
| Item, une table, de noyer de hazard | 15 L. |
| Item, deux coffres, de noyer de hazard | 40 L. |

| | |
|---|---|
| Item, une petite caisse, à bouquet en acajou | 30 L. |
| Item, un dessus de marbre griotte, pour un secrétaire | 30 L. |
| Item, un dessus de console, vert de mer, | 40 L. |
| Item, un marbre rond de marquetterie, de trente pouces | 120 L. |
| Item, cinquante livres de cuivre ouvragé | 150 L. |
| Item, quatre garnitures de sceaux argentés, pour des servantes | 96 L. |
| Item, vingt cinq livres de cuivre, non ouvragé | 25 L. |
| Item, cent pieds de moulure de cuivre repoli | 100 L. |

Il a été vacqué depuis lad. heure de huit jusqu'à celle de deux sonnées par double vacation........

La vacation pour la continuation du présent inventaire a été remise et indiqué aujourd'hui trois heures

Sintz, Trompette, Molitor, Fessard, Anger, Raguideau, Rouen

Est led. jour ... à la continuation du présent inventaire de la manière et ainsi qu'il suit...

(*suivent les papiers et appels ...*)

Premièrement une pièce c'est l'expédition d'un parchemin du contrat de mariage dud. Bernard Molitor...

Item deux pièces ce sont deux extraits de livre en langue latin l'un mortuaire de Nicolas Molitor père du comparant suivi aux regetus de la paroisse de Machtum Duché de Luxembourg le vingt sept avril 1787. L'autre est Mortuaire de Margueritte Lemmer, mère du comparant suivant aux registres et église paroissiale de Betzdorf Duché de Luxembourg à la date du 14 juillet 1776.

Lesquelles p... D E U X

Item deux pièces, la première est un extrait inscription sur le grand livre de la dette publique non viagère du 11 messidor de l'an 3 de la république française., suivant portée

Reg. M Vol/0 sous le N° II,035 de deux cent quatre vingt six Livres et promil annuel au nom dud. Bernard Molitor

La seconde, est une lettre de la comission des revenues nationaux relative à la remise du certificat de propriété sur lequel lad. inscription précedement inventorié a été expédiée ces deux pièces ont été inventorié.... T R O I S

Observe led. Molitor, que cette inscription représente le prix des ouvrages fait par lui, pour la liste civile et qu'il n'a encore rien touché sur cette inscription dont les produits lui sont dus depuis qu'ils en coure.

Item quatre pièces en sous N° trois pancartes d'actions de la caisse d'Epargne et de bienfaisance dit en la farge de la susnommé société en date le deux premières du 25 septembre 1793 la troisième du 26 du même mois,... signées vises versifiés... led. pancartes ensemble de dix actions enumerotées depuis et compris 96,232 jusques et compris 96,241... savoir les quatre premières actions sur la tête et au profit dud. Bernard Molitor né a Betzdorf pays de Luxembourg le 22 septembre 1755, les trois suivantes sur la tête et au profit de lad. défunte femme de Molitor né à Fontainebleau le 28 février 1758, enfin les trois dernières au profit dud. Bernard Molitor et sa femme sur la tête de lad. Anne Julie Molitor leur fille mineure née à Paris le 15 avril 1789 des quelles dix actions les numeré 96,232 sur la tête et au profit dud. Molitor père porte rente 2. et une petite note indicative que le certificat de vie a été fourni le 8 messidor de l'an 4 de la république française.

Lesquelles pièces... Q U A T R E

Item vingt deux pièces ce sont notes, borderaux et pièces le tout pouvant servir de renseignements sur l'affaire de l'état du Molitor notament avec, Lavieuville, Lacharte, Beauregard, Maurice de Caramant, Margueritte, Lafayette, Tessé, Crosbie, Revielle, Vaudemont, Fitz James, Mondavie, Dupré, Lasue, Mirpoix, Boigelin, Bonnecarrere et Ambassadeur de Suède.

Dont du tout de la réquisition en presse des parties il n'a été fait aucun autre détail, pour accélérer led. pièce fut collées... C I N Q

Observe led. Molitor qu'il a entre les mains du citoyen Guyot rue Montmartre près celle des vieux augustins diverses papiers qui peuvent comprendre, et venir a l'appuie d'aucunes de ceux qui viennent d'être inventoriées, mais comme il ne lui en a pas fait la remise; ils n'ont pus être compris au présent inventaire.

Item, quatre pièces ce sont quatre registres, dont trois de grandeur moyenne et le quatrième plus grand, trois couvert en parchemin fauve, le premier desd. registres écrit en totalité avec addition des deux cahiers de papier ordinaire, parallèlement écrits en totalité, mais le tout en partie raturé, contiennent divers façons d'ouvrages, fournitures, indications notes et objets de l'état dud. Molitor.

Le second écrit jusqu'environ les deux tiers et ensuite sur le verso de la dernière rayé et le reste et quatre lignes du verso d'une feuille de papier ordinaire même grandeur ajouté contient le détail et l'Etat du journées d'ouvrier employé par led. Molitor dans son état.

Le troisième, écrit jusqu'environ le tiers contient le détail de factures d'ouvrages, fournitures notes et objets de l'état dud. Molitor la majeure partie des articles raturés.

Enfin le quatrième, dont la feuillete sont timbrées et écrit seulement sur les douze premières feuilles de suite, sans interruption et sans rature et du tout de la Réquisition expresse des Parties il n'a point été fait d'autre Description (de la réquisition expresse des Parties), pour accélérer et le tout pouvant correspondre d'ailleurs aux pièces inventorié sous la côte cinq du présent inventaire.

Lesquelles quatre pièces ont été inventorié collées... SIX

observe que lesd. Registres ont été inventorié, collées paraphées seulement en tête et en fin des Portions écrites.

Item, deux pièces ce sont deux quittances du loyer de lieux, ou est procédé au présent inventaire signé dud. citoyen Trompette l'un des experts qui a procédé cy devant en ces présentes; propriétaire de la maison, en date du 1 juillet 1795 et 13 août 1796 de chacun huit cent Livres, pour chacune une année de loyer échu le premier juillet de chacune desd. années.

Les deux pièces... SEPT

Observe led. Molitor qu'il la doit que le terme courant de son loyer ainsi qu'il résulte desd. quittances et qu'il est locataire sans bail.

Item huit pièces; la première est la patente audit Molitor pour l'année 1791 délivrée le 18 may aud. an service arrondissement N°460 due... signées en forme, ... soixante quinze Livres

La seconde est pareille patente pour l'année 1792 délivrée le 7 septembre 1793, N°212, 14ᵉ arrondissement 4 ded. N°58 du rôle de la contribution mobiliaire moyennant cent Livres

La troisième est une quittance signe Bernard, receveur de la contribution patriotique et des impositions de sixième département du Paris le 12 juin 1792 de dix-huit Livres aud. Molitor pour la totalité de sa contribution patriotique sous le N°166.

Item, pièce la première est un certificat du Directoire du Département de Paris, délivre en bonne forme le 8 septembre 1793 sous le N°23 aud. Molitor constatant qu'il n'est porté sur aucune liste d' Emigrée, les deux suivantes sont certificats de résidence de trois témoins délivrés par la section de la Fontaine de Grenelle le vingt trois Pluviose de l'an trois de la République Française se sous le N°619, aud. Molitor, constatant sa résidence depuis le Premier Mai 1792, ce certificat visé par le Directoire du Département le 24 dud. mois. La troisième pièce est le certificat de Civisme dud. Molitor délivre par l'Assemblée générale de la Section de la Fontaine de Grenelle le 15 septembre 1793.

Les autres pièces sont Certificats de Prestations de serment, quittances de Dons à la Section, Certificat de Service de Garde Nationale et autres devoirs civiques dont du tout de la réquisition expresse des Parties il n'a point été fait d'autre description lesd. Pièces ont été collées... NEUF

Item dix sept pièces ce sont quittances de marchands, fournisseurs, ouvriers dont du tout de la réquisition expresse des Parties pour accélerer il n'a été fait aucune autre description... DIX

( suivent )

... l'acte de décès de lad. défunte femme Molitor...

... quittance des frais funéraires...

Item pièce la Première est un mémoire d'ouvrages faite pour led. Molitor, dans le courant des mois de Fructidor de l'an IV de la république française, par Berder, marbrier rue de Sevres N°1275, montant en demande a 110 Livres.

La seconde, est un mémoire d'ouvrages et fournitures, fait aud. Molitor par John, tailleur, le premier Vendemiaire de l'an cinq de la république française, montant en demande 73 Livres.

La troisième, est un Mémoire d'ouvrage en fournitures faites pour led. Molitor par Demay, Menuisier, rue de Cléry N°259 montant en demande de 447 Livres; les ouvrages faits dans le courant de Fructidor an quatre.

La quatrième, est un mémoire de fournitures faites aud. Molitor, par Virieux, serrurier montant en demande a 29 Livres au dessous du quel est un reçu de 15 Livres du premier Vendemiaire an Cinq de la république française.

Lesdites pièces... T R E I Z E

Déclare led. Molitor qu'entre les mémoires et sauf a regler s'il y a lieu sur leur montant (...) du aud. Michel Molitor dessus nommé en intitulé du présent inventaire une somme d'environ 1500 Livres pour fournier d'ouvrages depuis 1791 jusqu' à ce jour, ne lui ayant jamais reçu paye depuis qu'il travaille chez lui.

aud. Chaille faubourg St. Denis fournisseur en acier poli une somme de 150 Livres pour ouvrages de son état fait en l'année 1793

Au dessinateur 36 Livres, au tourneur de cuivre 18 liv. au tourneur en bois 8 liv., ces trois articles en numéraire....

a la garde malade de la défunte 21 liv.

au médecin 48 liv.

a l'apothicaire, enfin a son boulanger 9 liv.

Ce fait ne s'étant plus rien trouvé à dire, comprendre et déclarer

Et ont signé sous toutes les réserves prestations et ......

ont soussignés Molitor, C. Fessard, Rouen, Raguideau

A. N. Min. LXXI - 126

**Document 5**

Justice de Paix Saisseval contre Molitor

L'an dix de la République française le dix neuf vendemiaire (11.10.1801)

Par devant de bureau de paix de la division des Champs Elysées, canton de Paris département de la Seine

Est comparant le citoyen Jossé Bouillon demeurant à Paris rue Vantadout....(pour le) citoyen Claude Louis Saisseval .... demeurant à Paris rue de Lille.

........ Becure son constituant a fait cité à comparaître à ces jour, lieu et heure le citoyen Molitor ébéniste, demeurant à Paris rue du Faubourg St. Honoré entre la rue des Champs Elysées et celle de la Concorde. Pour se concilier se faire si peut avec le requérant sur la demande qu'il y propose de former contre le surnommé.

Pour dire que faute par lui d'avoir satisfait à la formation du onze du présent mois et suivant celle d'avoir remit au requérant les deux armoires dont il s'agit, qu'il sera condamné à rendre et remettre au requérant la somme de mille quatre cent livres tournois que le requérant lui a payé pour la façon desdites deux armoires sans préjudice et sous la réserve de demander la valeur de la matière première remise par le requérant au surnommé qui l'avait mise en réserve. Le tout avec intérêts et dépenses.

Et a signé Jossé Bouillon.

Et aussi comparant le Sieur Bernard Molitor, ébéniste, patenté pour l'an neuf sous le N°20, le 9 Nivôse, demeurant à paris rue et porte St. Honoré N°17.

Lequel a dit que la demande du citoyen Saisseval a d'autant plus lieu de la surprendre, qu'il n'a jamais refusé de remettre l'armoire qui lui restait, ni le prix de celle qu'il a vendu. Que ces deux armoires étant un ouvrage de fantaisie, ont cessé tout à coup d'être du goût du citoyen Saisseval, qui a invité le comparu après en avoir soldé en presque totalité et la façon et les fournitures, à les lui vendre au meilleur prix possible. En conséquence led. Molitor proposa de les vendre à plusieurs personnes et en trouva enfin la somme de trois cent soixante livres, que malgrè qu'il eut la permission de les vendre à quelqu'un prix que ce fut, il en voula point prendre sur lui aucun engagement sans en avoir prévenu le citoyen Saisseval, qui consentit à ce qu'elle fut donné pour le prix offert.

Le citoyen Molitor vendit donc une desdites armoires au citoyen Fachet pour la somme de trois cent soixante francs, que cedit citoyen ne lui a jamais payé. Qu'il est prêt de remettre au citoyen Saisseval trois cent soixante livres de prix de l'armoire vendue, ou si mieux il n'aime à lui en faire une pareille. Plus à lui rendre aussi celle qui lui reste et qu'il la fait conduire chez ledit citoyen Saisseval aussitôt que cedit lui a par sa soumission manifesté l'intention de l'avoir.

Et a signé sous toutes réserves de droit MOLITOR.

Archives de la Seine, Paris: D 1U <sup>1</sup>-11, Justice de Paix.

**Document 6**

*Inventaire après décès de Michel Molitor*, 21.5.1810

L'an mil huit cent dix, le lundi vingt et un mai onze heures du matin

A la requête de Monsieur Bernard Molitor, fabricant d'ébénisterie, demeurant à Paris, rue Neuve du Luxembourg N°37 division de la Place Vendôme, premier arrondissement.

Habille à se dire et porter seul représentation, et unique héritier de Michel Molitor, ébéniste, célibataire, son cousin germain étant fils de Bernard Molitor, lequel était frère de Nicolas Molitor père du requérant.

...(*description*)... de la sucession dudit Michel Molitor trouvés et étant dans une chambre au deuxième étage de la maison dans laquelle demeure ledit sieur Bernard Molitor, rue Neuve du Luxembourg N°37, et donc est principal locataire Monsieur Lemoine, libraire. Dans laquelle chambre dont ledit Bernard Molitor laissait la jouissance audit sieur Michel Molitor, celui-ci est décédé le douze du présent mois.

Sur la présentation et mise en évidence qui seront faites du tous aux notaires par ledit sieur Molitor, après serment par lui prêté entre les mains de Maître Rouen....

... La prisée des choses y sujetés sera faite par Monsieur Louis Guillaume Bouchy, commissaire priseur à Paris demeurant rue Neuve des petits Champs. ...

Dans ladite chambre ci-devant désignée et éclairée par une croisée sur la cour.

Premièrement une couchette en bois peint à deux dossiers et roulettes à pivots et à barre, trois matelas de laine couverts de toile à carreaux, un lit, un traversin de coutil, remplis de plumes et une mauvaise toile à paillasse, une vieille table de nuit en bois de noyer et son vase en fayence, prisés ...70 francs

Item deux petites tablettes à livres formant armoire par bas à deux petits vantaux, ferrures, serrures et clefs, vingt volumes de livres sujets de dévotion, un mauvais tableau peint sur toile et vingt petites gravures, sujets de dévotion, prisés ... 8 francs.

Une malle, une cassette, une boîte en bois, un petit coffre garni en cuivre, deux cartons, une cruche de grés et trente pièces de poterie et verrerie ne méritant description, prisés...3 F

Item deux couvertures de laine un vieux couvre pied, reprisé avec une mauvaise chaise foncé paille, un parapluie en taffetas vert une canne commune ...6 F

Item une boîte en fer blanc, un entonnoir aussi en fer blanc, un rasoir, une boîte à savonnette et autres mêmes objets ne méritant description prisés .. 3F

Item deux petits miroirs de toilette, un autre cassé, une brosse, un petit chandelier en fer, un éteignoir, tabatière en bois, un petit mortier en verre avec son pilon cassé, une paire de lunettes, une boîte garnie de quatre vieux rasoirs, un tire-bouchon, un petit tamin, dix flacons de gros verre de diverses grandeurs, un pot a eau à fleurs prisés ...6 F

Dans les malle et cassette ci-devant inventoriées trois vieux draps, quatre mauvaises serviettes, six vieilles chemises, cinq vieux mouchoirs et huit paires de bas de coton et chinés, quatre cols en mousseline et un paquet de vieux linges, coupons d'étoffes et autres débris ne méritant description prisés ... 30 F

Item un habit en étoffe couleur grisâtre et un autre en drap commun vert, un habit d'uniforme nationale en drap bleu doublé de blanc, veste en étoffe de laine, deux vieilles culottes en velours de coton, deux vieilles redingotes et une veste de travail, un sac en velours presque hors de service, six paires de vieilles chaussures et une paire de pantoufles le tout prisé avec deux cuillers et une fourchette en étain (et) un vieux chapeau de forme ronde ...40 F

Item une agrafe de col en argent prisé avec une paire de boucles de jarretières en acier ...3 F

Il ne s'est trouvé aucun papier à inventorier.

déclare Monsieur Molitor, qu'au moment du décès il s'est trouvé dans une des poches du défunt deux pièces en or de vingt quatre livres et en menue monnaie, et quatorze livres dix-huit sous, lequel argent a servi d'autant à payer ses frais d'inhumation et cérémonies du culte donc l'excédent a été avancé par M. Molitor ensemble les frais de maladie et autres dépenses donc il justifiera quand et ainsi qu'il appartiendra.

Monsieur Molitor observe encore qu'il a appris que le défunt avait déposé chez M. Baudoin au magasin de meubles, ancien Hôtel de la guerre, rue Grange Bâtelière, différents meubles lui appartenant. Le composant de deux commodes en marquetterie, à dessus de marbre, un chiffonnier en bois de rose, et deux tables à écrire formant bureaux aussi en bois de rose. Que pour retirer ces objets il y a à acquitter chez M. Baudoin les frais de magazinage et droits par lui réclamé, qu'en conséquence M. Molitor se dispose à retirer lesdits meubles lesquels aussi après leur transports dans les lieux où est présentment procédé seront comprises au présent inventaire après avoir été décrits et prisés ... signé Molitor

......La continuation du présent inventaire à cause des objets à reprendre chez M. Baudoin est remise au jour et heure qui seront ultérieurement indiqués et à ledit Sieur Molitor signé sous toutes réserves de droit .... Molitor

A.N. Min. LXXI - 169

## Document 7

*Livraison et Registre des livraisons du Garde-Meuble Impérial,* 5-1-1810
ENTREE
5608 - (12x) Du 5 janvier 1810 par M. Molitor, ébéniste pour le service des bureaux de la Trésorerie autorisation du 18.12. 1809 fond de réserve 1809
-       Douze Chaises, bois de noyer dossiers à planche, couvertes en peau jaune avec clous dorés leur galon faux à 36.09 ... 433,20 Francs
SORTIE
6.1.1810 Par Mogé Concierge Palais des Tuileries pour le Service des Bureaux de la Trésorerie, 5608 12x ....433,20 Francs
A.N. 0.2.610 fN° l.54

## Document 8

Garde-Meuble de la Couronne
Soumission du Sieur Molitor,
Rue Neuve du Luxembourg

Je soussigné promets et m'engage à fournir et livrer au Garde-Meuble les meubles portés en la présente soumission et aux prix qui y sont stipulés. Je m'engage de plus à confectionner ou faire confectionner dans mes ateliers lesdits meubles dans l'espace de deux ou trois mois en y employant le plus d'ouvriers possible, sans qu'il me soit permis de fournir pour la présente soumission aucun des meubles existant actuellement dans mes magasins ou ateliers.

Enfin je m'engage à établir lesdits meubles conformément aux modèles qui me seront présentés par M. l'Administrateur du Mobilier de la Couronne, de reprendre pour mon compte lesdits meubles, s'ils ne sont pas établis suivant les conditions, comme aussi de me soumettre aux vérification et règlement de M. le Vérificateur du Garde-Meuble.

Chaque meuble sera de plus poinçonné de mon nom dans toutes ses parties qui se séparent, comme commodes, etc.
Savoir:
Six tables à manger en acajou de forme ovale à abattant de cinq pieds, 250......1500 F
Deux consoles en acajou à dessus de marbre de 4 pieds 1/2, pieds de devant à double balustre, pieds de derrière à pilastres profilé de moulures, tablette

| | |
|---|---:|
| d'entrejambe en acajou massif, le marbre petit granit à 300 | 600 F |
| Quatre idem de 5 pieds à 350 | 1400 F |
| Quatre idem de 5 pieds 1/2 à 400 | 1600 F |

| | |
|---|---|
| Quatre tables en acajou à quadrille garnies de leur drap, 100 | 400 F |
| Deux tables de bouillotte id., 120 | 240 F |

Total :... 5740 F

Paris le 20 mai 1811

*Verso:*

Approuvé la présente soumission... Chartres, le 2 juin 1811.

L'Intendant Général de la Maison de l'Empereur.

(A.N. 02.513 fol.90)

Soumission du Sieur Molitor

Menuisier-ébéniste,

boulevard de la Magdeleine 37

Je soussigné promets et m'engage à fournir et livrer au Garde-Meuble de la Couronne...

Savoir:

Deux commodes en bois d'orme de 4 pieds à colonnes dans les angles, chapiteaux et base ciselés et dorés, à quatre tiroirs,boutons en cuivre doré marbre petit granit à 450: 900 F

Deux secrétaires idem à 450: 900 F

Total : 1 800 F

Paris, le 31 mai 1811,

Molitor

Accepte la présente soumission montant à dix-huit cents francs, Paris le 4 juin 1811, L'administrateur du Mobilier Impérial,

Desmazis

*Verso:*

Approuvé la présente soumission montant à la somme de 1 800 F. pour être executée selon sa forme et teneur. A Saint-Cloud, le 7 juin 1811, l'Intendant Général de la Maison de l'Empereur.

(A.N. 02.513 pièce N°124)

**Document 9**

*Recommandation adressée par le Baron Bourlet de Saint Aubin au Baron de Ville-d'Avray,* 28.2.1818

Madame de Kersalaim, fille de M. de Verdun, m'a prié mon cher Parent, de donner a M. Molitor un mot pour vous, afin que vous ayez la bonté de le recevoir. Vous le connaissez déja, et Madame de Villeneuve vous en a je crois, parlé. Je ne connais point le mérite de M. Molitor, ni la qualité de ses meubles, et je m'acquitte seulement de ce que j'ai promis. Ce petit billet d'introduction auprès de vous, va vous porter, et vous le recevrez, j'en suis sûr, avec plaisir, les expressions de mon sincère attachement.....

(Annotation sur la même feuille par le baron de Ville-d'Avray)

...Molitor ébéniste rue du Faubourg St. Honoré N°9, je pris M. Veytard d'y passer et de juger si les meubles qu'il désire céder au Garde Meuble pourraient nous convenir.

A.N. 0.3.1885

**Document 10**

*Première liste des meubles proposés par Molitor :*

Note demandée par Monsieur le Baron de Ville d'Avray à Molitor du prix des meubles désignés ci dessous:

Savoir :

- deux secrétaires formant bonheur du jour, en laque du japon, richement ornés en bronze ciselé et doré or mat et couvert de chaqu'un deux marbre vert de mer
- plus un autre secrétaire idem, en marqueterie orné idem, couvert d'un marbre griotte ...pour les trois : ensemble ...10 000 F
- deux consoles en bois d'orme, ornées de bronzes ciselés et dorés or mat, une glace dans le fond et le dessus d'un marbre blanc pour les deux : ensemble...1 800 F
- une petite table en bois d'acajou à quatre colonnes formant balustre, avec un tiroir,

richement orné idem, le dessus de marbre granite grise prisée....500 F

-      un grand bonheur du jour en bois d'acajou formant bijoutier, le haut fermant à deux portes très richement orné de bronzes idem, le dessus de marbre vert de mer, et un idem dans le dessous, prisée ...1 200 F

-      deux jardinières en bois d'acajou, montées sur quatre jarets à griffes et le haut en cygnes le tout doré, le dessus de marbre bleu turquin pour les deux : ensemble... 800 F
Total : ... 14 300F

(*Annotation sur la même feuille:*)

... Je le pris de conserver cette note. J'ai vu les meubles. Ils sont beaux et paraissent bien établis, mais ce n'est qu'a la fin de l'année qu'il serait possible de connaître quelque seront les montants disponibles applicables à une acquisition qui n'est point urgente.
A.N. 0.3.1885

## Document 11

*Recommandation, de la comtesse Clarac, pour l' Intendant du Garde Meuble de la Couronne, Baron de Ville-d'Avray,* 1.12.1818

... Je me suis présentée chez Monsieur le baron de Ville-d'Avray pour avoir le plaisir de le voir et pour lui recommander un fort bien et fort brave homme d'ébéniste, nomme Molitor, dont je lui ai déja parlé, il desirerait beaucoup que Monsieur de Ville d'Avray voulut lui acheter les meubles dont je lui laisse la note. -

    Ils sont très beau, et il en a vendu de pareils au Roi de Prusse et au Duc de Wellington, - il ne seroit pas très pressé d'avoir de l'argent, mais ce qu'il désirerait pouvoir faire sortir ces meubles d'un dépôt ou il les a placés, et dont il craint que le marchand ne fasse bientôt banqueroute...

Je prie, Monsieur de Ville d'Avray de me pardonner mon importunité mais c'est pour obliger un brave homme qui travaillait autrefois pour la Reine (Marie-Antoinette) et de lui renouveller l'attirance de tous nos anciens sentiments d'attachement.
Comtesse de Clarac

*Réponse par le baron Ville d'Avray,* 1.12.1818, *dicté en note sur le même feuillet :*

... Que j'ai bien du regret de ne pas m'être trouvé chez moi, lorsque Madame de Clarac a pris la peine d'y passer ; je ne puis me prêter à des acquisitions que les besoins du service n'indiquent pas, il se présentent trop de dépenses urgentes pour en entreprendre d'inutiles, une occasion extraordinaire pourrait seule me mettre dans le cas de satisfaire M. Molitor, mais je ne peux la prévoir.

Madame de Clarac ne peut douter du plaisir que j'aurais à me rendre à vos désirs.

Agréer je vous prie, Madame, l'assurance des sentiments respectueux avec lesquels....
Baron Ville d'Avray.

(*Annotation:*) Aquisitions proposées ou saisir l'occasion si elle se présente, de tâcher faire le sieur Molitor quelque commande.
A.N. 03-1891

## Document 12

*Le comte de Forbin, Directeur Géneral des Musées Royaux à Monsieur le Baron de Ville d'Avray Intendant du Garde-Meuble,* 21.12.1818

Monsieur le Baron,

    J'ai l'honneur de vous adresser un état de meubles précieux que M. Molitor désire céder au Garde Meuble de la Couronne.

    La description de ces objets ainsi que l'indication des matières qui les composent m'ont fait penser que leur acquisition serait d'autant plus avantageuse que M. Molitor est tout à fait disposé à faire un sacrifice sur la valeur. Je prends donc la liberté, Monsieur le Baron de vous recommander cette proposition, et vous prie de croire que je regarderai ce que vous voudrez bien faire en cette circonstance comme un service que je m'empresserai de reconnaitre toutes les fois que vous m'en offrirez l'occasion. Recevez .... le Comte de Forbin

(*Annotation Ville d'Avray sur la même feuille:*)

Monsieur Nanteuil, c'est pour le même objet que m'écrivait dernièrement Monsieur le

Comte de Clarac, répondez à Monsieur de Forbin à peu près de la même manière: y ad-jointes seulement un peu plus d'obligeance en lui écrivant qu'il ne peut douter du désir que j'aurais de faire quelque chose qui lui fut agréable, qu'il doit concevoir combien il est diffi-cile de trouver des fonds pour des acquisitions que n'indiquant pas les besoins du service, quand il est déja difficile de satisfaire aux acquisitions indispensables....22-12-1818
A.N. 0.3 .1891

**Document 13**

*Lettre autographe de Molitor adressée au Comte de Clarac,* Paris le 27.12.1819
Monsieur le Comte,
Connaissant l'interêt que vous m'avez toujours porté j'ose m'adresser à vous, pour vous prier de m 'être utile dans ce moment-ci, s'il vous est possible.
Il m'est resté des meubles assez jolis de ma fabrique, vous les connaissez; je desirerois pouvoir les placer au garde meuble. J'ai eu l'honneur d'écrire à ce sujet à Monsieur L'Inten-dant, je n'ai pu réussir jusqu'à ce jour; peut-être que par votre intercession serai-je plus heureux.

S'il étoit nécessaire pour parvenir à mon but de faire part de ce que j'ai eu occasion de faire dans une circonstance malheureuse au départ de nos princes au 20 mars: vous le savez. Monsieur le Comte, je vous l'ai dit verbalement; je reçus chez moi tous leurs effets et papiers précieux et les garder jusqu'à leur retour, sans considérer le danger où je m'exposais demeurant en face de la mairie et entouré de bonapartistes, en voyant entrer chez moi plus de quarante malles de différentes grandeurs: mais le plaisir que j'avais dans ce cruel moment de pouvoir faire quelque chose pour des princes que j'ai toujours chéris, l'emporta sur tout autre sentiment: je suis loin de vouloir faire valoir ce que le hazard me fit faire, tout honnête homme à ma place en eut fait autant.

Vous savez aussi Monsieur le Comte, j'ai eu l'honneur de vous le dire, j'ai rendu à l'an-cienne cour des services qui m'ont fait traduire au tribunal révolutionnaire, c'est un miracle de la providence si je m'en suis sauvé.
J'ose croire Monsieur le Comte que vous me connoissez assez pour être persuadé de la vérité de ce que j'ai l'honneur de vous dire : mais si vous en doutiez un instant vous pourriez vous en informer à M. le Barron Bourlet, il est venu plusieurs fois chez moi éplucher les papiers.

Enfin Monsieur le Comte, j'espère beaucoup de votre obligeance, je vous prie instam-ment de faire tout ce qu'il sera possible pour me faire placer mes meubles, je vous en aurai une grande obligation, en voici les détails :
un magnifique cabinet en bois de rose et mosaïques sur quatre colonnes, très richement orné de beaux bronzes ciselés et dorés au mat, avec trois grands panneaux et trois médail-lons ovales en marqueterie d'un travail parfait. Le dessus est un marbre griotte d'Italie. L'intérieur est en bois de rose et d'acajou, à tiroirs avec panneau en marqueterie, prise 4000 F.

deux cabinets en ancien laque du Japon, sur quatre pilastres ornés de cariatides, guir-landes, châpiteaux et moulures en bronze ciselé et doré au mat ; le dessus est en marbre vert de mer. L'intérieur en bois d'ébène et d'acajou avec tiroirs en laque 5 000 F

une commode en ancien laque richement garnie de bronzes dorés, ouvrant à trois portes. L'intérieur à douze tiroirs en bois satiné et le dessus en marbre blanc prix estimé 1800 Fpar le marchant je le laisse à 1500 F.

deux jardinières montées sur quatre jarrets sculptés et dorés ; le dessus en marbre bleu turquin avec galerie dorée prix 800 F.

une table à écrire en bois d'acajou, le dessus en marbre granite d'Egypte, ornée de bronze ciselé et doré au mat 550 F.

Pardon M. le Compte de la liberté que je prends d'oser vous importuner, veuillez je vous prie m'excuser et me croire avec la plus parfaite reconnaissance et la plus haute considération.
Votre très humble et soumis serviteur, Molitor.
Paris le 27 décembre 1819.
A.N. 03 - 1891

*Lettre de recommandation par le Comte de Clarac adressée à l'intendant du Garde Meuble le Baron de Ville d'Avray,*
29.12.1819
Je viens encore vous importuner mon cher Baron, il y a cependant longtemps que je vous laisse tranquille - tachez donc de faire quelque chose pour ce brave homme de Molitor - voici la lettre qu'il m'a écrit et je n'ai rien à ajouter à tout ce que je vous ai dit de lui et pour lui - vous me ferez un grand plaisir si vous pouvez rendre service à cet habile et honnête ébéniste qui le mérite de toutes manières ce qui serait excellent à employer pour le Garde Meuble tant par son goût, son amour pour les ouvrages bien faits que par sa probile - mais je ne veux pas vous retenir plus longtemps ...
*Annotation du Baron Ville d'Avray sur le même feuillet :*
Veytard, je désire bien qu'il puisse trouver l'occasion de prendre quelques meubles à Monsieur Molitor, notre voisin, ou de lui confier quelques travaux.
31.12.1819
A.N. 0.3.1891

## Document 14

*Rapport de l' Inspecteur Veytard,* 6.5.1820
Le Sieur Molitor l'un des ébénistes les plus distingués de Paris a exécuté, d'après les ordres de la feue Reine Marie Antoinette qui l'honorait de sa bienveillance, six meubles de la plus grande beauté en marqueterie, laque ancien et acajou, ornés de bronzes dorés au mat: ces meubles dont il avait reçu la commande en 1790, ne purent être terminés qu'en 1793 et les événements douloureux de cette époque empêchèrent le Sieur Molitor d'en effectuer la livraison: ils sont restés dans ses magasins ; trop beaux pour être vendus dans le commerce ou à des particuliers, ils ne peuvent convenir qu'au Roi. Le Sieur Molitor demande aujourd'huy que le garde meuble, en considération de l'auguste personne à laquelle ils étaient destinés, veuille bien en faire l'acquisition. Ils devaient lui être payés 18 000 F il s'est restreint successivement à 15 000 F, 12 000F et 11 300 F, j'ai obtenu en dernier lieu une diminution de 1 300 F.

Ci-joint devis de la dépense s'élevant à la somme de dix mille francs. Il comprend trois secrétaires dit bonheurs du jour dont un en marqueterie et les deux autres en laque ancien du japon, une commode en laque et deux jardinières en acajou, forme octogône.

Ces meubles ne laissent rien à désirer sous le rapport de la beauté des bois, de la richesse des ornements et de la perfection du travail: ils pourront être convenablement placés soit dans les appartements de S.A.R. Madame la Duchesse d'Angoulême au château des Tuileries, soit dans celui de S.A.R. Monsieur au Château de Fontainebleau, dont Monsieur l'Intendant a ordonné la restauration...
*Accroché à cette lettre se trouve une nouvelle liste de meubles proposés :*
Intendance du Garde Meuble de la Couronne, devis de la dépense relative à l'acquisition de divers meubles en laque et marqueterie offerte par le Sieur Molitor.
- Un secrétaire à abattant, dit bonheur du jour, en bois de rose sur quatre colonnes, richement ornées de cariatides en bronze ciselé et doré au mat, trois grands panneaux et trois médaillons ovales en marqueterie; un dessus en marbre griotte d'Italie; l'intérieur en bois de rose et d'acajou; tiroirs en acajou, panneaux en marqueterie... 3000 F
- Deux secrétaires à abattant dits bonheur du jour, en laque ancien du japon, sur quatre pilastres ornées de cariatides, guirlandes, chapitaux et moulures en bronze ciselé et doré au mat ; le dessus en marbre vert de mer.
L'intérieur en bois d'ébène et acajou, tiroirs en laque à 2500 F chaque....5000 F
- Une commode en laque ancien, richement garnie de bronzes ciselés et dorés au mat, ouvrant à trois portes. L'intérieur à douze tiroirs en bois satiné ; le desus en marbre blanc....1200 F
- Deux jardinières en acajou forme octogone, cygnes ailés, dorés au mat et très riches. Le dessus en marbre bleu turquin à 400 F chaque....800 F

Arrêté le présent devis à la somme de dix mille francs pour être soumis à Monsieur l'Intendant.

Paris, le 5 mai 1820

Veytard

25 mai 1820, proposition d'achat de deux secrétaires en laques offerts par le Sieur Molitor.

(*Annotation par le Baron Ville d'Avray*)

Monsieur Nanteuil, motivez l'acquisition sur la beauté de ces meubles leur destination primitive et l'intérêt que mérite la conduite politique de M. Molitor, en relisant les pièces et la correspondance M. Nanteuil retrouvera des traces du motif que j'indique.

A.N. 03.2104

## Document 15

11 décembre 1833, février 1834

INVENTAIRE, après décès M. Molitor, propriétaire à Fontainebleau

L'An mil huit cent trente trois, le mercredi, onze décembre huit heure du matin.

A la requête :

de Madame Renée Catherine Miray, veuve de Monsieur Bernard Molitor, propriétaire à Fontainebleau, lad. dame y demeurant rue Marrier N°7.

2nd de Madame Anne Julie Molitor, veuve de Monsieur Dominique Jean Philippe Eloy, à son vivant juge de paix des canton et ville de Fontainebleau, lad. dame demeurant rue basse N°13

3è Monsieur Pierre Joseph Debionne, juge de paix des canton et ville de Fontainebleau et Madame Elisabeth Molitor son épouse qu'il autorise, demeurant ensemble à Fontainebleau, rue Basse N°3.

4è et Mademoiselle Honorine Molitor, sans profession, célibataire majeure, demeurant à Fontainebleau rue marrier, chez madame sa mère.

Il va être par M. Louis François Bouchonnet, notaire à Fontainebleau soussigné, procédé à l'Inventaire.

La prisée de ceux des dits objets qu'y seraient objets sera traité par M. Charles Nicolas Hamel, commissaire priseur demeurant à Fontainebleau patenté.

Suit la Prisée

Dans une cave

(*suivent les cuvées*) Dans un bâtiment etant à droite de la porte cochère et dans lequel est pratique un petit cabinet en bois

Dans ce cabinet:

12.   une chaise longue en bois peint en gris, garni d'un coussin fourré en crin et de son oreiller fonce en plume le tout recouvert de vieux damas a grande fleurs ... 25 F

13.   une petite bibliotheque en bois d'acajou, deux chaises en bois d'acajou fourré en crin recouverts en toile verte, une petite table en bois de noyers, montees sur ses quatre pieds, une encoignure de bois de citronnier ...19 F

14.   un porte liqueurs en bois noirci, garni de deux caraffes et de six petits verres, deux paniers a verres contenant douze verres base, deux petits rideaux de colicot teint, un vieux tapis de pieds, deux serviette de toilette un peignoir de bain, une autre serviette de toilette une couverture de laine blanche une seringue, en etain garnie de ses deux mirroirs en fayence blanche le tout ...20 F

(*Suivent*) le vestibule, un office, la cuisine ...

Dans la salle a Manger éclairée par une croisée sur le jardin

28.   une table ronde en acajou, un petit gueridon aussi en acajou, deux servantes en bois d'acajou ...35 F

29.   un poêle en faïence à dessus de marbre, garnie de sa colonne et de ses tuyaux, deux petites encoignures en acajou, douze chaises en bois de noyer... 70 F

30.   un tableau et dix gravures de différents grandeurs sous verre et dans leur cadre de bois noirci, un petit miroir de toilette et un petit cartel en cuivre ...25 F

Dans l'Antichambre

31.   deux encoignures en bois d'acajou une table à jouer, aussi en acajou, une autre petite table en bois d'acajou, une chaise en bois de noyer ...40 F

32.   un écritoire en bois noirci, cinq tableaux peintes, douze gravures de différentes grandeurs dans leur cadre et sous verre une pincette et une pelle ...18 F

Dans un placard à droite de la porte de milieu et dans celui à gauche

33.   dix douzaines d'assiettes en porcelaine... et de différentes sortes, deux douzaines d'assiettes aussi en porcelaine ornées de raies bleues, deux saussières, deux- battaux, six plats, un saladier, une théière, un sucrier, une corbeille, une soupière, douze tasses à café et leurs soucoupes unies, un moutardier, douze coquetiers, douze pots à crème. Le tout en porcelaine uni ...45 F

34.   douze tasses à café et leurs soucoupes, trois autres tasses, un sucrier en porcelaine à filets dorés, un pot à crème un sucrier, trois coupes à thé, deux tasses et leurs soucoupes en porcelaine unie ...4 F

35.   trente assiettes, une théière, un sucrier, trois caraffes, quatre selliers, un poivrier à verre avec sept verres un huillier avec ses flacons, douze petits verres à liqueur, douze autres verres à vin de champagne un bocal deux cuvettes en cuivre argenté ... 8 F

Dans le Salon

36.   un guéridon en bois d'if, avec garnitures de cuivre doré or à dessus de marbre, deux tables à jouer en acajou, une petite table ployante aussi en acajou, deux jardinières en bois d'if ...220 F

37.   un meuble composé d'un canapé, garni de deux coussins et deux oreillers, deux bergères, garnies de leurs coussins, quatre fauteuils, six chaises, le tout en bois d'acajou et recouvert de velours d'Utrecht jaune, cinq carreaux recouverts de pareille velours et deux autres en tapisserie, deux petits tapis de pied ...600F

38.   un écran en bois d'acajou, un devant de cheminée en laque de la Chine, une pelle et une pincette deux chenets à fonte un souffleur, un petit balai ...15 F

39.   une pendule en cuivre doré sous globe de verre et sur son socle de bois d'acajou, deux vases en cuivre doré avec bouquets artificiels, sous globe de verre et socle en bois d'acajou, deux flambeaux en cuivre doreé ...250 F

40.   deux vases (comme les précédents), quatre flambeaux en bois d'acajou, un lustre en albâtre, une lampe en fer blanc peint ...37 F

41.   deux boîtes à jeu, dont une en bois d'if garnie de ses pièces et jetons, une petite boîte a thé en bois d'acajou, deux paires de mouchettes et leurs plateaux ...15 F

42.   deux tableaux peints, trente deux gravures sous verre, et dans leur cadres de bois doré, de différentes grandeurs, deux tableaux dont un en marqueterie et l'autre en mosaïque ...35 F

43.   une glace en son cadre de bois doré portant cent quarante centimètres de hauteur sur un mètre vingt quatre millimètres de large ... 400 F

44.   une autre glace ainsi dans son cadre de bois doré portant un mètre quatre vingt quatre millimètres de hauteur sur un mètre vingt quatre millimètres de large ...750 F

45.   deux glaces pareilles portant chacune soixante deux centimètres de hauteur, sur quarante deux centimètres de large à chacune ... 160 F

46.   et une autre glace portant cent soixantet reize centimètres de hauteur, sur cent vingt un centimètre ...400 F

47.   deux grands rideaux de croisée en calicot et deux de croisée en badin deux tringles en bois doré avec huit paternes une tringle en fer et deux rideaux de mousseline ...5 F

Dans le grenier

Dans une chambre à coucher ayant vue sur la rue et à gauche du corridor, au premier étage

54.   deux couchettes en bois d'acajou, sur lesquelles deux sommiers, foncés en crin quatre matelas et drap de lits deux traversins et deux oreillers fournis de plumes, deux couvertures de coton, deux couvre-pieds en bazin, deux édredons couverts en soie une table de nuit en acajou et à dessus de marbre, son vase, deux tapis de pieds, le tout prisé trois cent soixante francs ...360 F

55.   un guéridon en bois d'acajou à dessus de marbre, un fauteuil et trois chaises en bois d'acajou foncé en crin et recouvert en soie, un carreau en tapisserie et un tapis de pieds ...58 F

56.  deux chenets garnis en cuivre une pelle une pincette, un soufflet un petit balai d'âtre ...10 F

57.  une pendule en bois de citron en garniture de cuivre doré deux flambeaux en acajou, deux autres en cuivre argenté, deux petits flacons en cristal ... 95 F

58.  un chiffonnier en bois d'acajou, ouvrant à deux vantaux et sept tiroirs ... 80 F

59.  une glace dans son cadre doré, portande ...30 F

Dans la chambre en face de la précédente

60.  trois petits matelas, une couverture de laine et une autre, un traversin, une table de nuit en mauvais état, un couvre-pieds en calicot jaune, deux petits rideaux de croisée en mousseline, avec un balai de crin ...40 F

61.  deux chaises en bois de noyer foncés de paille avec une cuvette et son pot en fayence ...6 F

Dans une Chambre à coucher faisant suite à la première et ayant entrée à gauche du corridor et vue sur la rue.

62.  une couchette en bois d'acajou, un sommier fourré de crin, trois matelas couverts en toile de futaine, un traversin foncé de plumes recouvert de coutil blanc, une couverture de coton une édredon couvert en soie ...300 F

63.  une table de nuit en acajou ...18 F

64.  un petit lavabo en acajou garni de sa cuvette, une table à ouvrage, une chaise percée, un fauteuil et trois chaises en bois d'acajou, foncés de crin ..55 F

65.  deux flambeaux en cuivre, deux caraffes, deux autres flambeaux en cuivre argenté, deux chenets en fonte à pommes de cuivre un soufflet et un petit balai d'hêtre, prisée le tout avec un pot à eau et sa cuvette en fayence ...14 F

66.  cinq tableaux peints, quatre petites gravures un crucifix en cuivre ...6 F

67.  une glace dans son parquet de bois doré portant quatre vingt douze centimètres de hauteur sur quatre vingt centimètres de largeur ...45 F

Dans un cabinet ...

Dans la Chambre à coucher au bout du corridor, éclairée sur le jardin et sur la rue.

71.  une pelle, une autre pelle et deux pincettes, deux petits chenets et une barre en fer, une cheminée garnie de ses bouches de châleur et de son cendrier ...60 F

72.  quatre flambeaux de cuivre doré garnis de leur bobèches en cristal ...20 F

73.  deux candelabres en cuivre doré ...36 F

74.  quatre gravures sous verre dans leurs cadres de bois doré ...8 F

75.  quatre chaises en bois de merisier foncées en paille blanche...10 F

76.  six chaises et un fauteuil en bois de frêne foncées en crin et couvert en étoffe de laine bleu de ciel ...130 F

77.  un chiffonnier en bois d'acajou ouvrant à sept grands tiroirs...90 F

78.  une petite table en bois d'acajou ...6 F

79.  une armoire en bois d'acajou de forme carrée ouvrant à deux abattants ...200 F

80.  un guéridon en bois d'acajou couvert d'un marbre en blanc turquin orné d'une galerie en cuivre ...45 F

81.  un secrétaire-chiffonnier en bois de citron, ouvrant, dans ses parties inférieures à trois grands tiroirs, à bascule dans sa partie du milieu et à deux vantaux dans sa partie supérieure...100 F

82.  une commode en bois de frêne ouvrant à quatre grands tiroirs et à bascule dans sa partie supérieure ...80 F

83.  un coffre à argenterie en bois d'acajou et à compartiments ...30 F

84.  deux couchettes en bois de rapport, à roulettes à équerre et à fond sanglé, deux tables de nuit en bois de frêne revêtus d'un marbre blanc veiné, un porte manteau en pareil bois, monté sur son pied en forme de colonne, six sommiers foncés en crin et recouverts en futaine blanche, deux lits deux traversins et un oreiller foncés en plume et recouverts d'un coutil rayé de bleu et de blanc, quatre matelas en laine blanche recouverts en toile à carreaux bleus et blancs, quatre couvertures en coton, deux couvre-pieds en calicot et un recouvert de taffetas ...835 F

85.  deux tapis de lits, quatre petits rideaux de croisées en mousseline claire, deux rideaux et une draperie d'alcôve, deux autres rideaux de croisée et leurs draperies en taffetas quinze

seize, bleu de ciel garni de franges de soie de couleur, un tringle d'alcôve en fer ...60 F

86.    une pendule en cuivre doré représentant « Diane chasseresse », à cadran d'émail et sans verre monté sur son socle en bois d'acajou et sous sa cage de verre bombée ... 200 F

87.    une glace dans son parquet en bois doré portant un mètre trente millimètres de hauteur sur quatre vingt dix sept centimètres de largeur ..270F

Dans une chambre au second étage

88.    une petite table, trois chaises, une table de nuit en bois de noyer, deux chaises foncées de crin, une bassine en cuivre rouge, une pareillement en cuivre rouge, trois pincettes, une pelle, un garde feu, deux paires de chenets en fer avec ornements de cuivre, un sommier un matelas un lit de sangle, deux couvertures de coton ...79 F

89.    un morceau de glace ...10 F

Dans une autre chambre en face, éclairée sur la rue

90.    un bas bibliothèque en bois d'acajou et ouvrant à deux vantaux, un casier pareillement en bois d'acajou, garni de onze cartons de bureau, une couchette en bois d'acajou à fond sanglé en sommier, un matelas un lit de plumes un traversin deux chaises foncées en paille commune le tout estimé avec un morceau de glace cintré et un petit rideau en mousseline claire ...180 F

Dans une piece au fond du corridor à gauche, ayant vue sur la rue.

91.    une table en bois d'acajou, une table à jouer en bois de noyer, de forme longue, une table de nuit en bois d'acajou, à dessus de marbre St. Anne une peinture dans son cadre en bois d'acajou un fauteuil foncé en crin, un autre fauteuil en bois peint en gris une chaise en bois de merisier foncé en crin et recouverte en velours d'Utrecht ...46 F

92.    un sommier foncé en crin deux matelas foncés en futaine, le tout recouvert en futaine blanche, un lit, un traversin foncé de plumes et un autre traversin foncé aussi en plumes, le tout ...135 F

93.    une couchette en bois d'acajou à batteau et à têtes bronzées ...55 F

94.    deux petits rideaux de croisée en mousseline une vieille caisse prisée vingt sous si ...1 F

Dans une chambre a côté de la précédente.

95.    une table de toilette en bois de noyer, un pot et sa cuvette en faïence blanche, une table de nuit en bois de noyer dessus de marbre St. Anne, sept chaises et un fauteuil en bois de merisier foncés en crin, et recouverts en velours d'Utrecht, deux petits rideaux de croisée en mousseline claire, une paire de flambeaux...50 F

96.    un secrétaire en bois de marqueterie, ouvrant en sa partie supérieure à bascule, surmontée d'un grand tiroir et garni d'un marbre vert ...30 F

97.    une glace dans son cadre de bois doré ...30 F

98.    une couchette en bois fruit, à deux dessus et à fond sanglé, un sommier en crin et draps de toile à carreaux et un matelas foncé en laine blanche, et un lit, un traversin de plumes une courtepointe en toile blanche, un petit tapis de lit prisée avec un autre rideau de mousseline claire...108 F

Il a été vaqué à tout ce que depuis lad. heure de huit le matin jusqu'à lad. cinq de relevée, sans autre interruption fait que celle fait pour le dejeuner...

8 836,30 F

Est le douze décembre Mil huit cent trente trois cinq heures du jour.

Suite de la prisée:

99.    trente paires de draps ... *(linge de maison..)*

Argenterie:

110. dix couverts à filets portant le chiffre A.B.M. marqués au poinçon de Paris, pésant ... sept marcs ... estimés à raison de cinquante francs les vingt quatre décigrammes quarante six décigrammes (ou le marc) la somme de trois cent quatre vingt sept francs cinquante centimes ...387,50 F

111. neuf cuillers et huit fourchettes unies, un couvert d'enfant, cinq petites cuillers à café unies, six cuillers à café à filets, estimés ...331,25 F

112. cinq cuillers à Ragoûts et une fourchette à découper ...185,18 F

113. une cuiller à Ragoûts et deux cuillere à potage mêmes chiffres ...164,06 F 114. une grande casserole, deux autres petites casseroles, dont une avec couvercle, deux timbales, une soupière avec son couvercle, un plat long et huit plats ronds, le tout marqué au même

chiffre ...1507,03 F

115. un huillier, deux doubles salières et un moutardier, marqués aux mêmes chiffres ...156,08 F

116. une petite cafetière à trois pieds avec son couvercle et son manche en ébène ...55,05 F

117. une cafetière en plaque avec son couvercle aussi en plaque et son anse en ébène ...10 F

Bijoux:

118. une montre à répétition à timbre dans sa boîte en argent ...30 F

119. une montre dans sa boîte en or ...45 F

120. une autre montre dans sa boîte en or, garnie de sa chaîne en or, et de son cachet ... 132 F

121. un lorgnon en argent doré ...10 F

122. une chaîne d'or ...90 F

123. et deux boutons de chemise, en or ... 4 F

Total de la prisée : 12 905,45 Francs.

*Suit l'inventaire des papiers et documents* .............

Il a été vaqué ...

...les parties signé avec M. Hamel ; les témoins et le notaire après lecture faite suivant la loi. R.C. Miray ; H. Molitor; A.J. Molitor; Hamel ; Debionne ; E. Molitor, Haye ; Foulon; Bouchonnet;

Archiv. Etude Maître Danré, Fontainebleau.

# Notes

Figure references in the notes refer to illustrations in the text unless otherwise stated.

1    See E. Erpelding, *Les Moulins du Luxembourg*, Luxemburg, 1981. This book also includes information on the Betzdorf mill, p. 144.

2    Betzdorf church register, *Archives Nationale de Luxembourg*.

3    See the Declaration concerning the fief by Baron P.E. Mohr de Waldt, in 1760, as noted by N. Majerus, *Les Communes du Luxembourg*, Luxemburg, 1956.

4    Nicolas Molitor's daughter Anne-Marie was born in 1744. The date of birth of Mathias, however, is unknown. He is listed in the 1766 census when the Molitor family, including the apprentice Frantz, comprised eight members.

5    In 1744 Bernard Molitor Senior became the godfather of the *ébéniste's* sister, Anne-Marie. He died in 1776.

6    A.N.Y 14 100. Many thanks to M. Dominique Augarde for the information about Michel Molitor cited in Foullet's inventory.

7    B.N. V. 28290.

8    Bernard and Michel Molitor's linguistic difficulties are apparent from the 1788 police report concerning the workshop robbery (see p.36) when the services of the interpreter Vogt were necessary *A.N.* Y-14436, (*doc* 2).

9    Lelièvre rented the building himself from M. de Gondin, the holder of the Royal Patent. He subsequently subletted many of the rooms. *Bibliothèque de l'Arsenal*, MSS 4012 p.249.

10    Founded in 1767 by Louis XV, The *Ecole Gratuite de Dessin* offered courses taught by the professors of the Academy of Fine Arts and other teachers. The school gave a basic foundation training in favour of trades relative to the Arts, for fifteen hundred students to whom were taught the elementary principles of practical geometry, architecture, stone cutting, perspective and different aspects of drawing, such as figures, animals, flowers and ornaments. *Almanach Royal*, 1788.

11    The *cabinet de retraite* constitutes one of the last works made for the Queen before 1789, and represent the zenith of the *goût étrusque*. The furniture, inlaid with pewter, steel and mother-of-pearl, was made by Riesener.

12    A.N. Y 9395.

13    The joiner Etienne Trompette, with whom Molitor had worked at Fontainebleau, was temporary President of the Guild at this time. The collection of 120 volumes on modern architecture and *Le traité de menuiserie* by Roubo itemized in the inventory drawn up after the joiner's death, are evidence that Trompette showed interest in such subjects which were related to his profession. Since he and Molitor lived in the same house, it is possible that Molitor had access to the library. A.N.M.C. LXXI–256, (24 October, 1829).

14    A.D.S. Consulat D6 V3 10, reports, cart 27.

15    See Pierre Verlet, *Möbel von J.H. Riesener*, Darmstadt, (n.d.). See Pierre Verlet, 'Le Boudoir de Marie-Antoinette à Fontainbleau,' *Art de France*, 1, 1961, p. 161.

16    A.N.M.C. LXXXV–710: When he married in 1749, Œben's fortune amounted to 600 *livres*; Riesener's, in 1767, to 1,200 *livres* and Weisweiler's, in 1777, to 1,500 *livres*.

17    Anne-Julie Molitor, 15 April 1789–3 March 1882, during a holiday in Nice.

18    Buying order A.N.M.C. XCVI, 9 Vendemière year IX (2 October 1800).

19    Trompette, Grevenich and the Marquis de Saisseval (as was before the Revolution) were also on the list. *Liste des citoyens actifs de la Section de la Grenelle, 1790*, B.N.

20    On 7 October 1793, during Marie-Antoinette's trial, the architect Renard, Molitor's co-tenant, was suspected of having organised the flight from the Tuileries on the night of 20–21 June 1791. *Actes du Tribunal Révolutionnaire*, Mercure de France, 1968, p. 79. Since Renard, the joiner Trompette and Molitor executed commissions for the Crown until 1792, it is possile that Molitor was in contact with the Royal Family when they were planning their flight, such a connection might have caused Molitor difficulties.

21    According to its definition, the *Contribution Patriotique* was an optional tax voted by the National Assembly with the aim of rescuing State finances.

**22** Other *ébénistes* were similarly taxed, particularly those who had worked for the nobility before the Revolution. Hence, we know that after his denunciation in the spring of 1794, George Jacob donated 500 mahogany rifle butts to the Republic to save himself. See H. Lefuel, *George Jacob – Ebéniste du 18ème siècle*, Paris, 1923, pp. 81–3.

**23** A.N. T514.

**24** In his estate, twenty prayer books and an oil painting, as well as twenty religious engravings were listed. A.N.M.C. LXXI–169, 21 October 1810, (*doc.* 6).

**25** See Dominique Augarde, 'Signaturen französischer Möbel,' *Kunst und Antiquitäten* I, 1984.

**26** See Michael Stürmer. *Handwerk und höfische Kultur*, Munich, 1982, pp. 135–50.

**27** Report by M. Dallande, Assemblée Nationale, 15 Feb, 1791. As quoted by Lespinasse, *Histoire générale de Paris – Les Métiers de Paris*, I, 1882.

**28** *Moniteur*, VIII reprint, 1847, p. 662.

**29** The same was true for the *ébéniste* Claude Chapuis who worked in Paris from approximately 1792.

**30** *Archives Départementales du Calvados* 8 E 3128.

**31** Besides Anne-Julie and her grandfather Miray from Caen, also present at the twins' baptism were Pierre Joseph Zimmermann, harpsichord maker, and the jeweller Milbrord Veyder, whose address was given as 10 rue des Deux Portes, Saint-Sauveur. Molitor's daughter Hortense died soon after her birth. Honorine, who never married, lived with her parents until her death in 1830. Baptismal register, *Archives paroissiales de La Madeleine*, Paris.

**32** A.N.M.C. LXXI–139, 22 March 1803.

**33** A.N.M.C. LXXI–164.

**34** A.N.M.C. LXXI–610 (*doc* 6).

**35** A.N.M.C. XCV–511.

**36** *Archives Départementales du Seine et Marne 18ᵉ* 212, 4 July 1828.

**37** A.N.M.C. LXXV–1113.

**38** *Archives Départementales du Seine et Marne* 5 Mi. 3956 Fontainebleau.

**39** Succession inventory. Archives of Maître Danré, Notary, Fontainebleau (*doc* 15).

**40** In the inventory of Elisabeth Molitor, dated November 1869, there are many pieces of furniture already listed in the 1833 inventory. Here the period is noted; hence Molitor's older pieces can be identified by the designation 'd'époque Louis XVI' or 'Empire'. Archives of Maître Danré.

**41** With the death of Bernard Molitor, the male side of the family was extinguished. There are, however, records of direct descendents until the beginning of the present century, since when, Molitor's descendents have been dispersed throughout a large number of families.

**42** Date of publication of the first advertisement appearing in *Les petites annonces, affiches et avis divers*.

**43** List of tenants, Arsenal Mss. 4045 p. 405.

**44** After the completion of the work on the building, premises C were issued to M. Demazis. When the building became vacant in August 1776, it was allotted to Monsieur de Gondin, *Capitaine de Dragon*, according to the terms of the Royal Patent. He never resided there himself but rented it to Lelièvre from 1 January 1778, who then sublet it to six different occupants. A.N.M.C. CV11 587.

**45** A.N.Y 14436 31 December 1787, (*doc* 2).

**46** Sébastien Mercier gives a description of the Faubourg in *Tableau de Paris* as does Thierry in his *Nouveau Guide de Paris*, 1787, P. 591. The house where Molitor lived no longer exists. In its place, there is a subway entrance on the plaza in front of the Musée d'Orsay.
Contemporary details of the site and area are known from a drawing by Meunier engraved by Née (see 24.) The engraving illustrates the Hôtel de Salm before 19 June, 1791, when the coat of arms of the prince de Salm was destroyed. In the background, Trompette's two houses are visible.

**47** In the guardianship documents concerning Anne-Julie, Jacques Raveneau declared that he resided on rue Bourbon.

**48**  The *ébéniste* Joseph Baumhauer also had eight workbenches in his workshop. In Adam Weisweiler's workshop there were six; Guillaume Beneman, an *ébéniste* to the Crown had 16. See Michael Stürmer, *Handwerk und höfische Kultur*, Munich, 1982 pp. 75ff.

**49**  On 2 Fructidor year II (19 August 1794) a plot of land which comprised an apartment building and a courtyard, formerly the property of the arrested prince de Salm, was offered for rent in *Les petites affiches* .... It adjoined Trompette's property, where Molitor had his wood depot at that time.

**50**  This large number is significant since the furniture is now difficult to identify. The stamps were placed on the upper edge of the top rail before assembly to the top and were only discovered by accident when restoration was undertaken.

**51**  Works by Riesener and Weisweiler, now in the Musée du Louvre and the Château de Fontainebleau, had already been ornamented with steel.

**52**  Trompette, *Menuisier et Entrepreneur des Bâtiments du Roi*, is a representative example of a craftsman ruined by the Revolution. Until 1792, he had executed work at the Château de Fontainebleau, Versailles and the Tuileries. The contents of his workshop, 60 workbenches and tools, were sold at auction on 18 August 1798. Henceforth, Trompette limited his activities to the retail sale of wood for construction and heating (*Petites annonces, affiches et avis divers*, BN–V28419). Much later, in compensation for his numerous unpaid bills, the State offered him a house at 141 Saint-Honoré. (See also footnote 13.)

**53**  A.N.M.C. XCVI–602.
The exact date is mentioned on two consecutive notarized meetings: A.N.M.C. LXXI–136; V 882.

**54**  Detrez, *Le Faubourg St. Honoré*, Paris, 1957.

**55**  These rooms are mentioned by Constance Martine, *La rue de Lille-l'Hôtel de Salm*. Institut Néerlandais exhibition catalogue, 7–28 February 1983, p. 123.

**56**  A.N.M.C. LXXI–139.

**57**  Two tax offices on the rue Neuve du Luxembourg dispensing fiscal stamps were listed in the 1791 Almanach Royal.

**58**  At this point the boulevard was 30 metres wide. Shaded by four lines of trees, the wide sidewalks attracted Parisian strollers, and were welcome relief for a population who often lived in small, poorly-lit quarters. A contemporary English traveller commented, 'It is by far the cleanest and most lively place in Paris. In reality the terms that I use do not give an idea of their beauty and elegance'. H. Redhead-Yorke, *Paris et la France sous le Consulat*, London 1804.

**59**  Many boutiques were renowned for their location on the Boulevard de la Madeleine. The celebrated upholsterer and *marchand-mercier* Morillon traded at number 27. The abolition of the Guild after the Revolution, brought about a rapid development of the retail trade in Paris. The manner of representing merchandise progressed. Also *marchands-merciers* elaborated the new fashion for display in boutiques, echoing the first shops with show windows in the Palais Royal, launched by the duc d'Orléans. Sebastien Mercier, *Paris pendant la Revolution*, Paris, 1862, p. 301.

**60**  *L'Almanach de Commerce* for 1813 gives Molitor's address as the Faubourg Saint-Honoré again.

**61**  A.N.M.C. LXXV 1108.

**62**  A workbench with press and clamp valued at 5 francs.
A box containing instruments for reproduction valued at 6 francs.
The interior of a Chinese cabinet, a box containing pieces of veneer and other wood,
A pair of Empire andirons, valued at 10 francs.
A lathe with tools and accessories valued at 25 francs.
A small workbench with vice valued at 6 francs.
Nine saws of diferent sizes, a lot of trying planes, planes and other tools which do not merit description, in poor condition, valued at 5 francs.
A small round earthenware stove with its pipe, a lot of scrap iron, copper articles and old tools without value, valued at 3 francs.
A lot of wood for turning, valued at 2 francs.
Document for the inventory drawn up after the death of Elizabeth Molitor 22 November

1869, Archives of Maître Danré, Fontainebleau.

Rental contract 7 June 1846, A.N.M.C. XXV 159.

63   A.N. 02–504. See D. Ledoux-Lebard, *Les ébénistes parisiens, leurs oeuvres et leurs marques 1795–1870*, 1984, p. 545. The table is conserved in the Musée National du Château de Malmaison. (See the tea caddy for comparison 125).

64   Rémond's workshop owed its success largely to numerous commissions from the *Garde-Meuble* during the Restoration.

65   It is probable that Demay supplied Molitor with the sculpted wooden elements *en rond de bosse*, or with hock legs and caryatids. Stylistically they are reminiscent of other pieces of work by Demay.

66   The corresponding file is missing in the *Archives Nationales*; the report now only exists in the notary's registers. A.N.M.C. LXXI Rép.

67   A.S. D6 U3.10 The reasons for the dispute arose from Bellanger's refusal to pay the sum of 2,150 *livres* to Hindermeyer for a marquetry commode. After a detailed examination of the facts, the four experts decided in favour of Hindermeyer.

68   A.N.M.C. V 882.

69   Molitor is not mentioned in the Daguerre's succession inventory. See P. Lemonnier, *Weisweiler*, Paris, 1983, p. 162.

70   Molitor normally advertised twice a year. The following dates of advertisements have been verified: 6 April 1779; 3 September 1779; 20 April 1780; 20 May 1780; 27 December 1781; 12 December 1782; 23 June 1782; 9 September 1786; 1 January 1787; 1 June 1787; 26 October 1787.

71   Whether Etienne Trompette, a former *député* of the Guild, or the Fessards, a family concern working for the Crown, intervened in the *ébéniste's* favour remains a matter of conjecture, since both worked at Fontainebleau in 1787.

72   *Almanach de commerce de Paris* – 'containing the names and addresses of the principal artists, merchants, manufacturers [...] it was decided to mention in each class only those who are the best known for their talents or the importance of their trade.' Besides Molitor, the other *ébénistes* named are Magnien, Moreau, Ohneberg, Roussel, Schmidt and Thouvenin: *Almanach de Paris*, II, 1789. Ed. Lesclapart.

73   A.N.M.C. LXXI–139.

74   On 9 Floréal year XIII (29 April 1805), Molitor lent 4,200 francs to the comte de Médavy which he only recovered in 1815 following the court decision of 26 August 1812 which ordered the sale of all the comte's belongings. A.N.M.C. XXXVI–651; XIV–620. On 27 August 1807 he lent the sum of 14,000 francs to his father-in-law Londe – A.N.M.C. LXXI–158.

75   Sale contract, A.N.M.C. XCV–499.

76   *Archives Départementales du Calvados* 8 E 8552, 7 February 1817.

77   *Archives Départementales du Seine et Marne* 18^E 241/242, Maître Lemoine.

78   The queens of France had a budget for their personal expenses. The considerable expenses incurred by Marie-Antoinette were public knowledge and certainly led to the judicious destruction of the supporting documents between 1789–92.

79   For the period from 1793 to 1803, in the absence of documents, we will limit ourselves to comparisons with signed pieces by other *ébénistes*, and with contemporary engravings and written descriptions.

80   Pierre Rousseau, 1751–1829, architect of the Hôtel de Salm, now the Musée de la légion d'Honneur (1785). Nicolas-Marie Potain, architect, former Guild Master, was then father-in-law to Pierre Rousseau, (d. 1829).

81   C. Samoyault Verlet, 'Les travaux de Pierre Rousseau à Fontainebleau', *Antologia di Belle Arti*, II, Rome, June 1977, p. 157.

82   Pierre Verlet, *Styles, meubles, décors du Moyen Age à nos jours, vol II, de Louis XVI à nos jours*, Paris, 1972, p. 98.
Pierre Verlet, *Les bronzes dorées françaises*, Fribourg, 1987, p. 78.
M. Beurdeley, *La France à l'encan*, Fribourg, 1981, p. 208.

83   Renard's nomination as the *Deuxième architect du roi per choix du roi* and *Inspecteur principal de bâtiments* was only announced on 10 March, 1792, five months before the fall

of the Royal Family. Molitor's contract must have been carried out between March and August 1792, since the Monarchy was abolished and the Royal Family transferred to the Temple on 13 August. A.N. 01–1933a.

**84** Also known as *La Liste Civile*, the accounts registers where finished but unpaid commissions received under the *ancien régime* were listed during the Revolution.

**85** A.N. 02–396.

**86** A.N. 02–412.

**87** The description of the doors delivered by Molitor on 14 Messidor year III (2 July, 1795): '*2 superbes portes d'acajou à deux vantaux de 10 pieds 2 pouces 6 lignes de haut, sur 4 pieds 8 pouces de large, 8 frises et 8 rosettes en cuivre ciselé, suivant la note ci-joint*'. A.N. 02–470. *doc.* 20.

**88** G. Vauthier, 'Le Directoire et le Garde Meuble,' *Annales Révolutionnaires*, XXXXI, 1914, p. 24.

Crowned with success during the 1780s, the *ébéniste* Riesener had to abandon his workshop between 1796 and 1800, following a desperate and bankrupting attempt to buy back at auction the pieces he had made for the Royal Family.

**89** The acquisition of works of *ébénisterie* made by Audry, Molitor, Mauter and Vassou. Other furniture, including seat furniture, was supplied by Lependu, Lignereux, Adam and the Jacob *frères* . . . Biennais sold *tables à jeux*. Most of the ormolu mounts were from Galle. B.N. MSS 5–6583.

**90** Jacob-Desmalter and the Marcion workshops achieved great success; they executed important commissions for the *Garde-Meuble*. Jacob-Desmalter employed as many as 350 workers before the Blockade, but during the crisis, after 1807, no more than 100 workers. Source, see note 91.

**91** A.N. AF IV 1060.

**92** A.N. 02 610.

**93** A.N. 02 513, 522; U. Leben, 'Une commande Impériale à Bernard Molitor,' *L'Estampille*, 12, 1986, p. 42.

**94** A.N. F12–2282.

**95** Already on 10 May 1793, the former inspector of the *Garde-Meuble*, M. Bayard, wrote in a report concerning the innumerable pieces of furniture coming from the reserves of the Royal furnishings that, 'the last Tyrant had them built . . . to be cherished by the residents of the Faubourg Saint-Antoine'. A.N. 02–470.

**96** As a result of the special budget, other commissions arrived on 29 June and 3 December of the same year.

**97** Besides Molitor, other *ébénistes* such as Marcion, Rémond, Papst, Bellanger and Demay participated in the special employment programme.

**98** A.N. 02 513, Mobilier Impérial Soumission no. 71 (*doc.* 8). Le Sieur Frichet, residing at 42 rue du Faubourg Saint-Denis, executed sketches of various pieces of furniture for the *Garde-Meuble*. On 8 July 1811, he received the sum of 78 francs for '13 dessins de différents modèles de meubles, à 6 francs'. A.N. 02 522 (*doc.* 5).

**99** A.N. 02 513, Soumission no. 124.

**100** Bellanger supplied furniture for a value of 12,530 francs, Demay, 5,974 francs; Marcion, 20,152 francs; Lerpscher, 15,460 francs. A *secrétaire* made by Martin was valued at 500 francs. Conversely, prices could also be lower than those announced. A.N. 02 522.

**101** D. Ledoux-Lebard, *Les ébénistes parisiens*, 1984, p. 988. Here is listed the furniture identified by the *Mobilier National Français* without giving the details of their provenance: M 531, catalogue no. 63A G.M.F. 7143, catalogue no. 63B G.M.F. 7142, catalogue no. 25 G.M.F. 7192.

**102** A.N. 02–586, 02–616.

**103** A.N. 02 627.

**104** A.N. 02 627.

**105** A.N. 02 601.

**106** A.N. 02 627.

**107** A.N. 03–2082, AJ 19–306.

**108** See B. Foucart, 'Attirance et réaction dans les relations artistiques Franco-Allemandes entre 1800 et 1815,' *Francia* 1972, p. 607; Georg Himmelheber, 'Die Kunst des deutschen Möbels', *Klassissismus, Historismus, Jugendstil III, Munich, 1973, p. 80.*

**109** Two World Wars have erased practically all traces of the original interior design.

**110** While visiting Kassel, the painter-decorator Friedrich Maurer remarked on the annoyance engendered by Jérome among his subjects due to his heavy taxations. See W. Meyer *Elend und Aufstieg in den Tagen des Biedermeier, Erinnerungen und Tagebuchblätter von Friedrich Maurer,* Stuttgart, 1969. For a while, Napoleon entertained the idea of developing Kassel, an important, centrally-located city, with the aim of making it the new capital of occupied Germany.

**111** *Landesarchiv-Hessen,* Marburg; 75 Royaume du Westphalie II-b-7.

**112** See catalogue, *92A* and *92B; 93A–D.* Furniture with probable origins: catalogue *33A–D, 111* and *112, 153B.* Besides Molitor, Jacob-Desmalter also produced furniture for Kassel. See H. Lefuel, *François Honoré et George Jacob-Desmalter – Ebénistes de Napoléon et de Louis XVIII,* Paris, 1926; A. Maze-Sencier, *Les Fournisseurs de Napoleon I,* Paris, 1853, p. 122.

**113** Presently, the furniture is dispersed in several different châteaux. I have located some pieces in Kassel, Schloss Wilhelshöhe, Bad Homburg vor der Höhe, Schloss Fasanerie in Fulda and the Neues Palais in Potsdam.

**114** There would seem to be a correlation between Molitor's wish for a rapid sale of the furniture and the closing of the workshop in 1817. From 1818, the *ébéniste* and *fabricant de meubles* no longer appears in the list of tradesmen, but in the list of the ten thousand principal gentlemen of Paris who were not actually producing anything. *Almanach de Commerce,* Tynna, 1817, 1819 and 1820.

**115** Mme de Kersalaim, daughter of M de Verdun, who prior to 1789 was *Surintendant des finances* of Monsieur, comte d'Artois, the King's brother. Mme de Villeneuve, probably the wife or a relative of the *Inspecteur du garde-meuble* of the same name, named in 1784, brother-in-law de Thierry de Ville d'Avray.

**116** In 1814–1815, considering the economic crisis and the repeated damage caused by the occupying troops, the *Garde-Meuble* had more pressing matters at hand with the restoration of the châteaux and ministries than the acquisition of *ébénisterie.*

**117** The furniture acquired by the Duke of Wellington for the future George IV in 1816 and delivered to Carlton House, had been commissioned from Molitor through the intermediary of M. Wattier. The pieces are now in Buckingham Palace. (See 34 and 35). There is however no trace of the cabinets sold to the King of Prussia, Friedrich Wilhelm III.

**118** A.N. 03–2104. We know from numerous sources that bargaining over prices was a comon practice between clients and *ébénistes.*

**119** A.N. AJ19–300.

**120** Receipts from the comtesse de La Marck for commissions executed and delivered to Saint-Germain, between April 1792 and June 1793. A.N.T. 769 *doc* 3. Many thanks to M Patrick Leperllier for this information.

**121** A.N.M.C. XIII–474 'Union of the Creditors (Udc) of Victor Maurice Riquet Carament', 27 September 1793; A.N.M.C. XIII–479 'Udc Louis François Chamillard de la Suze' 15–17 October 1793; A.N.M.C. XIII–479 'Udc Thiroux Médavy 4 November 1793; A.N.M.C. XIII–479 'Udc Jules François Arnaud Polignac and spouse', 6 November 1793.

**122** Molitor supplied a large console table to the comtesse on 13 February 1793. In the succession inventory dated 7 August 1793, the console table is listed under the reference number 146 and described, *Une grande console de bois de rapport à dessus de marbre blanc garni d'un tiroir et de deux tablettes, garnis de balustrades dorées d'or moulu* valued at 120 *livres.* The console table was to be sold at auction on 2 September 1793 for 349,19 *livres* under the no. 1855. Archives Départment des Yvelines: E.S. Germain en Laye Odiot/Plantelin 140/1 1793.

**123** When he left the country, the ambassador owed 72 *livres* to Molitor. He also had debts to other *ébénistes:* Roussel, Jacob and Leclerc; A.N.T. 1245. Nunèz was a client of Daguerre. Many thanks to Mlle Patricia Lemonnie for this information.

**124** Probably Bonnecarère, the representative of the Archbishop of Liège in Paris, according to the memoires of Madame La Tour du Pin, and not the citizen and president of the *Section de la fontaine de Grenelle,* Guillaume Bonnecarère.

**125** Upon his return from America, marquis de La Fayette acquired an hôtel on rue de Lille, which he continued to decorate until the beginning of the Revolution. La Fayette and his family were forced to flee Paris after the abolition of the monarchy in August 1792. The following year, during the Terror, their property was requisitioned and the furniture sold at auction. The documents containing exact details of the state of the interior and the furniture when the family left are still inaccessible to the public at the Fondation Josée et Renée Chambrun. See: *La rue de Lille – l'Hôtel de Salm*, p. 96.

**126**   We also come across the name of the marquis de Beauregard a fortune seeker and adventurer from the post-Revolutionary years who was really the former wigmaker. Leuthereau, who lodged in the former hôtel of the prince de Salm in 1795, opposite the *ébéniste*, until he was sent to prison for being unable to meet his debts.

**127**   Table 62 and 73.

**128**   Lits de repôs 27 and 68.

After his promotion to Colonel – then to General, the comte resided regularly in his hôtel in Paris from 1806–12.

**129**   The marquis de Saisseval resided in an *hôtel* on rue de Lille. Although he was a marquis, he was referred to as 'citoyen' in the 1801 document, following the abolition of the nobility. The marquise de Saisseval had been lady-in-waiting to Madame Victoire, daughter of Louis XV.

**130**   Succession inventory of Madame de Jaucourt, *née* Elisabeth de la Chastre. A.N.M.C. XCI–1405; XIII–528.

**131**   It is certain that in 1808 there was furniture supplied by Molitor at Auteuil. The modern ebony furniture in the duc and duchesse's rented apartment at Saint-Germain en Laye could have also been produced by the *ébéniste*.

**132**   A.N.M.C. LVIII–638, 639, 739, 768, 847, LIV–1369, XLVIII–989, 765.

**133**   *Journal des Dames*, 30 Messidor year XII (1805); *Zeitung für die elegant Welt*, 62, Leipzig, 23 May 1805.

**134**   See also Günther Bandmann. 'Das exotische in der europäischen Kunst,' *Der Mensch und die Künste, Festschrift Heinrich Lützeler*, Düsseldorf, 1962, p. 337.

**135**   10–12, 34, 35, 53–54, 65, 66, 75 (*docs.* 4 and 11).

**136**   The *Journal des Luxus und der Moden*, edited by Friedrich Justus Bertuch (1742–1822) in Weimar, was a monthly magazine with a large circulation throughout Germany. In presenting new ideas, Bertuch played the role of mediator and disseminator rather than creator. He gave structure to the trends reported from his correspondents in the major European capitals: Paris, London and Berlin. Besides original contemporary literature, critical reviews of theatre and opera performances throughout Germany, and travel commentaries, there were always articles on fashion, interior decoration and furnishings. The magazine enjoyed a wide success during the thirty years of its existence.

**137**   *Do.* A. *Département des Yvelines*, E. Saint Germain en Laye, Odiot/Plantelin 140/1–1793. See *doc. 3*.

**138**   *Journal des Luxus und der Moden*, April 1794.

**139**   Jacques Antoine Courbin, *Serrurier ordinaire des meubles de la Couronne à Paris*. A.N. 01 3634.

**140**   See Stürmer, *Handwerk und höfische Kultur*, p. 112; C. Witt-Döring, 'Tradition und Wirklichkeit – Das Wiener Biedermeier,' *Parnaß Sonderheft* IV, Linz, 1987, p. 24 ff.

**141**   Gambier received 72 *livres* for the creation of designs. The same design was listed on three occasions during January 1788. Many thanks to M. Christian Baulet for this information.

**142**   D. Ledoux-Lebard, 'Le destin extraordinaire de deux bronziers,' *L'Estampille* CCXXIII, 1989.

**143**   Kunstbibliothek Berlin, HDZ 4642.

**144**   Cauvet Album 69.690.1. p.18 verso. Metropolitan Museum of Art, New York.

**145**   'L'Amour désarmé,' 1788, Catalogue de Sèvres no. L.C.31, p. 34; 'Leçon à l'Amour,' 1790, Catalogue no. Vc 4 B.29, p. 52 *Archives de la Manufacture de Sèvres*.

**146**   A.N.M.C., Et. LVIII–638, 768 XLVIII–738, 765.

**147**   See M. Praz, *A History of Interior Decoration* London, 1990, pl 168, p. 201.

**148**   Several designs by Dugourc in the above-mentioned style from the Tassinari and

Chatel Collection were sold at auction at the Etude Arcole, Paris on 3 June, 1988.

**149** Sébastien Mercier, *Tableau de Paris*, Amsterdam, 1788, VIII, p. 81; XII, p. 110.

**150** For the development of Neo-classicism and the *goût étrusque*, see S. Erickson, *Early Neoclassicism*, London, 1972 and Ottomeyer, 'Vergoldeten Bronsen' *Groteskenstil 1.4* Munich, 1986, I, p. 216.

**151** H. Lefuel, *Georges Jacob* Paris, 1923, p. 141.
Antique furniture is also depicted in the following paintings by Jean-Louis David: *Le Serment des Horaces*, (1784); *La Mort de Socrate*, (1788); *Paris et Hélène*, (1789); *Brutus*, (1789); *Madame Récamier* (1800). See A. Boime, *Art in the Age of Revolution 1750–1800*, Chicago/London, 1987, p. 150.

**152** For his publications Willemin used engravings of complete collections which had already been published in other countries. His appendices refer to more than 18 different editions by Kirchner, Winkelmann and Tischbein. Nicolas Xavier Willemin, *Collection de plus beaux ouverages de l'antiquité*, Paris. (Since the book was 'A.P.R.', 'Avec privilege du Roi' it must have been published before the abolition of the monarchy in 1792.)

**153** Concerning mysticism and occultism in the 1780s, see Robert Darnton. *Der Mesmerismus und des Ende der Aufktärung in Frankreich*, Berlin, 1985.

**154** Premièred in Vienna, 1782.

**155** C. Baulez, 'Le goût turc,' *L'Objet d'art*, 2, 1987.

**156** A. Young, *Voyage en France 1787–1789*, Paris, 1976.

**157** A. Pradère, 'Le mobilier du marquis de Marigny,' *L'Estampille*, CLXXXXIII, 1986.
A Gordon, 'The Marquis de Marigny's purchases of English furniture and objects,' *FHS* XXV, 1989.

**158** E. Joy, *English Furniture 1800–1850*, London, 1977, p. 37.
Some of the furniture for Carlton House was executed in Paris by Weisweiler after designs by Holland.

**159** J. Starobinski, *1789 – Les emblèmes de la Révolution*, Paris, 1979, p. 50.

**160** Tocqueville expressed on several occasions in 1835 his apparent rejection of outward show and display, '. . . but the apparent brilliance of power is not necessary for the course of state affairs; it is rather offensive to the public eye.' '. . . they act like a Lord who dresses soberly in order to teach the disdain of luxury to simple *bourgeois*.'
A. de Tocqueville, *De la démocratie en Amérique*, Paris, 1835 – modern edition, Stuttgart, 1985, p. 121 and p. 253.

**161** *Tableau général du goût des modes et costumes de Paris*, vol 1 1797, p. 89.

**162** *Journal des Luxus und der Moden*, December 1790–January 1791.

**163** J.F. Reichardt, *Briefè aus Paris*, Hamburg, 1804, p. 95.

**164** To understand this desire for the creation of new forms: 'The public monuments of free people should have no resemblance with despots' palaces'. After Caraffe, a pupil of David, quoted in H. Ottomeyer, *Des frühe Werk Charles Percier (1782–1800)*, doctoral dissertation, Munich, 1981, p. 134.

**165** *Tableau général du goût des modes et costumes de Paris* 1797, pl. 15.

**166** G. Vauthier, 'Le Directoire et le Garde Meuble,' *Annales Révolutionnaires*, XXXXI, Paris, 1914. Robert Rey, *Histoire du Mobilier du Palais de Fontainebleau*, Paris, 1936.

**167** Concerning the date of *Recueil . . .*, see H. Ottomeyer, 'Das Fühe Werk *Charles Percier (1782–1800)*' doctoral dissertation, Munich, 1981 p. 196.

**168** A.N. 01–1437. Molitor was due to be paid 7,549.13 *livres* for his work at Fontainebleau. He only received 3,500 during 1787–8 (A.N. 01–1444, Do. 231; 01–2424). We do not know if he was ever paid the outstanding amount, but the debt to the *ébéniste* was noted several times during 1787–90 in the annual accounts of the Crown. (A.N. 01–2804, 01–2805). In the last account, 7 August 1791, Molitor had still not been paid. (A.N. 01–1444, 01–1446 Do. 237, 01–3601.)

**169** G. Wilson, 'A pair of cabinets for Louis XVI,' *Furniture History*, XXI, 1985, p. 39.

**170** The history of the porcelain plaques has been studied by Gillian Wilson and David Cohen. See cabinet *69*. Also, 'New Information on French furniture at the Henry E. Huntington Library and Art Gallery', *The J. Paul Getty Journal*, IV, 1977, p. 29;
D.H. Cohen, 'Four Guéridon tables by Sèvres', *Antologia di Belle Arti*, XIII/XIV, Rome, 1980.

# Glossary

*Armoire* A large cupboard or press with either shelves or drawers enclosed behind hinged doors.

*Assignat* A promissory note issued by the French Revolutionary government, 1790–96.

*Baguette* A french word for a type of moulding or fillet.

*Bas d'armoire* A low cupboard with one or two doors.

*Bibliothèque* Bookcase or stand.

*Boiserie* Decorative, carved wooden panelling of a room.

*Bonheur-du-jour* A small, lady's desk, sometimes raised on high, slender legs and often fitted with drawers, a cupboard or shelves hidden behind a fall-front serving as a writing desk. (See also *secrétaire à abattant*.)

*Bun foot* Foot in the shape of a flattened ball.

*Bureau* Writing desk or table.

*Bureau à cylindre* (also *secrétaire à cylindre*) Roll-top desk.

*Bureau de dame* (also *secrétaire de dame*) Lady's writing desk.

*Bureau plat* Table intended to be used as a writing desk with drawers in the frieze.

*Cabinet turc* Small room decorated in an Oriental (or what was thought to be an Oriental) style.

*En caisson* Decorative, carved wooden panel in the *boiserie* of a room, within a frame.

*Chaufferette* Foot or hand warmer often in the form of a book.

*Chiffonier* Tall, but not normally very deep piece of furniture, often raised on legs, containing numerous drawers arranged one above another.

*Coiffeuse d'homme* Gentleman's dressing table.

*Commode* Chest of drawers. Originally the commode was designed to store clothes in a bedroom, but later it was placed in private rooms and towards the end of the eighteenth century in reception rooms where it served no clear function other than decorative.

*Console table* A side table which is undecorated at the back being designed to stand against a wall. Often designed in pairs and given marble tops.

*Cul-de-lampe* Bracket or corbel.

*Cyma recta frieze* A moulding composed of a double frieze – the upper part of which is concave and the lower convex.

*Desserte* French word for a sideboard; a table that was originally used to display plate but gradually evolved and was sometimes given drawers and a cupboard.

*Dossiers à planche* Shaped panel of wood forming the backrest of a chair in the antique style.

*Doucine allongée* Decorative moulding—convex above and concave below.

*Drawers à l'Anglaise* Drawers which are designed with fronts that can be lowered to reveal the contents – usually clothes.

*Escutcheon* Derived originally from heraldry, decorative carving inspired by designs, sometimes used on the pediments of large pieces of case furniture. Also, the decorative metal plate surrounding and protecting the keyhole on drawers or desks.

*Estampille* The official stamp of an *ébéniste* or Guild applied to verify the authorship of pieces of furniture.

*Fauteuil* French term for an arm-chair with arm-rests and open sides.

*Fillett* A narrow, flat band used to separate two mouldings or to terminate a series of mouldings.

*Flambeau* French word for a torch, used as a decorative motif.

*Garde-Meuble* Official body in France initially set up in the middle ages to administer the furnishings of French royal palaces.

*Gerbe-motif* Decorative motif composed of carved bound ears of corn.

*Guéridon* Initially introduced in France in the mid-seventeenth century as a small stand on a tripod base, often in pairs, to support candelabra. Later it refered to any round or oval table, normally with three legs or on a tripod base.

*Jardinière* Ornamental container designed to hold growing, rather than cut plants, normally raised on a decorative stand or legs.

*Lambrequin* Valance or pelmet, also a carved moulding inspired by draped fabric, which is a schematic rendering of a scalloped edge.

*Lit de repos* Day-bed with a mattress and upholstered for a salon.

*Ovoli frieze* (also egg and dart) A decorative moulding based on alternating arrow-heads and egg forms.

*Point de diamond* Small, decorative element, carved in the form of a square-based pyramid.

*Pupitre à lecture/à music* Raised book or music stand for lecturing or reading music, the latter often decorated with a lyre motif, the former generally more plain.

*Pupitre à voyage* Small writing desk designed for travellers, normally in two pieces and with handles to facilitate transportation.

*Rinceau* Foliated scroll.

*En rond de bosse* Three-dimensional decorative carving.

*Scotia* Term for the concave moulding at the base of a column.

*Secrétaire à abattant, secrétaire* (also *secrétaire en armoire* or *bonheur-du-jour*) Upright secretary, with a drawer and a fall-front in the upper part and doors or (rarely) drawers in the lower part.

*Secrétaire à cylindre* (see *bureau à cylindre*)

*Secrétaire de dame* (see *bureau de dame*)

*Semainier* A tall, narrow piece of furnture, composed of seven drawers, one for each day of the week as implied by the name.

*Stanchion* An upright bar, stay or support.

*Table à brelan* Gaming table for a particular game called brelan.

*Table de chevet* Table placed beside the bed for books, candle and chambre pot.

*Table écrire* Writing desk.

*Table à écritoire* Type of writing table with a drawer for writing equipment.

*Table à en cas* Gate-leg table.

*Table à étagere* Table divided into several levels to display decorative objects.

*Table à jeux* Gaming table.

*Table à pompadour* Old-fashioned term for a lady's toilette or writing table, usually placed in a bedroom.

*Table à café* Small normally round table with a marble top, on which to place cups of coffee in a salon.

*Table à thé* Large round *guéridon*, usually with a central stand on which to put the samovar when serving tea in a salon.

*Table de toilette* Table to hold a looking glass, toilet equipment and hair brushes.

*Table de travaille* Needlework table.

*Table à tric-trac* Gaming table for a particular game called tric-trac.

*Table vide-poche* Small table, normally used as a knitting table.

*Talon* (see fillet).

*Term* A pedestal tapering towards the base and usually supporting a bust or merging at the top into a human, animal or mythological figure.

# Photographic acknowledgements

Figures refer to the number of the page on which the reproduction appears. Positioning of the reproductions on the page are shown: (t) top, (m) middle, (b) bottom, (l) left, (r) right.

The drawings on 44 (A.N. F34 45/118) 165, 189, 194 are by Titus Köhler.
The author would especially like to thank M. E. Erpelding for kindly allowing the illustration on 13.
All black and white photographs were taken by Jêrome Letellier unless otherwise stated.

England

**London**
Alexander & Behrendt 203 (b)
Blairman and Sons 165 (t)
Partridge and Sons 202 (t)
Royal Collection, By Kind Permission of Her Majesty the Queen 47 (l and r), 87
Sotheby's 159, 193 (b), 194, 201 (t)
Philip Wilson Publishers 80, 91 (t), 121
Christie's Colour Library 113, 166
Wallace Collection 20, 34, 53 (photograph Douglas Cooper)

France

**Grasse**
Appolot 162 (b)
**Paris**
*Institutions*
Archives Nationales 16, 45 (F 31 74), 135 (01 1437) (photographs the author)
Bibliothèque des Arts Décoratifs, Collection Maciet 17, 86, 106, 108, 112, 202
Bibliothèque Historique de la Ville 33 (photograph the author)
Bibliothèque Nationale 70, 76, 84, 97, 101 (t), 109, 116 (t and b), 117 (t), 118, 131 (t), 134, 148, 158, 159, 161 (b), 164
Drouot S.A. Documentation 46 (b), 114, 154, 169, 178, 182 (b), 184 (t), 191, 196, 198, 200 (m), 201 (b)
Musée des Arts Décoratifs 98 (bl), 181 (photograph M.A.D./Sully-Jaulmes)
Réunion des musées nationaux 90, 118
*Private galleries:*
Galerie Didier Aaron 71, 193 (m), 199 (b)
Etude Ader-Picard-Tajan 163
Galerie Aveline 108 (t)
Etude Binoche et Godeau 155 (t and b)
Galerie G. David 62
Galerie Fabre et fils 69
Galerie Roger Imbert 63
Galerie Claude Levy 160 (r)
Galerie Mancel-Coti 99
Galerie J. Perrin 140
Etude Daussy Ricqlès 180 (t)
Galerie B. B. Steinitz 41, 81, 130
*Photographers*
Edi Media 179, 200 (b) (Photograph Bonnefoy-Connaissance des Arts)
Vincent Godeau 28, 134 (r), 192
Jêrome Letellier 35, 37, 60, 66, 75, 78, 79, 85, 101 (b), 136, 144, 157, 171 (t), 173, 180, 188, 189, 205
Benedicte Petit 120
Jean Yves and Nicolas Dubois 26, 31, 57, 67, 74, 85 (b), 94 (m), 95 (b), 96 (t), 104, 127 (b), 132, 133, 172, 204, 206

*Author's photographs*
12, 15, 16, 28 (l), 29, 45, 48, 51, 72 (t), 93, 95, 96 (b), 100, 103, 108, 110, 115, 121, 122, 130 (b), 131 (b), 135, 156 (t), 161, 171 (b), 162 (t), 184 (b), 185 (b), 197, 204 (t)

Germany

**Berlin**
Galerie Pels Leusden, Villa Grisebach 155
**Cologne**
Lothar Schnepf 25 (l), 38, 39, 42, 43, 46 (t), 83, 123, 125, 126, 127 (t), 145
**Hessen**
Verwaltung der Staatlichen Schlösser und Gärten Bad Homburg v.d. Höhe, 156, 165, 183, 198, 203 (t)
**Kassel**
Dieter Schwerdtle 61, 64, 167
**Munich**
Galerie Daxer & Marshall 129

Italy

**Florence**
Sotheby's 187 (t)
**Venice**
Franco Semenzato 88, 89, 105

Monaco

Christie's 82, 137, 141, 184 (m)
Sotheby's 49, 50 (detail), 52, 59, 116 (m), 160 (l), 174, 176, 184 (b), 186

Portugal

**Lisbon**
Fondacion Galouste Gulbenkian 153

United States of America

**Cleveland**
Cleveland Museum of Art 30, 186
**Malibu**
The J. Paul Getty Museum 22, 23, 91, 92, 151, 152,
**New York**
Documentation T. Dell 117
Christie's 124, 146, 148 (b), 176
Sotheby's 119, 120, 124, 147, 148, 168, 170, 176, 185 (t)
**Pittsburg**
The Carnegie Art Institute 25 (r), 182 (t), 203 (m)
**San Marino**
The Huntington Library and Art Collection 149, 200 (t)
**Toledo**
The Toledo Museum of Art 21

# Bibliography

Bibliography

Ananoff, Alexandre. *Boucher Werkkatalog*, Lausanne, 1976.

Apra, Nicole. *Il mobile Impero*, Novara, 1970.

Avril, Paul. *L'ameublement parisien pendant la Révolution*, Paris, 1924.

Beauvallet and Normand. *Fragments d'ornements dans le style antique*, Paris, 1820.

Beurdeley, Michel. *La France à l'encan*, Fribourg, 1981.

Bizot, Chantal. *Mobilier Directoire et Empire*, Paris, (n.d.).

Boime, A. *Art in the Age of Revolution 1750–1800*. Chicago/London, 1987.

Brunhammer, Fayet. *Meubles et Ensembles Directoires et Empire*, Paris, 1965.

Brunhammer, Yvonne. *Le Mobilier Louis XVI*, Paris, 1965.

Burckhard, M. *Le Mobilier Louis XVI*, Paris, (n.d.).

Cauvet *Recueil de vases, meubles, lambris*, Paris, 1777.

Chanson, L. *Traité d'ébénisterie*, Paris, 1988.

Cooper, D. *Trésors d'art français dans les grandes collections*, Zurich, 1965.

———. *Trésors d'art français dans des collections privées*, Zurich, 1963.

Coornaert, E. *Les Corporations en France avant 1789*, Paris, 1941.

Daremberg *Dictionnaire des Antiquités grecs et romains*, Paris, 1904.

Darnton, Robert. *Der Mesmerismus und das Ende der Aufklärung in Frankreich*, Berlin, 1985.

*Décorations intérieurs et meubles d'époques Louis XV, Louis XVI et Empire*, 2 vols, Paris, 1907–1909.

De Groer, Leon. *Les arts décoratifs de 1790–1860*, Fribourg, 1983.

Detrez *Le Faubourg St Honoré*, Paris, 1957.

Devinoy, P. and Jarry, M. *Le siège français*, Fribourg, 1973.

de Diesbach, Ghislain. *Histoire de l'Emigration*, Paris, 1984.

Edwards, Ralph. *Dictionary of English Furniture*, 3 vols, Woodbridge, 1986.

Egger, G. *Beschläge und Schlösser an alten Möbeln*, Munich, 1977.

Elias, Norbert. *Die höfische Gesellschaft*, Darmstadt, 1983.

Eriksen, Svend. *Early Neoclassicism*, London, 1972.

Favelac, P. M. *Aujourd'hui s'installer en Directoire – Empire*, Paris, *c.* 1960.

Foley, Edwin. *The Book of Decorative Furniture*, 2 vols, London, 1910–11.

Forty, Jean-Francois. *Œuvres de sculpture en bronze, contenant girandoles flambeaux, feux pendules, bras, cartels*, Paris, *c.* 1780.

Fregnac, C. *Les styles françaises*, Paris, 1976.

Furet, François and Richet, Denis. *La Revolution Française*, Paris, 1965 and Frankfurt, 1973.

de Goncourt, Edmond and Jules. *Histoire de la société française sous le Directoire*, Paris, 1855.

———. *Histoire de la société française pendant la Révolution*, Paris, 1854.

Gonzalez-Palacios, Alvar. *Gli ebanisti del Louis XVI*, Milan, 1966.

Grandjean, Serge. *Empire Furniture 1800–1825*, London, 1966.

Hamilton, W. *Antiquités étrusques et romaines tirées du cabinet de M. Hamilton envoyé extraordinaire de S. M. Britannique en cour de Naples*, Paris, 1766.

Hancarville and Tischbein *Antiquités étrusques, grecques et romaines gravées par F. A. David*, 5 vols, 1785–1788 (French edition of the Hamilton Collection).

Harris, John. *Regency Furniture Designs from Contemporary Source Books, 1803–1826*, London, 1961.

Harris, Eileen. *The Furniture of Robert Adam*, London, 1963.

Havard, H. *Dictionnaire de l'ameublement et de la décoration depuis le XIIIème siècle jusqu'à nos jours*, Paris, 1887–90.

Hepplewhite, George. *The Cabinet-Maker and Upholsterers' Guide*, London, 1789; 3rd ed. 1794.

Hessling, E. and W. *Le Style Directoire*, Paris, 1914.

Honour, Hugh. *Neoclassicism*, London, 1968.

———. *Meister der Möbelkunst*, Pawlak, 1976.

Huth, Hans. *Roentgen Furniture – Abraham and David Roentgen European Cabinet-Makers*, London/New York, 1974.

Janneau, Guillaume. *Le style Directoire, Mobilier et Décoration*, Paris, 1938.

_____ . *Les meubles de style Louis XVI au style*, Paris, 1944.

_____ . *Le siège*, Paris 1974.

_____ . *Le meuble d'ébénisterie*, Paris, 1974.

Janneau, Guillaume and Jarry, M. *Le siège en France du Moyen Age à nos jours*, Paris, 1948.

Jèze *Tableau de Paris*, Paris, 1760.

Jones, A. M. *A Handbook of the Decorative Arts in the J. Paul Getty Museum*, Malibu, 1965.

Joy, Edward. *English Furniture 1800–1850*, London, 1977.

Junquera y Mato, Juan José. *Meublos Franceses en los Palacios Reales*, Madrid, 1975.

Karamsin, Nicolas. *Briefe eines russischen Reisenden*, East Berlin, 1981.

Keim, Albert. *Le beau meuble en France*, Paris, 1928.

Kimball, Fiske. *The Creators after the Chippendale Style*, New York, 1929.

_____ . *Le Style Louis XV*, Paris, 1949.

Kjelleberg, P. *Le Mobilier Français*, Paris, 1980.

von Kotzebue, August. *Meine Flucht nach Paris im Winter 1790*, Leipzig, 1791.

_____ . *Souvenirs de Paris*, Leipzig, 1805.

Krafft and Ransonette. *Plan, coupe, élévation des plus belles maisons*, Paris, 1800.

Lacroix, Paul. *Directoire, Consulat, Empire*, Paris, 1884.

Lafond, Paul. *L'art décoratif et le mobilier sous la République et l'Empire*, Paris, 1900.

Laking, G. Francis. *The Furniture of Windsor Castle*, London, 1905.

La Malmaison, *Le passeport de l'art*, Paris, 1984.

La Tour du Pin, Marquise de. *Souvenirs d'une femme de cinquante ans*, Paris, 1982.

Ledoux-Lebard, Denise. *Le grand Trianon – Meubles et objets d'art*, Paris, 1975.

_____ . *Les ébénistes parisiens, leurs œuvres et leurs marques 1795–1870*, Paris, 1984.

Lefebre, G. *Le Directoire*, Paris, 1971.

Lemonnier, Patricia. *Weisweiler*, Paris, 1983.

*Les ébénistes du XVIII siècle*, (author unknown) Paris, 1963.

*Les ébénistes du XVIII siècle*, (author unknown) Paris, 1965.

*Les matinées à Paris*, (author unknown) Lausanne, 1800.

Lespinasse. *Histoire générale de Paris – Les Métiers de Paris*, Paris 1882.

Lever, Jill. *Architects' Designs for Furniture*, London, 1982.

Luthmer, Ferdinand. *Sammlung von Innenraümen, Möbeln und Geräten im Louis XVI und Empire Stil*, Stuttgart, 1897.

Marmottan Paul. *Les arts en Toscane sous Napoléon – La Princesse Elise*, Paris, 1901.

_____ . *Le style Empire*, Paris, 1927.

Maze-Sencier, *Alphonse. Le livre des fournisseurs de Napoléon I*, Paris, 1893.

Meister, Henri. *Mon dernier voyage à Paris, 1795*, Paris, 1910.

Mercier, Sébastien. *Tableau de Paris*, Amsterdam, 1782.

_____ . *Nouveau tableau de Paris*, Paris, 1798.

_____ . *Paris pendant la Révolution*, Paris, 1862.

*Merveilles des Châteaux de Normandie*, (author unknown), Paris, 1966.

Meyer, W. Hrag. *Elend und Aufstieg in den Tagen des Biedermeier, Erinnerungen und Tagebuchblätter von Friedrich Maurer*, Stuttgart, 1969.

Mottheau, J. *Meubles et ensembles Directoire et Empire*, Paris, 1958.

Niclausse, Juliette. *Thomire, Fondeur Ciseleur*, Paris, 1947.

Nicolay, J. *L'art et la manière des maîtres ébénistes français du XVIIIème siècle*, Paris, 1956.

Nonenfant-Feymans A. M. *Jean-Jacques Chapuis, ébéniste parisien de Bruxelles*, Paris, (n.d.).

Normand, Charles. *Nouveau recueil de divers genres d'ornements*, Paris, 1803.

Oberkirch. *Souvenirs de la baronne d'Oberkirch*, Paris, 1979.

Packer, Charles. *Paris Furniture*, London, 1956.

Pary, E. *Guide des Corps des Marchands et des Communautés*, Paris, 1766.

Percier, Charles and Fontaine. *Recueil de Décorations Intérieures comprenant tout ce qui a rapport à l'Ameublement*, Paris, 1801–1812.

Petitclerc, Fréderique. *Ebenisten der Louis XVI Möbel*, Munich, 1972.

Piranesi, Giovanni Battisti. *Diverse maniere d'adornare i camini*, Rome, 1769.

Praz, Mario. *L'ameublement, psychologie et évolution de la décoration intérieure*, Paris, 1964.

_____ . *A History of Interior Decoration*, London, 1990.

Redhead-Yorke, Henri. *Paris et la France sous le Consulat*, Paris, 1804.

Rènouvier, M. J. *Histoire de l'art pendant la Révolution*, Paris, 1863.

Rey, Robert. *Histoire du Mobilier du Palais de Fontainebleau*, Paris, 1936.

de Ricci, Seymour. *Der Stil Louis XVI*, Stuttgart, 1913.

Ripault. *Une soirée de Paris an V*, Paris, 1797.

_____ . *Une soirée de bonne compagnie, an XII*, Paris, 1804.

de Rothschild, Alfred, Charles. *A Description of the Works of Art forming the Collection of Alfred de Rothschild*, London, 1884.

Roubo, Jacob, A. *L'Art de Menuisier*, 5 vols, Paris, 1769–1775.

Rubiera, José. *Encyclopedia of French Period Furniture Designs*, New York, 1983.

Salverte, comte de. *Les ébénistes du XVIII siècle*, Paris, 1934.

_____ . *Le meuble français d'après les ornemaniste de 1660 à 1789*, Paris/Brussels, 1930.

Schmitz, Hermann. *Deutsche Möbel des Klassizismus*, Stuttgart, 1914.

Schulz, Friedrich. *Über Paris und die Pariser*, Berlin, 1791.

Sennett, Richard. *Verfall und Ende des öffentlichen Lebens – Die Tyrannei der Intimität*, Frankfurt, 1982.

Sheraton, Thomas. *The Cabinet-Maker and Upholsterers' Drawing Book*, London, 1791–1794.

_____ . *The Cabinet Dictionary*, London, 1803.

Siguret, Philippe. *Le style Louis XVI*, (date unknown).

Smith, G. *A Collection of Designs of Household Furniture*, London, 1808.

Sombart, Werner. *Liebe Luxus und Kapitalismus; Krieg und Kapitalismus*, 2 vols, Leipzig, 1912 and Munich, 1967.

Starobinski, Jean. *1789 – Les emblèmes de la Révolution*, Paris, 1979.

Stone, Anne. *Antique Furniture*, London, 1982.

Stürmer, Michael. *Herbst des Alten Handwerks*, Munich, 1979.

_____ . *Handwerk und höfische Kultur*, Munich, 1982.

*Tableau général du goût des Modes . . .*, Paris, 1797, (doc. B.N.).

Theunissen, A. *Meubles et siège du XVIIIème siècle*, Paris, 1934.

Thierry. *Nouveau Guide de Paris*, Paris, 1787.

Thornton, Peter. *L'époque et son style 1620–1920*, Paris, 1984.

Tischbein Wilhelm. *Recueil de gravures d'apres des vases, etrusques*, Paris, 1797.

de Tocqueville, Alexis. *L'Ancien Régime et la Révolution*, Paris, 1967.

de Tourzel, Duchesse. *Souvenirs de la gouvernante des enfants de France 1789–1795*, Paris, 1980.

Vacquier, Jacques. *Le Style Empire*, Paris, 1911.

Verlet, Pierre. *La maison du XVIIIème siècle en France*, Fribourg, 1966.

_____ . *Möbel von J. H. Riesener*, Darmstadt (n.d.).

_____ . *Styles, meubles, décors du Moyen Age à nos jours*, vol. II: *de Louis XVI a nos jours*, Paris 1972.

_____ . *Les bronzes dorées françaises*, Fribourg, 1987.

Vigée Lebrun, Elisabeth. *Souvenirs de Elisabeth Vigée Lebrun*, Paris, 1984.

Watson, Francis, J. B. *Le mobilier Louis XVI*, Paris, 1983.

Willemin, Nicolas Xavier. *Choix de costumes civils et militaires de peuples d l'antiquité*, 2 vols, Paris, 1798–1802.

Winkelmann, Joachim. *Histoire de l'art de l'antiquité*, Leipzig, 1781.

Young, Arthur. *Voyage en France 1787–1789*, Paris, 1976.

*Zeitung für die elegante Welt*, 62, Leipzig, 1805.

**Journals, documents and dissertations**

*Actes du Tribunal Révolutionnaire*, Paris, 1968.

*Almanach de Paris*, 2 vols, Paris, 1789.

*Almanach de Commerce*, Paris, 1797–1820.

Augarde, Dominique. 'Signaturen französischer Möbel', *Kunst und Antiquitaten*, I, Munich, 1984.

_____ . 'Le Mobilier de Saint Cloud et du Palais du Temple au temps du Comte d'Artois', *L'Estampille*, ccxv, June 1988, p. 20.

Bandmann, Günther. 'Das exotische in der europäischen Kunst', *Der Mensch und die Künste, Festschrift Heinrich Lützeler*, Düsseldorf, 1962.

Baulez, Christian. 'Le choix de citoyen Alcan', *Drouot Annual Report, 1984–85*, Paris, 1986.

_____ . 'Un Médailler de Louis XVI à Versailles', *Revue du Louvre*, March 1987, pp. 172ff.

_____ . 'Le goût turc', *L'Objet d'art*, 1987.

de Bellaigue, Geoffrey. 'The Royal Collections: George IV and French Furniture', *The Connoisseur*, June 1977.

Bertuch, ed. *Journal des Luxus und der Moden*, Weimar, 1786–1810.

Boutemy, A. 'Les secrétaires en cabinets'. *Bulletin de la société de l'histoire de l'art français 1970*, Paris, 1972.

Cohen, David Harris. 'Four tables guéridons by Sèvres', *Antologia delle belli Arti*, xiii and xiv, Rome, 1980.

_____ . 'Pierre Philippe Thomire Unternehmer und 'Künstler', *Vergoldete Bronzen*, Ottomeyer/Pröschel, Munich, 1986.

Curl, J. S. 'Du Nil à la Seine', *Connaissance des Arts*, cdxi, 1986.

de Diesbach, Ghislain 'Le Château de Wallenried', *Connaissance des Arts*, ii, 1968.

Dugourc, Jean Demosthène. 'Autobiographie de Dugourc', *Nouvelles Archives de l'art Français*, Paris, 1877.

Dumonthier, E. 'Les tables styles Louis XVI et Empire', *Documents d'Art – Mobilier National Français*, Morance, 1924.

_____ . *'Les plus beaux meubles des ministères et administrations publiques'*, (n.d.).

Foucart, Bruno. 'Attirance et réaction dans les relations artistiques Franco-Allemandes entre 1800 et 1815', *Francia: Schriften des deutschen Historischen Instituts* 1972.

Gonzalez-Palacios, Alvar. 'Arredi Francesi da Parma à Firenze', *Richerche di Storia dell'Arte*, iv, Milan, 1977.

Gordon, A. 'The Marquis de Marigny's purchases of English Furniture and objects' *F.H.S.*, xxv, 1989.

Guillaume Brulon, Dorothée. 'Les cabinets en porcelaine', *L'Estampille*, Paris, Nov. 1983.

Guth, Paul. 'Fortune et infortune d'un intendant plein d'initiative, Thierry de Ville d'Avray', *Connaissance des Arts*, Paris, June 1956.

_____ . La carrière brisée d'un ébéniste d'avant-garde B. Molitor *Connaissance des Arts*, VI, Paris, 1957.

_____ . 'La Château de Villarsceaux', *Connaissance des Arts*, civ, Paris, 1960.

Hartmann, Simone. 'Jean Dugourc – ornemaniste précurseur de l'Empire', *L'Estampille*, lxxxxviii, Paris, 1978.

Higgs, David. *Nobles, titrés, aristocrates en France après la Révolution, 1800–1870*, Paris, 1990.

Himmelheber, George. 'Die Kunst des deutschen Möbels' vol. 3, *Klassiszismus, Historismus, Jugendstil*, Munich, 1973.

Huth, Hans. 'Lacquer of the West – History of a Craft and an Industry 1550–1950', *Art Bulletin*, lv, London, 1973, p. 305.

*Journal de la Mode et du Goût*, Paris 1790–1802 (later called *Journal des dames et des modes*, Paris 1805–1836).

de La Mésangère, Pierre. *Collection de meubles et objets de goût au bureau du Journal des dames*, Paris, 1802–35.

_____ . ed. *Journal des dames et des modes*, 1797–1838.

*L'Arlequin – Journal de pièces et morceaux*, Paris, 1799 (B.N.).

Leben, Ulrich. 'L'atelier de Bernard Molitor sous la Révolution', *L'Estampille*, clxxvii, Paris, 1985.

_____ . 'B. Molitor: Leben und Werk eines Pariser Ebenisten', *Hemecht*, Luxemburg, 1986.

_____ . 'Une commande Impériale à Bernard Molitor,' *L'Estampille*, Dec., Paris, 1986.

_____ . 'Die Werkstatt B. Molitor', *Kunst und Antiquitäten*, iv, Paris, 1987.

_____ . *Bernard Molitor (1755–1833): Leben und Werk eines Pariser Kunsttischlers*, doctoral dissertation, University of Bonn, 1989.

_____ . 'La sobre élégance de B. Molitor', *Connaissance des Arts*, Feb., Paris, 1990.

Ledoux-Lebard, Denise. Les trois Bellangé, fournisseurs de la Cour', *Connaissance des Arts*, Nov., 1964.

\_\_\_\_\_ . 'Empire Furniture in *bois indigène'*, *The Connoisseur*, London, 1976.

Ledoux-Lebard, Denise and Youf, J. B. 'Un ebanista à Lucca' *Arte Illustrata*, Nov.–Dec., Florence, 1971.

\_\_\_\_\_ . 'Le destin extraordinaire de deux bronziers', *Estampille*, CCXXIII, 1989.

Lefuel, Hector. *Georges Jacob, Ebéniste du XVIIIe siècle*, Paris, 1923.

\_\_\_\_\_ . *François Honoré et George Jacob-Desmalter – Ebénistes de Napoléon et de Louis XVIII*, Paris, 1926.

'Les bustes en bronze doré', *Connaissance des Arts*, LV, Paris, 1956.

'Les tables à manger', *Trouvailles*, XLIII, Paris, 1983.

*Liste de citovens actifs dans le section de la fontaine de Grenelle*, Paris, 1791 (doc. B.N.).

*Magazin der Freunde des guten Geschmacks*, Leipzig, 1794–1797.

*Magazin des Luxus und des neuesten Geschmacks der vornehmen und feinen Welt*, Paris and Leipzig, 1800–1809.

*Moniteur*, VIII, reprint 1847.

Ottomeyer, Hans. *Das frühe Werk Charles Percier (1732–1800), Zu den Anfängen des Historismus in Frankreich, Altendorf D. Grabner 1981*, doctoral dissertation, University of Munich, 1981.

Piranesi, Giovanni Battisti. *Vasi, candelabri, sarcofagi, tripodi, lucerne ed ornamenti antichi*, Rome, 1778.

Pradère, Alexandre. 'Le mobilier du marquis de Marigny', *L'Estampille*, Paris, CLXXXXIII, Paris.

\_\_\_\_\_ . 'Boulle, du Louis XIV sous Louis XVI', *L'Objet d'Art*, IV, Paris, 1988.

Samoyault, Verlet, Colombe. 'Les travaux de Pierre Rousseau à Fontainebleau', *Antologia delle Belle Arti*, II, Rome, 1977.

Stratmann, Rosemarie. *Der Ebenist J. F. Œben*, doctoral dissertation, University of Heidelberg, 1971.

Van der Kemp, G. 'Contribution à l'étude deux *bonheurs-du-jour* de B. Molitor', *Archives de l'art français*, XXII, Paris, 1959.

Vauthier, G. 'Le Directoire et le Garde-Meuble', *Annales Révolutionnaires, XLI*, Paris, 1914.

Verlet, Pierre. 'Le Boudoir de Marie-Antoinette à Fontainebleau', *Art de France*, I, Paris, 1961.

Watson, Francis, J. B. 'The Great Duke's Taste for French Furniture', *Apollo*, London, July 1975.

Whitehead, John and Impey, Oliver. 'From Japanese Box to French Royal Furniture', *Apollo*, London, Sept. 1990.

Willemin, Nicolas Xavier. *Collection de plus beaux ouvrages de l'antiquité*, Paris, c. 1792.

Wilson, Gillian. 'New Information on French Furniture at the Henry E. Huntington Library and Art Gallery', *J. Paul Getty Museum Journal*, IX, 1977, Paris.

Witt-Döring, Christian. 'Tradition und Wirklichkeit – Das Wiener Biedermeier', *Parnaß Sonderheft*, IV, Linz, 1987.

Museum catalogues

Bauer, Marker. *Europäische Möbel von der Gotik bis zur Gegenwart*, cat. Kunstgewerbemuseums Frankfurt, Frankfurt, 1976.

Dreyfuss C. *Le mobilier français au Musée du Louvre*, cat., 1921.

Hubert, Gerard. *Malmaison*, cat., Paris, 1980.

Lefuel, Hector. *Catalogue du Musée Marmottan*, Paris, 1934.

Musée Nissim de Commondo. cat., Paris, 1983.

Wark, Robert. *French Decorative Art in the Huntington Collection*, cat., San Marino, 1961.

Watson, Francis J. B. 'The English as Collectors of French Furniture', *I, The Connoisseur*, London, 1974.

\_\_\_\_\_ . *Wallace Collection – Catalogue of Furniture*, London, 1956.

\_\_\_\_\_ . *The Wrightsman Collection, New York* (vol. I: *Furniture*), cat., New York, 1966.

Wilson, Gillian. *Decorative Arts in the J. Paul Getty Museum, Los Angeles*, cat., Los Angeles.

Exhibition catalogues

Academy of Berlin, *Meisterwerke aus preußischen Schlössern. Verwaltung des staatlichen Schlösser und Gärten*, Sept.–Nov. 1930, exhib. cat., Berlin, 1930.

*Biennale des Antiquaries au Grand Palais*, exhib. cat., Paris, 1972.

Institut Néerlandais. *Le palais Bourbon*, exhib. cat., Paris, 1987.

—— . *La rue de Lille – l'Hôtel de Salm*, exhib. cat., Paris, 1983.

*Les chefs-d'œuvre des grands ébénistes 1790–1850*, Musée des Arts Décoratifs. exhib. cat., Paris, 1951.

Musée Carnavalet. *L'Art de l'Estampe et de la Révolution*, exhib. cat., Paris, 1977.

—— . *De la place Louis XV à la place de la Concorde*, exhib. cat., Paris, 1982.

# List of names